The Many Faces of Maimonides

Emunot: Jewish Philosophy and Kabbalah

Series Editor
DOV SCHWARTZ (Bar-Ilan University, Ramat Gan)

Editorial board
ADA RAPOPORT ALBERT
(University College, London)

GAD FREUDENTHAL
(CNRS, Paris)

GIDEON FREUDENTHAL
(Tel Aviv University, Ramat Aviv)

MOSHE IDEL
(Hebrew University, Jerusalem)

RAPHAEL JOSPE
(Bar-Ilan University, Ramat Gan)

EPHRAIM KANARFOGEL
(Yeshiva University, New York)

MENACHEM KELLNER
(Haifa University, Haifa)

DANIEL LASKER
(Ben-Gurion University, Beer Sheva)

The Many Faces of Maimonides

DOV SCHWARTZ

Translated by Batya Stein

BOSTON
2018

Library of Congress Cataloging-in-Publication Data

Names: Schwartz, Dov, author. | Stein, Batya, translator.

Title: The many faces of Maimonides / Dov Schwartz ; translated by Batya Stein.

Description: Brighton, MA: Academic Studies Press, 2018.

Series: Emunot, Jewish philosophy and kabbalah | Collection of essays (some originally published in Hebrew). | Includes bibliographical references and index.

Identifiers: LCCN 2018006997 | ISBN 9781618117809 (hardcover)

Subjects: LCSH: Maimonides, Moses, 1135-1204. Dalåalat al-òhåa*iråin. | Judaism. | Jewish philosophy. | Philosophy, Medieval.

Classification: LCC B759.M34 S34 2018 | DDC 296.1/81—dc23

LC record available at https://lccn.loc.gov/2018006997

© **2018 Academic Studies Press**
All rights reserved.
ISBN 978-1-61811-780-9 (hardback); ISBN 978-1-61811-906-3 (paperback);
ISBN 978-1-61811-781-6 (electronic)

Book design by Kryon Publishing Services (P) Ltd.
www.kryonpublishing.com
Cover design by Ivan Grave

Published by Academic Studies Press in 2018
28 Montfern Avenue
Brighton, MA 02135, USA
press@academicstudiespress.com
www.academicstudiespress.com

Table of Contents

Introduction		vi
1.	The Passion for Metaphysics	1
2.	The Separate Intellects	61
3.	Astral Magic and the Law	90
4.	Idolatry as Mediation	104
5.	Immortality and Imagination	118
6.	Maimonides: A Philosophical Theologian	134
Epilogue		165
Bibliography		167
Index		182

Introduction

The present book will address mainly philosophical dimensions in Maimonides' thought, focusing on a new reading of several issues in *The Guide of the Perplexed*. A figure like Maimonides would obviously have a variety of interests and goals and his writing will certainly be diverse and multifaceted. Even an esoteric interest or political and religious goals and motives do not exhaust the pursuits of Maimonides, who both transcended and included all of these. I do not accept mystic explanations of his endeavor, and can only study his genius.

Medieval Jewish thought can be clearly split into two eras—before and after the appearance of *The Guide of the Perplexed*. No other philosophical treatise has ever evoked so many discussions, neither in the rabbinic nor in the scholarly literature, and no other work of Jewish philosophy has ever given rise to such polarized interpretations. *The Guide of the Perplexed* also had an essential influence on medieval (Christian) scholastic thought and, through it, on Western culture in general. My attempt in this introduction is to offer a brief outline of various reasons for this phenomenon.

The Guide of the Perplexed, which was completed in 1191, turned into a popular volume that, over centuries, gained acceptance not only among thinkers and scholars but also among the general public. This book's popularity is an impressive and paradoxical event, given that it absolutely contradicts its writer's original intention. At the end of his Introduction, Maimonides set a criterion—his book would please one in ten thousand readers:

> To sum up: I am the man who when the concern pressed him and his way was straitened and he could find no other device by which to teach a demonstrated truth other than by giving satisfaction to a single virtuous man while

displeasing ten thousand ignoramuses—I am he who prefers to address that single man by himself, and I do not heed the blame of those many creatures.[1]

Maimonides knew that most people in the Jewish community would not understand the claims of the *Guide*, and wrote the book with this purpose in mind. Indeed, he actively tried to distance ordinary readers from his book and therefore wrote it using deliberate contradictions, as he admitted in the introduction. Maimonides thus adopted all possible means to ensure the book would *not* be popular but to no avail.

The paradox of the book's acceptance is evident in the fact that it was written for a specific student, R. Joseph b. Judah. Contrary to Maimonides' previous large treatises, *Commentary to the Mishnah* and *Mishneh Torah*, which were written for the Jewish community in general, the *Guide* was tailored for Joseph: a scholar, interested in various scientific and philosophical fields, who had become perplexed. In the "Introduction to the First Part," Maimonides clarified that the work had been designed for one who is knowledgeable in Torah as well as in the theoretical and philosophical[2] sciences but has difficulty reconciling them. The rabbi's personal guidance to his student thus opened up possibilities of deeper knowledge to many. In this book, I focus mainly on the *Guide* and only in Chapters Three and Five consider his other writings.

Structure

Before attempting to consider the general principles of the *Guide*, I will briefly present its structure and its main conceptual approaches in the table below:

Part	Chapters	Content
I	1-49	*Negating corporeality*: lexicographical discussions, focusing on the negation of corporeality. Almost every chapter interpretsbiblical attributes of God in non-corporeal terms.
	50-70	*Attributes*: Denying any attributes to God, who is entirely indescribable.[3]
	71-76	*Dispute*: Polemic with Muslim theologians.

---

1 Moses Maimonides, *The Guide of the Perplexed*, trans. Shlomo Pines (Chicago: University of Chicago Press, 1963), 16. All further English citations of this work are from this translation (henceforth and throughout this book, *Guide*).
2 Today, the expertise of a "philosopher" is in a field entirely different from that of a "scientist," who deals with order in the material world. In the Middle Ages, however, there was no significant distinction between a theoretical scientist and a philosopher.
3 Maimonidean scholarship has discussed the extent of Maimonides' recourse to analogy in the description of God.

Part	Chapters	Content
II	1	*Demonstration*: A series of proofs of God's existence, unity, and non-corporeality.
	2-12	*The Spheres and the Angels* (separate intellects): The notion of emanation, which clarifies how the heavenly elements and the angels came into being.
	13-31	*Creation*: The impossibility of demonstrating scientifically either the creation or the eternity of the world. Reasons for preferring creation.
	32-48	*Prophecy*: Divine revelation is natural and subject to a set order. Its functions are political
III	1-7	*The Account of the Chariot*: A meteorological and physical interpretation of the biblical chapters on the chariot.
	8-24	*Providence and Knowledge*: God's providence protects only humans according to their level of knowledge. God knows the details from his knowledge of himself.
	25-50	*The Reasons for the Commandments*: Rational arguments for all the commandments
	51-54	*Perfection*: The ethos of worshipping the divine among those who attained perfection.

This division is only one way of presenting the contents of the *Guide*, but immediately raises questions about its structure and order, which have proven extremely controversial. For example, the polemic with the Muslim theologians is closer in its character and contents to the issue of creation than to the issue of negative attributes, but Maimonides nevertheless set it in Part I. Not only are the contents of the *Guide* puzzling, but so are the structure and order of the discussions. In the first two chapters of this book, I consider the structure and the order of two sets of chapters in the *Guide*, drawing lessons from them about Maimonides' philosophical writing in general.

The Legitimation of Scientific Philosophical Pursuits

A fundamental principle of the Maimonidean approach that appears already in the introductions to the *Guide* is the equation of *maʿaseh bereshit* [the Account of the Beginning] with physics, and of *maʿaseh merkavah* [the Account of the Chariot] with metaphysics. What is revolutionary in this equation? *Maʿaseh bereshit* and *maʿaseh merkavah* reflect the most esoteric concerns of tannaitic thought—the former referring to the secrets of creation, and the latter, based on the visions of Isaiah and Ezekiel, to the supreme revelations of prophecy. Maimonides, then, at one stroke, interpreted these two terms according to the Aristotelian science that he had come to know through the Arabic translations of the Greek philosopher and through the writings of Muslim philosophers—Alfārābī, Avicenna, Ibn Bājjah, Ibn Ṭufaīl, and others.[4] To Maimonides, *maʿaseh bereshit* conveys the physical order of the material world—the laws of motion, time, meteorology, and so forth—whereas *maʿaseh merkavah* conveys the order of the heavenly world—the movement of the spheres and their movers. In this daring interpretation, Maimonides pivoted the most secret traditions of the Oral Law on the scientific laws of his time.

Furthermore, Maimonides adopted in the *Guide* (I:71) the approach that ancient Jews had displayed wondrous expertise and creativity in various sciences. When the Jewish people went into exile, Gentile nations learned these sciences from the Jews who, over the centuries, had forgotten them due to the hardships and persecutions afflicting them. With this explanation, Maimonides instantly legitimized the study of philosophy from the books of Muslim thinkers. The study of the great Muslim philosophers merely returns a lost item to its rightful owners. Maimonides tells the scholar, as it were, that learning about scientific problems from Arabic sources is, in fact, a return to the rabbis' esoteric tradition.

The acquisition of scientific knowledge as the supreme human purpose is an approach that Maimonides endorses in all his writings. This notion is already developed systematically in his Introduction to *Commentary to the Mishnah* and is the basis for the discussions in the *Guide*. Maimonides emphasized that the Torah and its commandments aim at "the welfare of the soul and the welfare of the body."[5] By "welfare of the body" he meant imparting normative and ethical foundations for the existence of the society, and by "welfare of the soul"—the acquisition of general and proper scientific knowledge. For Maimonides, then, philosophical and religious ideals coalesce. The Torah is unique because it directs us to acquire knowledge and scientific learning.[6] Scientific knowledge, however, must be acquired from scientific sources, meaning Greek science through Muslim

---

[4] Maimonides greatly respected Alfārābī, and L. V. Berman has even referred to Maimonides as Alfārābī's "disciple." Currently, several scholars have pointed to various thinkers and philosophical traditions that have contributed to the shaping of the views in the *Guide*. See, for example, chapter 5 below.

[5] *Guide*, III:27, 510.

[6] Several scholars hold that Maimonides was a skeptic and an agnostic and, therefore, preferred political pursuits to the acquisition of metaphysical knowledge, but this approach has proved controversial and is not the one accepted in Maimonidean scholarship.

mediation, not from the Torah. In the following chapters, I consider the Muslim sources of the *Guide* and, specifically, the notion of idolatry as mediation that is manifest in Maimonides' attitude to astral magic and in his conception on the immortality of the intellect.

Maimonides was aware that many in the rabbinic world did not agree with the rationalist version he upheld. Indeed, toward the end of his life, a bitter polemic had already erupted regarding his thought, which would persist long after his death.

Scientific Truth *versus* Religious Truth

For Maimonides, as noted, the authoritative scientific sources were the writings of Muslim philosophers from Alfārābī onward. What about the two centuries of Jewish philosophizing that had preceded his birth? Systematic theological and philosophical treatises had been written before the appearance of the *Guide*—Saadia Gaon's *The Book of Beliefs and Opinions*, Bahya ibn Paquda's *The Duties of the Heart*, and Solomon Ibn Gabirol's *The Fountain of Life*. Maimonides did not flinch from controversy with his predecessors, and this matter requires an understanding of his view on the contrast between scientific and religious truth.

Maimonides sharply distinguished theologians, who focus on proving religious truths at any price, from philosophers, who seek scientific objective truth. Specifically, Maimonides addressed a phenomenon widespread in the Muslim world—the Kalām. The term "Kalām"—meaning thought, speech, logic, and so forth—denotes Muslim theological schools that strove to offer the truth of Islam in rational terms. These theologians used polemical and dialectic arguments to prove that reason supports Muslim religion. Since existing sciences did not meet the aims of the Kalām supporters (known as Mutakallimūn), they created an alternative science. The natural science of the Mutakallimūn relied on elements (atomism, the existence of a vacuum), which Maimonides strongly opposed. Interestingly, modern science accepts these elements, but the dominant paradigm in Maimonides' times was Aristotelian science, which negated them. Maimonides viewed Muslim theologians—and theologians in general—as self-serving and uninterested in objective truth, concerned only with the verification of their approach at any cost.[7] He argued that they first made presumptions

---

7   *Guide*, I:71. See chapter 6 below.

and only then turned to explain the reality facing them. By contrast, true scientists observe reality as is and then approach it to determine its laws.

A question could be raised—Maimonides is, after all, a religious man and he too wishes to verify the assumptions of religion. Theologians devoted their efforts to the endorsement of approaches such as creation and divine omnipotence, which were important to Maimonides himself. Why, then, not endorse the view of the Kalām theologians? Maimonides would answer that objective truth is the supreme value and, as such, does not contradict religious existence. He did not shy away from stating that not every religious belief can be scientifically proven. Given his fearless adherence to truth, he never hesitated to criticize his forebears, pointing out mistakes by talmudic sages who had claimed that heavenly elements make sounds in their motion.[8] He also criticized a group of thinkers whom he respected as halakhists and talmudists—the geonim. Maimonides noted that, when the geonim deal with conceptual and theological matters, they adopt the arguments of Muslim theologians (Mutakallimūn). Similarly, he was critical of Karaite thinkers because some of them had endorsed the Kalām natural science.[9] He had praise only for "Andalusian" thinkers, that is, for philosophers who lived in his own surroundings. Unfortunately, we have no way of identifying who these "Andalusians" were.

Maimonides, then, recognized the existence of an objective scientific truth and thereby displayed intellectual integrity. The implication, however, is not that Maimonides blindly followed the determinations of the scientists. He held that it is definitely possible to criticize assumptions adopted by scientists when these assumptions cannot be demonstrated and are merely intuitions. Because he clung to scientific truth, Maimonides turned directly to the scientific writings of his time, which were not Jewish sources. It is thus clear why, generally, he did not relate to the Jewish philosophical tradition that had preceded him.

The present book seeks to contribute to the understanding of modes of thought adopted mostly in the writing of *The Guide of the Perplexed* and to the knowledge of its sources. The last chapter acts as a summary, presenting

---

8   Ibid., II:8. See chapter 2 below.
9   Ibid., I:71. See chapter 6 below.

Maimonides as a "philosophical theologian" according to a model of his own design.[10]

Thanks to the translator and editor of this book, Batya Stein, whose involvement was crucial to the clarification of my thinking. She is a permanent partner to my thought and my work, and I am grateful for the opportunity of enjoying her collaboration.

---

10 Chapters 1 and 6 were written originally for this volume. Previous versions of chapters 2 to 5, translated from the Hebrew by Edward Levin, the late David Louvish, and Batya Stein appeared as "Sources of Maimonides' Concept of Idolatry as Mediation," with Eliezer Schossberg, *The Annual of Rabbinic Judaism* 1 (1998): 119-128; "The Separate Intellects and Maimonides' Argumentation," in *Between Rashi and Maimonides*, ed. Ephraim Kanarfogel and Moshe Sokolow (New York: Yeshiva University Press, 2010): 59-92; "Avicenna and Maimonides on Immortality: A Comparative Study," in *Medieval and Modern Perspectives on Muslim-Jewish Relations*, ed. Ronald Nettler, 185-197 (Oxford: Harwood Academic Publishers, 1995).

Chapter 1

The Passion for Metaphysics

The present chapter focuses on *Guide of the Perplexed* I:31-35. These five chapters, though constituting a unit apart, are still part of the discussion unfolding in the *Guide* and share its literary features. Dealing mainly with an educational and didactic question, this unit is concerned with the proper approach to the study of metaphysics as manifest in four aspects:

(1) The scientific aspect: The study of metaphysics must be preceded by the study of sciences (logic, mathematics, physics, and astronomy).
(2) The methodological aspect: Proper rules of thought must be preserved, proceeding cautiously and constantly examining the arguments.
(3) The ethical aspect: All attention must be focused on the study of these sciences, keeping away from material concerns.
(4) The political aspect: The multitudes must be attended to from both a negative and a positive perspective—from a negative perspective, ensuring they do not exceed the limited boundaries of their comprehension, and from a positive one, by providing them only a minimum of metaphysical assumptions.

The chapters in this unit thus consider the implications of this approach for the education of the multitude; in many respects, the discussion in them may be viewed as shifting from study to political conduct. Ultimately, the metaphysical formulations delivered to the public outline the manner of study suited to the perfect person.

Some of the *Guide*'s commentators and scholars have suggested adding Chapters 30 and 36 to this unit, speculating that they were connected to its topics. In literary and philosophical terms, however, attaching them to Chapters 31 to 35, which have their own thematic and stylistic foundation, does not seem inherently justified.

I will argue that, in this unit, Maimonides relies mainly on the profound emotional need, the almost uncontrollable urge, to reach the summits of knowledge. When issuing his complicated instructions for acquiring knowledge, Maimonides is guided by the principle of passion for metaphysics. I will further argue that Maimonides turned the passion for metaphysics into a powerful element, political as well as theological. The conclusion of the discussion will be that this unit is one of the most concentrated expressions of Maimonidean rationalism.

Introduction

In the *Guide*, we find several questions that appear recurrently. For example, almost every analysis of a specific conception raises the issue of Maimonides' aim in writing the book. Every one of these analyses sort exposes Maimonides' attitude toward science and its connection to revelation on the one hand, and toward biblical exegesis and rabbinic sources on the other. Additional questions touch on the character of the book (an exegetical work, a philosophical one, a polemic with the Kalām), the reason for the order of its chapters, the techniques of concealment, the identification of esoteric ideas, and so forth. One issue that raises many of these questions to the surface is the proper attitude toward the study of metaphysics.

Metaphysics in the Guide of the Perplexed

The widespread term for metaphysics in the Middle Ages was *elohiyot* or *hokhmah elohit* [divine wisdom]. In many respects, the *Guide of the Perplexed* was meant to pave the way for the intellectual to acquire metaphysical knowledge. Metaphysics was clearly an esoteric realm for Maimonides, and he held that the rabbis had referred to it as *ma'aseh merkavah* [the account of the Chariot] and, in some sense, also as *sitrei Torah* [mysteries of the Torah]. In the introduction to the *Guide*, Maimonides wrote that physics too, *ma'aseh bereshit* [the account of the Beginning], is included among the esoteric bodies of knowledge but, from the outset, concealment is naturally intended for metaphysics. For medieval scholars, metaphysics comprised mainly the discussion about the separate intellects and the divine attributes. Although this was the framework that Maimonides adopted concerning the contents of metaphysics, in the chapters dealing with the *merkavah* (*Guide* III:1-7), *ma'aseh merkavah* hardly relates to the separate intellects.

To prevent misunderstandings regarding the importance of metaphysics, Maimonides opens the *Guide* with a discussion of the divine attributes—first he validates the negation of anthropomorphism in the lexicographical chapters and then deals directly with the doctrine of the attributes. The *Guide* is thus built as an inverse pyramid regarding the quality of the sciences and the extent of their concealment: it opens with the most secret issues (attributes) and considers their substantive and hermeneutical aspects, and slowly descends into more "revealed" issues, from creation and prophecy to the reasons for the commandments and the practical conduct of the perfect human. This structure is meant to clarify the importance of metaphysics. Maimonides painstakingly explained that metaphysics cannot be approached as any other body of knowledge. He notes that analytical ability does not suffice to lay the foundations for theology or metaphysics and devotes considerable efforts to the conditions and the background required for its acquisition.

Within the lexicographical chapters in Part I of the *Guide*, therefore, Maimonides embedded a unit of five chapters dealing with a quasi-educational, ethical, and pedagogical preparation for the doctrine of divine attributes. In his view, one embarking on the study of this doctrine faces a kind of paradox: the doctrine of divine attributes is, on the one hand, the apex of the sciences. Were we asked to place this doctrine within a philosophical realm, the natural choice would be metaphysics that, for Maimonides, represents the summit of scientific thought. On the other hand, this doctrine leads to the negation of the attributes. Ultimately, God cannot be described in human thought through human language. The tension in the complex discussion of negative knowledge requires the student to acquire what in modern language is called "consciousness," that is, to be cognizant of the structure and traits of the personality and adapt them to the task of learning the doctrine of the attributes. The cognitive effort per se, however, is not enough. The dialectic of affirmation and negation of the divine attributes requires restraint and caution, as shown below, and it is for this purpose that Chapters 31 to 35 were included in Part I of the *Guide*.

The location of some of the chapters units in the *Guide* is not self-evident. One example is the unit in II:2-12, which deals with the separate intellects and their connection to earthly existence, which is placed between the proofs of the existence of God based on the eternity of the world and the chapters that refute eternity and assume creation. Commentators and scholars have dealt with the location of this unit, straining to connect it to the surrounding chapters.¹ Another example is the unit of the *merkavah* chapters in *Guide* III:1-7.² The unit in I:31-35 is also found between various lexicographical chapters and could have been placed right before or after them.

The Scholarly Research

Medieval interpretation was already aware of *Guide* I:31-35 as a freestanding unit. R. Moshe Narboni, for example, argued that these chapters are a kind of allegorical and personal interpretation of the Sinai epiphany. This interpretation also influenced the commentaries on these chapters by R. Shem Tov b. Isaac ibn Shem Tov and R. Mordekhai Komtiyano.

In many classic studies from the nineteenth and the first half of the twentieth century, the question of *Guide* I:31-35 was conflated with the discussion of the divine attributes. This decision seems understandable: the unit does not belong directly to the strong rejection of anthropomorphism in the lexicographic chapters, which attracted the attention of scholars engaged in biblical exegesis and, in particular, in philosophical biblical exegesis. Nor is the unit an integral part of the divine attributes doctrine, which attracted the interest of classic scholars such as David Kaufmann, Harry Austryn Wolfson, and Julius Guttmann. Other scholars who composed monographs on Maimonides, such as Fritz Bamberger, did not relate to this unit. The interim generation, which began publishing studies in the mid-twentieth century—including Shlomo Pines, L. V. Berman, and Herbert A. Davidson—discussed these chapters only incidentally.

Over time, however, research on Maimonides has expanded and, more recently, scholars have examined aspects of the chapters in this unit. A few examples follow: Joel Kraemer discusses the relation between Maimonides'

---

1 See Dov Schwartz, "The Separate Intellects and Maimonides' Argumentation," in *Between Rashi and Maimonides*, ed. Ephraim Kanarfogel and Moshe Sokolow (New York: Yeshiva University Press, 2010), 59-62. For an extended and revised version of this study, shee Chapter 2 below.
2 See, for example, Gad Freudenthal, "Maimonides on the Scope of Metaphysics *alias Ma'aseh Merkavah*: The Evolution of His Views," in *Maimonides y suépoca* , ed. Carlos del Valle, Santiago Garcia-Jalon, and Juan Pedro Monferrer (Madrid: Sociedad Estatal de Conmemoraciones Culturales, 2007), 221-30; idem, "Four Observations on Maimonides' Four Celestial Globes (*Guide* II:9-10)," in *Maimonides: Conservatism, Originality, Revolution*, ed. Aviezer Ravitzky (Jerusalem: Zalman Shazar Center, 2008), 499-527 [Heb].

scientific method and the passion for metaphysics[3]; Sarah Stroumsa presented the Muslim model fitting the figure of Elisha ben Abuyah set forth in Chapter 32[4]; Amira Eran studied the connection between Chapters 33 and 34 and the concept of "artifice"[5]; Sara Klein-Braslavy examined key terms in the unit as part of a general discussion of the *Guide's* esoteric methodology;[6] James Diamond explored the hermeneutical and conceptual background of Elisha ben Abuyah's character in Chapter 32;[7] Menachem Kellner examined the connection between Chapters 32 and 33 and how Maimonides grappled with mysticism,[8] and Armand Maurer discussed the relationship between these chapters and the definition of metaphysics.[9]

The Theses

I will seek to analyze and interpret Chapters I:31 to I:35 as a cohesive unit, examining its structure and leitmotifs. An initial look at these chapters reveals one formal characteristic of the unit—multiple numbered and unnumbered lists. An in-depth literary analysis of the chapters reveals additional lists. Almost in every chapter, Maimonides presented lists of factors, causes, and principles. Some of the lists are revealed while others are concealed, as follows:

(1) In Chapter 31 are three factors for the limitation of human reason regarding metaphysics (concealed), four causes of dispute (revealed), and four types of harm that result from crossing the bounds of apprehension (concealed).

(2) In Chapter 32 is a partial discussion of the four who entered the *pardes* [garden or orchard] (concealed).

---

3   Joel L. Kraemer, "Maimonides on Aristotle and Scientific Method," in *Moses Maimonides and His Time*, ed. Eric L. Ormsby (Washington, DC: Catholic University of America Press, 1989).
4   Sarah Stroumsa, "Elisha ben Abuyah and Muslim Heretics in Maimonides' Writings," *Maimonidean Studies* 3 (1992-1993): 175-183.
5   Amira Eran, "'Artifice' as a Device for the Study of the Divinity in the Writings of Maimonides and Averroes," *Pe'amim* 61 (1995): 109-131 [Heb].
6   Sara Klein-Braslavy, *King Solomon and Philosophical Esotericism in the Thought of Maimonides* (Jerusalem: Magnes, 1996), Part One [Heb].
7   James A. Diamond, "The Failed Theodicy of a Rabbinic Pariah: A Maimonidean Recasting of Elisha ben Abuyah," *Jewish Studies Quarterly* 9 (2003): 353-380.
8   Menachem M. Kellner, *Maimonides' Confrontation with Mysticism* (Oxford: Littman Library, 2006).
9   Armand A. Maurer, "Maimonides and Aquinas on the Study of Metaphysics," in *A Straight Path: Studies in Medieval Philosophy and Culture— Essays in Honor of Arthur Hyman*, ed. Ruth Link-Salinger (Washington, DC: Catholic University of America Press, 1988), 206-215.

(3) In Chapter 34 are five causes that prevent beginning with the study of metaphysics (revealed).
(4) In Chapter 35 are two dogmatic lists meant for the multitude (revealed and concealed), and one list of the "mysteries of the Torah" [sitrei Torah] for intellectuals (revealed).

Chapter 33 serves as a kind of transition from the discussion of educational and didactic aspects of metaphysical apprehension per se to the political discussion, which deals with imparting minimal truths to the multitude. Chapter 33 is, therefore, a transition from directives to the intellectual in the speculative sphere (who seeks intellectual perfection) to instructions to the intellectual in the political realm (the ruler).

The relationship between the chapters of the unit also touches on substantive motifs and on the dynamics of their disclosure. The Maimonidean discussion in these chapters (which are marked by a stable formal structure, as noted) is based on a number of concealed motifs that become revealed. The motifs relate to the human psyche (desires, cognitions, and the like) on the one hand, and to the proper political leadership on the other.

Turning now to the aspect that is distinctly conceptual, I will make the following arguments about the approach to the study of metaphysics that Maimonides conveys in the chapters of the unit:

(1) The student of metaphysics confronts a series of obstacles.
(2) The greatest and most dangerous obstacle is the passion for metaphysics, that is, the uncontrollable longing for universal knowledge.
(3) Sexual desire most accurately clarifies the nature of the passion for metaphysics.
(4) The passion for metaphysics characterizes all humans, by their very nature.[10]
(5) Balancing the passion for metaphysics in broad sections of the public requires political ability.
(6) The passion for metaphysics is the most accurate expression of Maimonidean rationalism.

---

10 The passion for metaphysics is indeed stronger in the consciousness of the religious person, who longs to know God at any cost. Unlike the classic philosopher, such as Aristotle, for whom God is an element of the system, meaning the assurance of the heavenly movement, for religious individuals in the Middle Ages, God is not only an object of knowledge but the source of the revealed commandment, intensifying this passion in their existence.

(7) To illustrate the dangers of the passion for metaphysics, Maimonides presented a partial and tendentious description of the sources of talmudic mysticism.

But why does the discussion of metaphysics in this chapter of the *Guide* not revolve entirely around content and hermeneutical considerations dealing with the divine attributes and the immaterial substances? Why address issues pertaining to human nature, such as the order of study, proper education, and so forth? If we take into account that the *Guide* was written for R. Joseph b. Judah, we will understand that he was a "perplexed" individual who had threatened to be disappointed by philosophy and favor theology instead (Kalām).[11] Maimonides wrote as follows about the nature of his relationship with R. Joseph (I have split the quote into four):

(1) "Thereupon I began to let you see certain flashes and to give you certain indications [*'ishārāt*]."
(2) "Then I saw that you demanded of me additional knowledge and asked me to make clear to you certain things pertaining to divine matters [= metaphysics],"
(3) "to inform you of the intentions of the Mutakallimūn in this respect, and to let you know whether their methods were demonstrative and, if not, to what art [*ṣināʿa*] they belonged."
(4) "As I also saw, you had already acquired some smattering of this subject from people other than myself; you were perplexed, as stupefaction had come over you."[12]

The purpose of the book, as Maimonides himself attests, is to dispel speculative doubts rather than provide educational, moral, or political guidance.[13] The discussion of the educational conditions for the study of metaphysics is thus seemingly superfluous. Maimonides apparently wanted to indicate to the reader that the speculative obstacle is sometimes due to causes that are in no way speculative. We may occasionally search for errors

---

11 On the letter accompanying the *Guide*, see below, Summary.
12 See Genesis 33:13. Citations are from *Guide*, 3-4. The source is Moses Maimonides, *Epistles*, ed. David Hartwig Baneth (Jerusalem: Magnes, 1985), 8 [Heb]. See also S. Rawidowitz, "The Structure of the 'Moreh Nebuchim,'" *Tarbiz* 6, 3 (*The Maimonides Book*) (1935), 45 [Heb] (= *Likkutei Tarbiz 5V: Studies in Maimonides* [Jerusalem: Magnes, 1985]; identical pagination). I discuss this content of the accompanying letter in Chapter 6 below.
13 See below, n. 16.

in the wrong place, looking for them in the realm of learning and in the material we are grappling with, when the reasons are to be found in psychological, ethical, and political realms.

I will argue that the central reason for error in metaphysics is psychological and hinges on the passion for metaphysics. For Maimonides, then, the human psyche bears the "blame" for the error.

The following arguments relate to the unit's literary aspects:

(1) An esoteric reading of the chapters in this unit will enable us to trace the concealed motifs, which grow increasingly stronger until they are fully revealed.
(2) These chapters convey Maimonides' hermeneutical approach to the sources of talmudic mysticism.
(3) Various aspects of R. Saadia Gaon's approach are challenged throughout the unit.

These literary aspects show that the study of metaphysics is a topic incorporating characteristics of the *Guide* as a whole and involving esoteric, hermeneutical (from both Scripture and Aggadah), and polemical dimensions.

Finally, note that commentators and thinkers in late medieval Spain and Provence devoted much attention to the issue at the center of the moral and pedagogical chapters—the proper attitude to metaphysics and to the "mysteries of the Torah."[14] This concern is quite understandable given that, for this era's rationalist, the proper approach to metaphysics was a momentous question. By contrast, modern scholarship has shown less interest in this matter than in other topics in Maimonidean thought. I turn now to the discussion of this unit of chapters.

The Limits of Apprehension

The first phase of Maimonides' discussion on the proper approach to the study of metaphysics is negative: the boundaries of the human intellect are impenetrable. Such a fundamental assumption must be a leitmotif

---

14 See Dov Schwartz, *Contradiction and Concealment in Medieval Jewish Thought* (Ramat-Gan: Bar-Ilan University, 2002), 218-257 [Heb]. Maimonides prescribed a rigorous order of study beginning with logic and culminating in metaphysics (221-222). Interestingly, for R. Judah Halevi, physics, psychology, and the theory of intellect sufficed ("matter and form"; "elements"; "nature"; "soul"; "intellect"; "metaphysics in general"). See Judah Halevi, *The Kuzari*, trans. Hartwig Hirschfeld (New York: Schocken, 1964), 5:2, 249. Halevi mixed together Aristotelian sciences and the Kalām, a matter deserving separate discussion.

for any student of metaphysics, to be disregarded at one's peril. This first phase appears in Chapters 31 and 32. Maimonides chose to elucidate the principles of this phase by drawing a parallel between the cognitive and physical planes, where knowledge is compared to sensory perception. The elements of the Maimonidean discussion on the boundaries of cognition are examined below.

Hierarchy

Chapter 31 deals with hindrances to the apprehension of metaphysics. Maimonides points to three factors that he ranks by their order of importance—from the cognitive intellectual factor, through the moral factor, and up to the political one. The three factors are:

(1) Apprehension and cognition: Maimonides writes of the limits of cognition relying on an analogy to sensory perception: just as the senses are limited in their ability, so is cognition. He also points to individual differences in the human powers of apprehension:

> The identical rule obtains with regard to human intellectual apprehensions. There are great differences in capacity between the individuals of the species. ... It may thus happen that whereas one individual discovers a certain notion by himself through his speculation, another individual is not able ever to understand that notion. Even if it were explained to him for a very long time by means of every sort of expression and parable, his mind would not penetrate to it in any way, but would turn back without understanding it.[15]

Lack of awareness regarding the limits of metaphysics precludes its apprehension.

(2) Will and longing (moral): The element of passion [*shawq*], which will prove to be a leitmotif of the entire unit, enters the discussion here for the first time. Besides awareness of the limits of cognition, humans are also required to control their will, longings, and desires. Maimonides

---

15 *Guide* I:31, 65. The Judeo-Arabic original is from *Dalālat al-Ḥaʾirīn*, ed. Salomon Munk and I. Yoel (Jerusalem: Yunovits, 1931) (henceforth and throughout this book, Munk and Yoel). Maimonides used *'idrāk* in this Chapter to denote apprehension (44, ln. 8). See Shlomo Pines, "The Limitations of Human Knowledge according to Al-Fārābī, ibn Bājja, and Maimonides," in *Studies in Medieval Jewish History and Literature*, vol. 2, ed. Isadore Twersky (Cambridge, MA: Harvard University Press, 1979), 100-104.

assumed that, by nature, humans are endowed with a passion for apprehension. Though not all topics are the object of such passion, metaphysical ones are certainly part of it: "On the other hand, there are things for the apprehension of which man will find that he has a great longing.[16] The sway of the intellect endeavoring to seek for, and to investigate, their true reality exists at every time and in every group of men engaged in speculation."[17] Longing interferes with metaphysical apprehension because zest leads to carelessness and to the omission of the distinction between proven, plausible, and erroneous assumptions.[18]

(3) Controversy (political and social): The longing for metaphysics leads to disputes.

> With regard to such things there is a multiplicity of opinions, disagreement arises between the men engaged in speculation, and doubts crop up; all this because the intellect is attached to an apprehension of these things, I mean to say because of its longing [*shawq*] for them; and also because everyone thinks that he has found a way by means of which he will know the true reality of the matter.[19]

---

16 "... *shawkahu 'ila 'idrākihā 'azīma*" (Munk and Yoel, 44, ln. 18). Al-Ghazālī mentions that apprehension (*'idrāk*) is the motive for love, and therefore precedes it. See the analysis of Binyamin Abrahamov, *Divine Love in Islamic Mysticism: The Teachings of al-Ghazālī and al-Dabbāgh* (London: Routledge Curzon, 2003), 44. On the possible influence of al-Ghazālī on Maimonides on this issue, see Steven Harvey, "The Meaning of Terms Designating Love in Judeo-Arabic Thought and Some Remarks on the Judeo-Arabic Interpretation of Maimonides," in *Judaeo-Arabic Studies: Proceedings of the Founding Conference of the Society for Jewish-Arabic Studies [Chicago, May 1984]*, ed. Norman Golb (Amsterdam: Harwood Academic Publishers, 1997), 188. Unlike al-Ghazālī, Maimonides discussed love or longing as preceding apprehension rather than ensuing from it.

17 *Guide* I:31, 66. In Chapter 34 (beginning of the third cause, 73-74), Maimonides lists the "things" that a person desires to know. See below.

18 In the "Epistle Dedicatory" at the opening of the *Guide*, Maimonides mentioned that R. Joseph had a "strong desire" (ḥirs) and a "powerful longing" (ishtiyāq) for speculative matters and a "longing" (*shawq*) for mathematics (*Epistles*, ed. Baneth, 7-8; *Guide*, 3). Maimonides, however, mentions that R. Joseph had channeled his longing in positive ways. He further writes that he had studied with R. Joseph "the science of astronomy," and before that, "the art of logic." R. Joseph, then, did not apply his longing to metaphysics but channeled it solely to the preliminary sciences. Maimonides therefore held that R. Joseph was capable of learning "the secrets of the prophetic books" (i.e., metaphysics), and, to some degree, physics as well. Already in the "Epistle Dedicatory," then, Maimonides had clearly hinted at the centrality of passion.

19 *Guide* I:31, 66.

In this context, Maimonides cites the causes of disagreement set forth by Alexander of Aphrodisias—(1) the inclination to dominate; (2) the complexity of the object of apprehension, and (3) the limitations of the one apprehending,[20]—to which he added a fourth cause of his own, habit.

The issue of disagreement requires some clarification. Pines argued in his classic essay on the sources of the *Guide* that Maimonides "contrasts his own times, which he seems to have held to be dominated by superstition ... with Greek antiquity, in which the philosophers who aspired to know the true nature of things did not have to struggle against the dead hand of traditional belief."[21] Pines introduced the element of religion into the discussion. Summarizing Alexander of Aphrodisias, Berman writes "that there were times in which people, due to their education, were not accustomed to things that contradict philosophical speculation."[22] Maimonides mentions the division into "desert" and urban centers ("towns"). Life in the desert is primitive ("the disorderliness of their life, the lack of pleasures, and the scarcity of food"), resulting in prejudices and superstition. He adds that such a reality is characteristic of his own time and contrasts with the ancient world, where Alexander of Aphrodisias had lived. "However, in our times there is a fourth cause that he did not mention because it did not exist among them."[23] Did Maimonides really seek to distinguish the Hellenistic from the Islamic period as regards their social culture? I hold that he meant to contrast the life of Jews in antiquity with their lives in exile. Maimonides, then, compared rabbinic activity in the Hellenistic world with his own time, meaning the time of Alexander of Aphrodisias (parallel to the late tannaitic period) with the twelfth century, when the Jewish people are in exile and the social and geographic structure of the Gentile surroundings influence Jewish society. This is the situation he is identifying when stating that "man is blind to the apprehension of the true realities and inclines toward the things to which he is habituated."[24] His frame of reference is

---

20 Here too, Maimonides uses the terminology of love: the first cause of the disagreement is "love [ḥubb] of domination and love of strife" (*Guide*, 66; Munk and Yoel, 44, ln. 30).
21 *Guide*, "Translator's Introduction," lxviii.
22 Lawrence V. Berman, *Ibn Bājjah and Maimonides* (PhD diss.: Hebrew University of Jerusalem, 1959), 108 [Heb]. See also Abraham Melamed, *On the Shoulders of Giants: The Debate between Moderns and Ancients in Medieval and Renaissance Jewish Thought* (Ramat-Gan: Bar-Ilan University, 2003), 97-98 [Heb].
23 *Guide* I:31, 67.
24 Ibid.

indeed the Jewish people and, indirectly, he enters into a discussion of the "decline of the generations" concept.[25]

Disagreement as a factor hindering metaphysical apprehension is undoubtedly a consequence of the passion for metaphysics. Maimonides explicitly states that the multiplicity of opinions and the disagreements follow from the strong desire to engage in metaphysics.[26] Here too, Maimonides created a ranking: "The things about which there is this perplexity are very numerous in divine matters [metaphysics], few in matters pertaining to natural science, and nonexistent in matters pertaining to mathematics."[27] Maimonides, then, was aware of human curiosity. The human urge to know is the cause of disagreements in almost every realm (except for the quantitative sciences, such as mathematics, geometry, and stereometry). Metaphysical curiosity, however, is exceptional because its intensity, together with the impossibility of adducing absolute proof for some or most of its arguments, lead to disagreements. Maimonides perhaps wanted to hint that the mixture of science and experiential religious interest is liable to be extremely dangerous. The lure of metaphysics has its basis in the religious personality; Maimonides occasionally referred to *al-Rabbānīn*,[28] and was critical of philosophical and theological approaches raised by Jewish thinkers who had preceded him.[29] Several times, however, Maimonides found the passion for metaphysics to be characteristic of humans as such rather than of religious individuals.

The mainstay of the ranking created by Maimonides, then, is the passion for the metaphysical. When discussing the immortality of the intellect, he introduced animated and emotional concepts into abstract speculative apprehension.[30] Maimonides continued this direction with the implicit argument that this longing is bound up with apprehension to such an extent that they can no longer be separated. Internalizing the limits of apprehension suggests awareness and control of this passion. Maimonides knew that, by slipping into the moral and educational sphere, he differed from Aristotelian philosophy, which had hardly devoted attention to personality

---

25 See Menachem M. Kellner, *Maimonides on the "Decline of the Generations" and the Nature of Rabbinic Authority* (Albany, NY: SUNY Press, 1996).
26 See the passage cited in n. 19, above.
27 *Guide* I:31, 66.
28 *al-Rabbānīn*. See *Guide*, Introduction (Munk and Yoel, 5, ln. 27); 3:43 (Munk and Yoel, 420, ln. 16). See also below.
29 See Dov Schwartz, "The Figure of Judah Halevi as Emerging from Maimonides' *Guide* I:71," *Daat* 61 (2007): 23-40 [Heb].
30 I am referring to *ladhdha*. See Chapter 5 below.

and to psychological preparation for the study of metaphysics, and certainly did not view it as a critical principle. Maimonides, therefore, summed up Chapter 31 with a declaration:

> Do not think that what we have said with regard to the insufficiency of the human intellect and its having a limit at which it stops is a statement made in order to conform to Law. For it is something that has already been said and truly grasped by the philosophers without their having concern for a particular doctrine or opinion. And it is a true thing that cannot be doubted except by an individual ignorant of what has already been demonstrated.[31]

Maimonides admitted that the limitation of apprehension is perceived as a "natural" characteristic of the *sharī'a*,[32] which Ibn Tibbon and al-Harizi translate as "Torah," and Pines as "Law." The religious approach emphasizes God's exaltation and transcendence, and also supports a moral and educational method for apprehending it. Maimonides, however, felt it necessary to add that philosophers also support the limitations of apprehension.

R. Shem Tov b. Joseph Ibn Falaquera continued in the course charted by Maimonides and, as usual in his interpretation of the *Guide*, sought support for the limitation of metaphysical apprehension in Aristotle's writings. Falaquera wrote:

> Aristotle said: Many times we believe the opposite of the truth in metaphysics [literally, divine things] because we were raised hearing it and have been accustomed to justify it. For on a thing that we had been accustomed to hear during childhood, we shall think differently from what we had not been accustomed to hear, it being distant and unknown. We will be able to learn the extent of the impression of habit and education on our believing something or its opposite when studying the laws, for you will find in them riddles or things close to deceits, but because we are accustomed to them, doubt will not cross our hearts, and this is one of the reasons that truth is hidden from people.[33]

Aristotle considered how the influence of what is said depends on the listener's conduct (ἔθη) and habits (εἰώθαμεν).[34] In other words, he related

---

31 *Guide* I:31, 67.
32 Munk and Yoel, 45, ln. 18. See, for example, Joel Kraemer, "*Sharī'a* and *Nomos* in the Philosophical Thought of Maimonides," *Te'uda: Studies in Judaica*, 6 (1986): 183-202 [Heb].
33 Shem Tov b. Joseph Ibn Falaquera, *Moreh ha-Moreh*, ed. Yair Shiffman (Jerusalem: World Union of Jewish Studies, 2001), 131, lns. 8-14 [Heb].
34 Aristotle, *The Metaphysics*, trans. Hugh Tredennick, II, 3, 995a (Cambridge, MA: Harvard University Press, 1947), 94-95.

to preconceptions and, particularly, to the willingness of individuals to internalize information in accordance with their nature. Aristotle clarified that some are impressed by mathematical precision and others by a poetic style. He distinguished between the methods of the natural sciences, such as physics, and the study of immaterial substances (μὴ ἔχουσιν ὕλην). These statements follow a discussion of the four causes (material, formal, efficient, final), in time and in infinity. In the late medieval discourse, nonmaterial entities became "divine things." Thinkers active in the religious world, then—in this case, Falaquera in the name of Averroes—incorporated metaphysics into the discussion on the limits of apprehension.

Aristotle did not intentionally ascribe passion to metaphysical matters. This factor took on additional significance mainly in the religious world even though, in Maimonides view, this passion was not necessarily religious but typical of humans as such, as shown below. In any event, Maimonides interpreted Aristotle as conveying far-reaching support for the risk or, alternatively, for the caution required when studying metaphysics. He implied that religious laws are the first and immediate step in a suitable preparation for metaphysics and that philosophers also advocate the need for such preparation, namely, educational and ethical preparation. The passion for metaphysics thus reemerges as a built-in component of the religious philosopher's existence.

Harm

Maimonides painstakingly emphasized the harm resulting from the improper study of metaphysics and exceeding the boundaries of apprehension. This emphasis directly reflects the danger he ascribed to the passion for metaphysics. Two topics show the harm of uncontrolled passion: the theory of the intellect, and the dichotomy of error.

First, the theory of the intellect. Occasionally, Maimonides drew a parallel between the soul and the intellect on the one hand, and the body and matter on the other. In his Introduction to Tractate Avot, he fashions a detailed parallel between healing the soul and healing the body. In Chapter 31, Maimonides used this parallel to clarify the limits of cognition, and in Chapter 32—to explore the harm that ensues from attempts to cross these boundaries. Not only is this effort unsuccessful but it is also harmful to one making the attempt. Maimonides illustrates this through the sense of sight—if we attempt to see beyond our ability, we harm our ability to see generally. He summed up:

> A similar discovery is made by everyone engaging in the speculative study of some science [*'ilm mā*] with respect to his state of reflection [*al-tafakkur*]. For if he applies himself to reflection and sets himself a task demanding his entire attention, he becomes dull and does not then understand even that which is within his scope to understand. For the condition of all bodily faculties [*al-quwa al-badaniyya kullahā*] is, in this respect, one and the same.[35]

According to this passage, the intellect is included in the definition of "bodily faculties." Maimonides did not hold that the material intellect is a force in the body. The material intellect is obviously connected, in a way that remained controversial, to some physical faculty (imagination, the soul as a whole, and the like). The intellect per se, however, is a potential, and is therefore described in philosophical terminology as "intellect *in potentia*" or "hylic intellect." But as soon as the intellect has acted, through the thought process, to transform the imagined forms into intellectual forms (intelligibles), it is certainly not a physical faculty. At times, the material intellect is said to be a "faculty,"[36] and at times it is juxtaposed to "matter" or "body."[37] The connection of the material intellect to the physical faculties was usually defined as "connection of existence," but not as "connection of admixture," precisely because the material intellect is not mixed with the soul's material faculties. Scholars dealing with the theory of the intellect explained that it is not a "material faculty" or a physical faculty.

In the passage cited, Maimonides explicitly referred to those "engaging in speculative study." He attempted to temper the problematic of including thought among the physical faculties by using the term *fikra* that usually

---

35 *Guide* I:32, 68. For parallels in Maimonides' writings, see Herbert A. Davidson, *Moses Maimonides: The Man and His Works* (Oxford: Oxford University Press, 2005), 343-344.

36 In both the senses of psychological faculty and potential. In his *Short Commentary* on *De Anima*, Averroes calls the potential of the hylic intellect "the faculty within him" (Moses of Narbonne, *Ma'amar bi-Shlemut ha-Nefesh (Treatise on the Perfection of the Soul)*, ed. Alfred L. Ivry [Jerusalem: Israel Academy of Sciences and Humanities, 1977], 120, ln. 12 [Heb]). Maimonides himself did not endorse an unequivocal stance on the identification of the material intellect. Moshe Narboni, for example, argued that his approach was that the intellect is a disposition (*Ma'amar bi-Shelemut ha-Nefesh*, 123, lns. 226-227). See below, Appendix B.

37 In Averroes' formulation. See, for example, Gitit Holzman, *The Theory of the Intellect and Soul in the Thought of Rabbi Moshe Narboni Based on His Commentaries on the Writings of Ibn Rushd, Ibn Tufayl, Ibn Bājja and al-Ghazālī* (PhD diss.: Hebrew University of Jerusalem, 1996), 45 [Heb].

denotes the capability of the practical intellect.[38] The context, however, is unmistakable: Maimonides referred to the acquisition of speculative knowledge ("some science"), but nevertheless included the intellect among the "bodily faculties." It is on these grounds, I hold, that he ended the Chapter with an outright declaration: "Do not criticize the terms applied to the intellect in this chapter and others. For the purpose here is to guide toward the intended notion and not to investigate the truth of the essence of the intellect; for other chapters are devoted to a precise account of this subject."[39] Maimonides' inclusion of the intellect among the "bodily faculties" was thus intentional.[40] This is one of the places in the *Guide* where Maimonides explicitly makes a declaration about the literary style of the work: an educational message at the expense of philosophical precision. The discerning reader who understands what is "the truth of the essence of the intellect," knows this to be imprecise. The ordinary reader, by contrast, will perceive a real danger here and grasp, through the illustration from the

---

38 See Abraham Nuriel, *Concealed and Revealed in Medieval Philosophy* (Jerusalem: Magnes, 2000), 144 [Heb]. Falaquera emphasized this approach when he wrote: "It seems to me that he is referring to the thinking power, which is prone to weakness" (*Moreh ha-Moreh*, ed. Shiffman, 132, ln. 13). Falaquera apparently referred to *cogitatio*, which is the judgment that the practical intellect applies to the imagination. Averroes wrote: "The movement of the imaginative faculty will increase during sleep, since it is released from the connection to the cognition and leaves its dominion" (*Kitzur Sefer ha-Hush ve-ha-Muhash le-Ibn Rushd* (*Averrois Cordubensis: Compendia Librorum Aristotelis qui Parva Naturalia vocantur*), ed. Henricus (Zevi) Blumberg [Cambridge, MA: Mediaeval Academy of America, 1954], 46, lns. 6-7 [Hebrew]).

39 *Guide* I:32, 70. Nowhere in his writings does Maimonides actually devote a methodical discussion to the concept of the material intellect, and he refers to it only incidentally.

40 Nevertheless, fourteenth- and fifteenth-century commentators base this Maimonidean statement on the parallel between sensory and intellectual perception. According to Efodi, Asher Crescas, and Shem Tov b. Joseph, at the stage of the intellect's realization—*intellect in habitu*—its apprehension, unlike that of the senses, is not limited. Thus, for example, Efodi wrote: "'Do not criticize the terms applied to the intellect, and so forth'—this means that when I said that the human intellect has a limit, do not think that I am referring to the *intellect in habitu*, for the acquired intelligible has no limit. Rather, I mention it because the disposition for acquiring intelligibles undoubtedly has a limit, but not the intellect as such" (*Sefer Moreh Nevukhim im Mefarshim* [Guide of the Perplexed with Commentators] [Jerusalem: offset, 1960], 51b). See also R. Isaac b. Shem Tov, *Lehem ha-Panim*, MS. London 912, 139b. Commentators ascribed to Maimonides the possibility of metaphysical knowledge, an issue that has been discussed at length. See, for example, Pines, "The Limitations of Human Knowledge"; Herbert A. Davidson, "Maimonides on Metaphysical Knowledge," *Maimonidean Studies* 3 (1992/1993): 49-103. Maimonides' primary intent was seemingly to define the potential intellect and not necessarily the parallel he indicated.

bodily realm, that the passion for metaphysics comes with a price and that it inflicts severe harm.

In sum: when reaching the beginning of Chapter 34, the reader faces four aspects of this insatiable longing and the harms it causes, as follows:

(1) The cognitive aspect: the attempt to attain metaphysical apprehensions harms the person's existing cognitive ability.
(2) The volitional-animative aspect: a passion that is not consummated will eventually harm the one who longs.
(3) The bodily aspect: using a sense (such as sight) for something that cannot be apprehended harms the sense itself (a parable for the cognitive aspect).
(4) The social aspect: an erroneous assessment of the cognitive ability will ultimately lead to disagreement.

Besides the ranking of factors that limit the intellect, then, Maimonides implicitly set a ranking of harms. These harms extend to all realms of human activity. The physical aspect, as noted, served Maimonides as a parable for the cognitive one. The result is a long list of harms caused by the will to exceed the limits of apprehension.

The Mysteries of the Rabbis: (1) Success vs. Failure

I turn now to the error dichotomy. The talmudic texts dealing with *ma'aseh merkavah* are the main basis for the Maimonidean discussions on the study of metaphysics. Beginning with Chapter 32, these texts are an authoritative source of information on the risks and harms confronting the student of metaphysics. In many respects, the passion for metaphysics can be seen as a hermeneutical key for talmudic esotericism.

In Chapter 32, Maimonides turned to the tradition of the four who entered the *pardes*,[41] which he explains in relation to the harm of studying metaphysics without the proper preparation.[42] This tradition points

---
41 Tosefta Hagigah 2:3; PT Hagigah 2:1, 77b; BT Hagigah 14b, and more.
42 I will offer only a brief comment on a matter that I will not be expanding upon here. Maimonides presented the narrative of the four who entered *pardes* in the sequence of Chapters dealing with the preparation for metaphysics, and R. Akiva is depicted as someone who had studied metaphysics ("divine matters") and succeeded in this endeavor. In *Guide* II:30 (353), however, Maimonides implies that R. Akiva had dealt only with meteorology, not with the world of the spheres, and definitely not with the separate intellects.

to degrees of harm: Ben Azzai gazed and died, Ben Zoma gazed and was stricken,[43] and Elisha ben Abuyah became an apostate. Maimonides, by contrast, disregarded the "ranking" of the mistaken and of the harms, choosing instead to offer a dichotomy: Rabbi Akiva, who entered unscathed and emerged unscathed, is contrasted with Elisha ben Abuyah, who lost his faith.[44] We may assume that Maimonides, who related to the conceptual statements of the geonim as an independent philosophical school,[45] was familiar with at least some of their discussions on the standing and the punishment of Ben Azzai and Ben Zoma. R. Hai Gaon, for example, wrote:

> Regarding what they taught, that Ben Azzai gazed and died, it was because his time to leave the world had come. Regarding what they taught, that Ben Zoma gazed and was stricken, they meant by "stricken" [*nifga*] that he became deranged by the distressing sights that his mind could not bear, resembling the Psalm against plagues [*pega'im*], "dwells in the secret place of the most High..."[46] This is [the meaning of] what they taught: Once, R. Joshua ben Hananiah stood on a step on the Temple Mount. Ben Zoma saw him but did not stand up before him. He [R. Joshua] said to him, "From where and to where Ben Zoma?" At the end of the mishnah [here, Tosefta], R. Joshua said to his students: "Ben Zoma is already outside,"[47] that is, he has gone out of his mind.[48]

According to the gaon, the harm had focused on Ben Zoma's "mind." In *The Kuzari*, R. Judah Halevi also comments on this ranking of Ben Azzai

---

On R. Akiva's apprehension in Maimonides' discussion of creation, see, e.g., Sara Klein-Braslavy, *Maimonides' Interpretation of the Story of Creation* (Jerusalem: Rubin Mass, 1987), 163-164 [Heb]; Y. Tzvi Langermann, "'The Making of the Firmament': R. Hayyim Israeli, R. Isaac Israeli and Maimonides," in *Shlomo Pines Jubilee Volume on the Occasion of His Eightieth Birthday*, vol. 1, ed. Moshe Idel, Warren Zev Harvey, and Eliezer Schweid (Jerusalem: Hebrew University, 1990), 473-475 [Heb]; Aviezer Ravitzky, "Aristotle's 'Meteorology' and the Maimonidean Modes of Interpreting the Account of Creation." *Aleph* 8 (2008): 361-400. This tension could project onto the nature of Maimonidean esotericism concerning the possibility of acquiring metaphysical knowledge. See above, n. 40.

43 In the parable of the palace (*Guide* III:51, 618-619), Maimonides referred to the status of Ben Zoma as one of those who "is still outside." That is, Ben Zoma had not mastered physics, but only the mathematical sciences. We can thereby understand Ben Zoma's error: he had attempted to study metaphysics without knowledge of physics.
44 See Kellner, *Maimonides' Confrontation with Mysticism*, 55-56.
45 *Guide* I:71.
46 Psalms 91:10; PT Eruvin 10:11, 26c; BT Shevuot 15b.
47 Tosefta Hagigah 2:2; BT Hagigah 15a.
48 B. M. Lewin, *Otzar ha-Geonim: Thesaurus of the Gaonic Responsa and Commentaries*, vol. 4, *Chagiga* (Jerusalem: Hebrew University Press Association, 1984), 14-15 [Heb]. On the spiritual decline of Ben Azzai and Ben Zoma, see Yehuda Liebes, *The Sin of Elisha* (Jerusalem: Hebrew University, 1986), chs. 7 and 8 [Heb].

and Ben Zoma. He avoided precise identification of the two by name, not only because of the differences between versions but also to clarify that there is a ranking here. He writes: "The one who died [Ben Azzai] was unable to bear the glance of the higher world, and his body collapsed. The second [Ben Zoma] lost his mind and whispered divine frenzy without benefiting mankind."[49] That is, the hierarchy of error and harm from Ben Azzai to Elisha ben Abuyah became a tradition. R. Abraham ibn Daud twice mentions the four sages who entered the *pardes*.[50] Maimonides presented this dichotomy in the style of a personal address, preaching to the reader:

> For if you stay your progress because of a dubious point; if you do not deceive yourself into believing that there is a demonstration with regard to matters that have not been demonstrated; if you do not hasten to reject and categorically to pronounce false any assertions whose contradictories have not been demonstrated; if, finally, you do not aspire to apprehend ['*idrāk*] that which you are unable to apprehend—you will have achieved human perfection and attained the rank of Rabbi Aqiba, peace be on him. ... If, on the other hand, you aspire to apprehend things that are beyond your apprehension; or if you hasten to pronounce false, assertions the contradictories of which have not been demonstrated or that are possible, though very remotely so—you will have joined Elisha Aher. That is, you will not only not be perfect, but will be the most deficient among the deficient; and it shall so fall out that you will be overcome by imaginings [*al-khiyālāt*] and by an inclination toward things defective, evil, and wicked—this resulting from the intellect's being preoccupied and its light's being extinguished. ... In this regard it is said: "Hast thou found honey? Eat so much as is sufficient for thee, lest thou be filled therewith and vomit it" [Proverbs 25:16]. In a similar way, the sages, may their memory be blessed, used this verse as a parable that they applied to Elisha Aher. How marvellous is this parable.[51]

Maimonides did not want to accept even "partial" or less serious harm. Therefore, he excluded Ben Azzai and Ben Zoma from his discussion and rejected ranking the gravity of their errors. For him, anyone who intends to engage in metaphysics without the proper preparation must take into account the possibility of the worst scenario, symbolized in the figure of Elisha ben

---

49 Halevi, *The Kuzari* 3:65, 190. See Diana Lobel, *Between Mysticism and Philosophy: Sufi Language of Religious Experience in Judah Ha-Levi's* Kuzari (Albany, NY: SUNY Press, 2000), 117-118.

50 Abraham ibn Daud, *Das Buch Emunah Ramah, oder Der Erhabene Glaube*, trans. Simson Weil (Frankfurt am Main: Druck, 1852), 2, 75.

51 *Guide* I:32, 68-69.

Abuyah.[52] Stroumsa has already clarified that Maimonides presented a singular interpretation of Elisha. She maintained that Maimonides "updated" the information on his character, and made it current in two respects: its connection to the conception of the eternity of the world,[53] and its affinity with heretics in the Islamic world, such as Ibn al-Rāwandī and al-Rāzī.[54] Maimonides feared the passion for metaphysics to the point of ignoring degrees of error and harm. The threat was the most severe form of heresy and the greatest harm was exclusion from the community of believers and the loss of immortality. The arresting fact is that Maimonides excluded Ben Azzai and Ben Zoma from the ranking, but his interpreters struggled to restore them.[55] Maimonides notes in his description the hierarchy of errors and harms as it comes forth in Elisha ben Abuyah's figure:

(1) The cognitive aspect: "you aspire to apprehend things that are beyond your apprehension; or if you hasten to pronounce false, assertions the contradictories of which have not been demonstrated or that are possible, though very remotely so."
(2) The volitional-animative aspect: "and it shall so fall out that you will be overcome by imaginings and by an inclination toward things defective, evil, and wicked."

---

52 See Diamond, "Failed Theodicy."
53 See Stroumsa, "Elisha ben Abuyah."
54 Ibid., 183-193.
55 For instance, see the commentaries of R. Moshe Narboni and of R. Mordekhai Komtiyano, who paraphrased R. Moshe Narboni. Both related to *Guide* I:31 and adapted the story of the four who entered the *pardes* to the four causes of disagreement. In his commentary on the *Guide*, Komtiyano wrote: "The rabbis alluded to this when they said: 'Four entered the *pardes*.' Elisha ben Abuyah was among those who love power and command, and thought that a demonstration existed for something that precludes such a demonstration by its very nature. 'He gazed and died' hints at the limitations of the one apprehending. 'He gazed and was stricken' hints at habit and custom, for there is no greater harm than this given that anyone left [alone] with his intellect, would know this properly. And if we were to consider his habits, we would [see] they prevent him, placing a veil, as it were, that precludes knowledge of the truth. R. Akiva, may he rest in peace, entered unscathed and emerged unscathed, and did not pronounce false assertions the contradictories of which have not been demonstrated" (MS. Cambridge, Trinity College F 12 36, fol. 15a). On the commentary by Komtiyano, see Dov Schwartz, "Understanding in Context: R. Mordekhai Komitiyano's Commentary on the *Guide of the Perplexed*," *Pe'amim* 133-134 (2013): 127-183 [Heb]. See also Dov Schwartz and Esti Eisenmann, *Commentary on Guide of the Perplexed: The Commentary of R. Mordekhai ben Eliezer Komtiyano on Maimonides' Guide of the Perplexed* (Ramat-Gan: Bar-Ilan University Press, 2016).

(3) The bodily aspect: "Hast thou found honey? Eat as much as is sufficient for thee, lest thou be filled therewith and vomit it" (parable).
(4) The social aspect: Maimonides does not mention this aspect here, and probably relied on the knowledge of the discerning reader concerning Elisha's bad influence on youth, a tradition presented in the same talmudic source.[56]

Elisha ben Abuyah is thus the classic model of one who sought to cross the boundaries of apprehension and suffered the greatest harm. Maimonides, as noted, chose to ignore "partial" damages. He presented, on the one hand, R. Akiva, who followed the proper instructions for studying metaphysics and successfully overcame the threatening hurdle and, on the other, Elisha ben Abuyah, who broke the rules and deteriorated into the worst of all.

The Mysteries of the Rabbis: (2) A Hidden Controversy

Maimonides continued to explore the esoteric traditions of Tractate Hagigah in order to clarify the harm of exceeding the limits of apprehension. He relied on the mishnah: "It were better for whoever gives his mind to four things if he had not come into the world: what is above? what is beneath? what was before? and what will be hereafter?"[57] An interesting comparison is that between Maimonides' interpretation and that of R. Saadia Gaon, to whom Maimonides refers a few times in his writings, albeit without mentioning his name. Generally, these references are critical. In the introduction to *The Book of Beliefs and Opinions*, Saadia approached this mishnah as potentially supporting the claim that intellectual inquiry is dangerous. In Saadia's view, the argument that one who engages in such inquiry will end up without faith relies on this rabbinic teaching. Saadia, therefore, maintains that a proper inquiry, rather than beginning from a freely chosen starting point, should be solely grounded in the words of the prophets.[58] For Maimonides, this claim is further evidence that Saadia followed the Kalām method, that is, his knowledge has an ulterior interest—the verification of religion. By contrast, Maimonides replaced the directive about the prophets' words with the orderly study of the sciences. Howard Kreisel accordingly wrote:

---

56 See BT Hagigah 15a-b.
57 M. Hagigah 2:1; Tosefta Hagigah 2:7; PT Hagigah 2:1, 76d; BT Hagigah 16a.
58 Saadia Gaon, *The Book of Beliefs and Opinions*, trans. Samuel Rosenblatt (New Haven, CT: Yale University Press, 1948), 18.

> Maimonides, heavily influenced by the Aristotelian philosophic tradition, sees in medieval Aristotelian metaphysics and natural science the requisite knowledge for attaining true love of God. R. Seʿadyah who borrows heavily from the theology of the Kalam, agrees with the Aristotelian philosophical position in regard to the unity of God, but not the structure of the world. Nor does he mention knowledge of the structure of the world as a necessary condition for attaining love of God.[59]

Saadia and Maimonides, then, agree that this mishnah points to the danger of crossing the boundaries of apprehension or that apprehension leads to heresy. Ultimately, however, Saadia did legitimize the inquiry into these four matters, insofar as it relies on revelation. In his understanding, the rabbis had warned against an inquiry that is not guided by prophetic teachings. Maimonides, however, holds that there are fields in metaphysics that human knowledge cannot reach at all, such as the depiction of God with essential and positive attributes. In his understanding, therefore, the warning of the rabbis is absolute. Maimonides could be implying in concealed ways a critique of Saadia's tendentious method, which is incompatible with Maimonidean rationalism. For Maimonides, the basic assumptions are not found in books of prophecy but in books of science.

The Primary Impulse

Maimonides' concern about unrestrained forms of study extended not only to method and fields of knowledge but also to disregard of the proper order. People are eager to begin immediately with the study of metaphysics, without first learning the preliminary sciences. Maimonides devoted two chapters (33 and 34) to cool the ardor for metaphysics and, in Chapter 33, he indeed explained that metaphysics should not be the opening subject. As shown below, however, he went beyond the negative statement and traced the proper course that study should take.

The Literary Structure

In Chapters 31 and 32, Maimonides deals with the limits of cognition. The sole practical educational instruction in these chapters is to grapple

---

59 Howard Kreisel, "The Love and Fear of God," in *Maimonides' Political Thought: Studies in Ethics, Law, and the Human Ideal* (Albany: SUNY Press, 1999), 232.

with the longing to cross these limits and overcome it. Chapters 33 to 35 determine that metaphysics is not to be studied without the order of sciences that precede it. What, then, is the relationship between Chapters 33 to 35 and Chapters 31 and 32? Two answers are possible. One is that Chapters 33 to 35 add information about the proper way of engaging in metaphysics. This answer expresses the exoteric level and suggests that the literary structure conceals no other messages. The other answer is that Chapters 33 to 35 detail the message of Chapters 31 and 32, redefining it more precisely. At times, Maimonides presents a general outline in a specific chapter of the *Guide*, followed by a more detailed discussion in later chapters that may lead to results slightly different from the general outline. One example is the discussion of providence in *Guide* III:17, where Maimonides expressed the general opinion that providence applies solely to humans as humans. In a detailed discussion in Chapter 18, he concludes that providence is determined according to the measure of knowledge a person acquires—the greater the knowledge, the greater the providence. Commentators and scholars have already explored the meaning of this "turnabout" and have pointed out that, contrary to the initial impression, the detailing is also the precision (III:17).

Regarding the attitude toward metaphysics as well, Maimonides presented in the first two chapters (31 and 32) a general statement on the boundaries of cognition and the harm to the one seeking to cross them. In Chapters 33-35, Maimonides explained a series of important specific matters deriving from the boundaries of cognition, which define in precise terms the harm resulting from their crossing, as follows:

(1) Harm occurs when the order of study is not maintained. Driven by their passion for it, people begin to study metaphysics and are consequently harmed.
(2) The multitude is, in any event, incapable of engaging in metaphysics and the order of study is therefore not relevant to it.
(3) The multitude does long for metaphysics, however, and should be the object of a special dogmatic "metaphysical" education.
(4) The individual may engage in metaphysics according to the study method set forth by Maimonides.

The central emphasis in these matters is political. Maimonides, then, made the political consideration accompanying the study of metaphysics essential. If Chapters 33 to 35 do indeed define Chapters 31 and 32 more precisely, quite a radical conclusion emerges, suited to the political dimension of Maimonidean esotericism. According to this alternative, the limits of apprehension set in Chapter 31 had not related primarily to the multitude, to begin with. Only a simple person would think of engaging in metaphysics without the foundation of the sciences. As shown below, engaging with politics is among the requirements of intellectual perfection. Maimonides consequently dealt at length with the attempt to prevent beginning one's studies with metaphysics, even though this emphasis applied mainly to the education of the multitude. According to the literary structure that I proposed, however, the warning against crossing the boundary was meant, from the outset, to distance the multitudes from the peak of the sciences. Maimonides' concealment move is the following:

(1) Chapter 31 is actually concerned with the multitude.
(2) Chapters 33 to 35 also deal mainly with the multitude, in the following structure:
   (i) Chapter 33: Opposition to begin with the study of metaphysics: (a) for the sage ("the headings of chapters may be transmitted to him")[60] and for the multitude ("the Torah speaks in the language of men").[61]
   (ii) Chapter 34: Opposition to begin with the study of metaphysics: (b) for the multitude.
   (iii) Chapter 35: the beliefs suitable for the multitude, such as the negation of anthropomorphism.
(3) Chapter 32 deals with the intellectual (R. Akiva and Elisha ben Abuyah).

On this basis, we can surmise Maimonides' technique of concealment. Chapter 32 is meant to obscure the central standing of the political factor in this unit of chapters. The man of the multitude is threatened by a presentation of the engagement with metaphysics as both a crossing of borders and a failure to preserve the order of the sciences. The central message of this unit addresses the need to regulate and balance the multitude driven by the passion for metaphysics. The perfect man, then, rules the masses in the following manner:

---

60 BT Hagigah 13a.
61 For example, BT Yevamot 71a; cited by Maimonides, *Guide* I:26, 56.

(1) He sets boundaries to prevent them from engaging in metaphysics.
(2) He is aware of their passion for metaphysics.
(3) He sets before them a minimum of metaphysical truths (such as the negation of anthropomorphism) that provide a release for their passion.

In his statements and directives, Maimonides addressed both the intellectual and the man of the multitude. Covertly, these messages are intended for the intellectual to attain control of a multitude driven by zeal and passion by supplying it with basic beliefs, such as the negation of anthropomorphism. Berman asserts that, on the one hand, Maimonides held that "youth, women, the people as a whole, must be left with the simple meanings of the rhetorical prophetic parables with which the prophetic books are replete, and the meanings of the parables are not to be explained to them," and, on the other, advised teaching the multitude the negation of anthropomorphism.[62] I find no tension here. Quite the contrary: the perfect man controls the multitude out of his own awareness of the passion for metaphysics and by satisfying it at the most basic level of negating anthropomorphism.[63] This, then, is the central political message that characterizes the perfect man. An additional political message, discussed immediately below, is that without political perfection the intellectual cannot conduct his own personal way of study properly.

Let us return to a close reading of the Maimonidean discussion. Maimonides explained in Chapter 32 that the study of metaphysics must be approached with caution. Such circumspection, as noted, was typical of R. Akiva, who was aware of the fields that can be demonstrated beside those that cannot, which led Maimonides to address the problematic nature of study as such. In Chapters 33 and 34, he explained that beginning with the study of metaphysics is precisely the Achilles' heel of the pursuit of this wisdom. Having clarified in Chapters 31 and 32 that metaphysics is an abstract science that requires skills, is it at all conceivable to embark on the study of metaphysics before that of the sciences?

Indirectly, Maimonides explained yet again that the passion for metaphysics fans the urge to begin one's study with it. This passion makes people irrational so that, even when they are aware of its intensity and of the need for caution and skill in the study of metaphysics, their passion may

---

62 Berman, "Ibn Bājjah and Maimonides," 108-109.
63 This resembles the notion of the "servant of God" (*hasid*) (*The Kuzari*, Book III), who controls his powers by partially satisfying their needs, in an analogy to the leader who satisfies the public's needs in a controlled manner.

drive them to commence their study with it. The real reason behind the mixing of (demonstrable and indemonstrable) fields, which Maimonides discusses in Chapters 31 and 32, is the urge to study metaphysics without suitable preparations. A personality flaw is an underlying cause for the failure of those longing for this pursuit. Maimonides diverted the discussion from the methodological, didactic, and educational realm to the emotional and the political.

Both the simple person and the intellectual experience the passion for metaphysics, so the need for setting limits to cognition easily applies to both. Reading between the lines, however, we learn that this message is primarily intended for the simple person (more precisely, for instructing the intellectual on how to lead the public), as Chapters 33 to 35 show. The political factor will be revealed, explicitly and implicitly, as a leitmotif in this unit of chapters.

Artifice

In Chapter 33, Maimonides describes the proper approach to the study of metaphysics, which emerges *via negativa* through a parable illustrating the stumbling block: feeding an infant who has not been weaned foods that are difficult to digest (such as bread, meat, and wine).[64] The parable reads:

> Similarly these true opinions were not hidden, enclosed in riddles, and treated by all men of knowledge with all sorts of artifice [*taḥayyul*][65] through

---

64 This parable highlights the central role of the eating motif in this unit. It also links the unit to the preceding chapter, Chapter 30, which deals with the many denotations of "eat" (*akhol*) and also to the conclusion of Chapter 34, where it is mentioned again. In Chapter 30, Maimonides emphasizes that eating has a destructive sense, "the destruction and disappearance of the thing eaten, I mean the corruption of its form that first takes place" (*Guide*, 63). He accordingly cites a series of Scriptural sources supporting the meaning of harm, cessation, and the collapse of matter into its components. The second denotation is that of wisdom and intellective apprehension. This Chapter prepares the reader for those in the unit in that the concern with metaphysics can be destructive on the one hand, and the summit of human apprehension on the other. The reader understands that engaging in the metaphysical means walking a tightrope requiring detailed preparations, which include science, moral attributes, and tradition. Eliezer Hadad noted the central place of the parable but understood it relying on the cunning of Providence, and apparently exaggerated when making it constitutive to the historical development of the Jewish people (Eliezer Hadad, *Torah and Nature in Maimonides' Writings* [Jerusalem: Magnes, 2011], 115-118 [Heb]). Although Maimonides refers to the standing of the Torah in the process of studying metaphysics, he repeatedly stressed that the inclination for the metaphysical is universal, and undoubtedly knew that *ta'wīl* as an interpretive method originates in *Mu'tazila*.

65 See Eran, "'Artifice,'" 109-131.

which they could teach them without expounding them explicitly, because of something bad being hidden in them, or because they undermine the foundations of Law, as is thought by ignorant people who deem that they have attained a rank suitable for speculation. Rather have they been hidden because at the outset the intellect is incapable of receiving them; only flashes of them are made to appear so that the perfect man should know them. On this account they are called "secrets" and "mysteries of the Torah," as we shall make clear.[66]

The proper study of metaphysics relies on two principles: esoteric language ("hidden," "riddles") and artifice. The esoteric language enables gradual study, and the riddles restrain the student by releasing knowledge gradually, contrary to systematic explanation. The artifices enable proper faith during the lengthy process of exploration. "Artifice" means validating imperfect cognition, usually out of an awareness that there are "worse" ones, even less perfect. As shown below, just as the language of riddles restrains, so the artifice balances and regulates the study of metaphysics.

The standing of the artifice in this context merits examination. The place of artifice for the individual is hard to determine. We are speaking of a student who attains perfection gradually and, at each step, creates for himself metaphors and distinctions that are not entirely true but are suited to his level. This level, however, changes as the student advances in the acquisition of knowledge. Between the lines, Maimonides poses the question: how can we understand what is an artifice for the perfect man? In order to explicate the way of the artifice, Maimonides shifts from the individual to the multitude: the artifice is more easily comprehensible as it pertains to the broad public, returning then to the individual.[67] The multitude lives with the artifice at the minimal, rough level, making the meaning of artifice easy to understand. Maimonides distinguishes here between essence and existence:

> This is the cause of the fact that the "Torah speaketh in the language of the sons of man," as we have made clear. This is so because it is presented in

---

[66] *Guide* I:33, 71. See Eran, "Artifice," 111 n. 10, 120-21.

[67] This move is reminiscent of Plato's parable of the larger and smaller letters in *The Republic*, one version of which Maimonides might have learned from *The Kuzari* (the *hasid* as ruler at the beginning of Book Three). On the possible influence of *The Kuzari* on the *Guide*, see Pines, *Studies*, 172; Howard Kreisel, "Judah Halevi's Influence on Maimonides: A Preliminary Appraisal," *Maimonidean Studies* 2 (1991): 95-121; Dov Schwartz, "The Figure of Judah Halevi as Emerging from Maimonides' *Guide*," *Daat* 61 (2007): 23-40 [Heb]. See also Isaac Shilat, *Between the Kuzari and Maimonides* (Ma'aleh Adumim: Shilat, 2011) [Heb].

such a manner as to make it possible for the young, the women, and all the people to begin with it and to learn it. Now it is not within their power to understand these matters as they truly are. Hence they are confined to accepting tradition with regard to all sound opinions that are of such a sort that it is preferable that they should be pronounced true and with regard to all representations of this kind—and this in such a manner that the mind is led toward the existence [*naḥwa wujūdihi*] of the objects of these opinions and representations but not toward grasping their essence [*māhiyyatahu*] as it truly is. When, however, a man grows perfect "and the mysteries of the Torah are communicated to him" either by somebody else or because he himself discovers them— in as much as some of them draw his attention to others—he attains a rank at which he pronounces the above-mentioned correct opinions to be true; and in order to arrive at this conclusion, he uses the veritable methods, namely, demonstration in cases where demonstration is possible or strong arguments where this is possible. In this way he represents to himself these matters, which had appeared to him as imaginings and parables, in their truth and understands their essence [*māhiyyatahā*].[68]

The distinction between essence and existence served Maimonides on several issues,[69] and the focus here is on its connection to the acquisition of knowledge. The artifice implies using metaphysical and theological concepts without understanding their content, and certainly without verifying them by recourse to evidence. Since Maimonides supported the distinction between essence and existence at the ontological level, he was able to transfer this distinction to the educational level as well.[70] Knowledge of a concept, such as "the non-corporeal God" or "the one God," expresses "existence"; knowledge of its content is the "essence." The action of the artifice is now clear. From here, we turn to the proper way for the individual to study metaphysics: at each stage, the individual assumes the existence of some concept. When he understands the essence of this concept, he assumes the existence of an additional concept, which is now more abstract and of higher quality than its predecessor, and the task now is to understand the essence of the new concept.

---

68 *Guide* I:33, 71-72. On the transition from the individual to the collective, see Eran, "'Artifice,'" 112.
69 See Alexander Altmann, *Studies in Religious Philosophy and Mysticism* (London: Routledge & Kegan Paul, 1969), 108-127.
70 In medieval thought, distinctions were usually transferred from one realm to another. For example, modal categories that were initially discussed in the ontological context (necessary by virtue of its causes though possible in itself), and were then transferred to the realm of freedom of will and free choice, that is, to the context of human activity.

When the intellectual understands this essence, he assumes the existence of a new abstract concept, and so forth. Existence is replaced by essence at each stage, just as one climbing a cliff drives in a piton and then relies on it to drive in a new one. In various topics in the *Guide*, Maimonides explained, explicitly or implicitly, that politics is an inherent requirement for the study of the sciences.[71] A person who adopts the proper habits and, certainly, one leading the public, will ultimately also acquire the proper way to study metaphysics.

In any event, Maimonides added a necessary condition—the student must be "sagacious by nature."[72] He thereby made the study of metaphysics dependent on human nature. True, this perception refers mainly to speed and quality in the absorption of knowledge, but human nature conditions study.

In Chapters 31 and 32, then, Maimonides presented the general principle, that is, the boundaries of apprehension and the need for cautious study, without illusions. In Chapter 33, he painstakingly clarified the method of study, as follows:

(1) In terms of the way of study, existence precedes essence. In terms of dogmatic belief, it is existence that outlines the concept in which we believe (artifice).
(2) From a personality perspective, self-control and caution are necessary regarding the passion for metaphysics. Only such passion can explain the inclination of human nature to study while disregarding the proper order, that is, to begin the study of metaphysics without proper preparation.

In practice, the method of study balances the personality. Preceding essence with existence enables gradual progress and control over the search

---

71 See, for example, *Guide* I:54, and see below.
72 *Guide* I:33, 72. In the original, *dhakiyy al-ṭabāʿiʿ* (Munk and Yoel, 48, ln. 24). R. Qafih rendered this in Hebrew as *tevaʿim zakim* (pure natures). Maimonides also used this phrase in the Introduction to his *Commentary to the Mishnah*, where the Hebrew translation is *harif ha-tevʿa* (*Maimonides' Introductions to the Mishnah*, ed. Isaac Shilat [Jerusalem: Maʿaliyot, 1992], 54 [Heb]). In the Hebrew translation of *The Guide of the Perplexed* by Michael Schwarz (Tel Aviv: Tel Aviv University Press, 2002)—henceforth and throughout the book Schwarz—it is rendered as *harif me-tivʿo*." Indeed, *dhakiyy* usually means cleverness. This term appears also in Chapter 34 (78)—"natural perspicacity and understanding." Klein-Braslavy, *King Solomon*, 94-95, interpreted this term as relating entirely to the cognitive realm. The Maimonidean use of *tevaʿ* (nature) extends to psychological traits as well. See, for example, Isadore Twersky, "Halakha and Science: Perspectives on the Epistemology of Maimonides," *Shenaton ha-Mishpat ha-Ivri: Annual of the Institute for Research in Jewish Law* 14-15 (1988-1989), 140-143 [Heb].

for knowledge. We learn, therefore, that the caution principle comes forth in the methods of study and in self-restraint. Sharpness of intellect and shrewdness convey the nature of the suitable student of metaphysics.

Eros and Politics

In Chapter 34, the longest in this unit, we find two parallel movements bringing together substantive, hermeneutical, and literary motifs. One movement compares the longing for metaphysics to sexual desire, possibly continuing and even formulating in extreme detail the rules set in Chapters 31 and 32—the comparison of the physical and intellectual planes. The other movement presents the political implications deriving from this passion. Maimonides hinted at this movement already at the opening: "The causes that prevent the commencement of instruction with divine science, the indication of things that ought to be indicated, and the presentation of this to the multitude, are five."[73] The causes that prevent the preservation of order in the study of the sciences, then, are the same causes that prevent the education of the multitude and, therefore, the political movement of Chapter 34 is explicit. By contrast, the movement of the sexual motif is concealed in the chapter's discussions. The course of these two movements is traced below.

The Sexual Movement

Moshe Idel briefly discussed medieval cosmoeroticism. He pointed to the description of natural processes in sexual terms, and mentioned the longing of the celestial spheres for the separate intellects:

> Maimonides' explanation of the movement of celestial spheres as part of their desire to become similar to God,[74] drawn from Aristotle, left an indelible imprint on medieval Jewish philosophy. He did not allow the possibility of emotional or, even less, sexual events in the supernal world, even in an allegorical sense.[75]

---

73 *Guide* I:34, 72. Beginning one's studies with metaphysics means violating the principle of the sciences' order. See, for example, what Efodi writes: "That is, the causes that prevent a person from beginning, at the start of his study, with metaphysics" (*Sefer Moreh Nevukhim im ... Perushim*, fol. 52b).
74 The desire to resemble God is present only in the approach that sets God as the First Mover, and only in regard to the first sphere. Indirectly, however, the intellects do indeed long for God.
75 Moshe Idel, *Kabbalah and Eros* (New Haven: Yale University Press, 2005), 182.

This issue is indirectly connected to learning since metaphysics deals with the separate intellects. Cosmoeroticism is not unique to the Maimonidean context. Steven Harvey argued that before Avicenna, theologians and philosophers had recoiled from using the sexual motif to denote love of God or intellectual conjunction.[76] Avicenna used the erotic motif to denote pleasure in the immortality of the soul,[77] and Amira Eran indicated that al-Ghazālī too resorted to this motif.[78] Maimonides used the erotic motif to denote man's pleasure in the uppermost stages of apprehension and of God's presence.[79] The sexual metaphor is thus meant to depict the path of the perfect individual. In this unit of chapters, the sexual image actually conveys the beginning of this path or, to be precise, its initial or primitive layers. This image expresses the urge to acquire a comprehensive knowledge of God and the world without any effort. In terms of the sexual image, the initial urge for comprehensive knowledge, inherent in humans, encounters the uppermost stage of intellectual conjunction.

Already in his *Commentary to the Mishnah*, Maimonides had alluded to the linkage between sexual passion and the passion for metaphysics. He wrote about *sitrei 'arayot* (literally, "the secrets of illicit sexual relations"): "Because of people's great desire [*sharāha*] in this matter, they will allow it to themselves when they have some doubt regarding what they heard from the rabbi, and will incline toward leniency."[80] He then states: "And it is known that every man thirsts [*yashtāq*] for all the sciences, whether he is a fool or a sage."[81] *Sharāha* means ardor or desire, while *yashtāq* means yearning and possibly longing for a loved one, but Maimonides hinted in this early composition to a connection between sexual desire and the thirst for metaphysics: both are threatened by an urge that is almost uncontrollable. The Mishnah prescribes that both topics, *arayot* and *ma'aseh merkavah*, should

---

76 See Harvey, "Meaning of Terms."
77 See ch. 5 below.
78 Amira Eran, "The Ladder of Delight in Al-Ghazālī's and Maimonides' Metaphors," in *Alei Asor: Proceedings of the Tenth Conference of the Society for Judaeo-Arabic Studies*, ed. Daniel J. Lasker and Haggai Ben-Shammai (Beer-Sheva: Ben-Gurion University of the Negev Press, 2008), 183-191 [Heb].
79 See Harvey, "Meaning of Terms." The features of Adam are also part of the degrees of perfection. See, for example, Warren Z. Harvey, "Sex and Health in Maimonides," in *Moses Maimonides: Physician, Scientist, and Philosopher*, ed. Fred Rosner and Samuel Kottek (Northvale, NJ: Jason Aronson, 1993), 36-37.
80 Maimonides, *Mishnah Im Perush Rabbenu Moshe ben Maimon* [Mishnah With the Commentary of Our Master Moses ben Maimon], ed. Yosef Qafih (Jerusalem: Mossad Harav Kook, 1963), M. Hagigah 2:1, 376 [Heb].
81 Ibid., 377.

be concealed. Maimonides' veiled interpretation connects them due to their shared ardor. An incidental element in the *Commentary to the Mishnah* thus becomes a leitmotif in the *Guide*.

In *Guide* I:34, Maimonides lists five reasons for not beginning one's course of study with metaphysics, and scholars such as Eran have already discussed them.[82] The text leads us from association to direct focus, and from an allusion to an explicit discussion. Sexuality is, at most, intimated associatively in the first cause and concealed even more in the second. In the third cause, however, it appears openly, to become even stronger in the fourth and fifth ones. Idel wrote a classic work on the connection between Maimonidean thought and *sitrei 'arayot*.[83] I will argue that the present unit is a powerful implementation of this connection.

I turn now to the analysis of the causes. The first cause relates to the complexity and profundity of metaphysics. Maimonides uses the parable of water:

> The first cause is the difficulty, subtlety, and obscurity of the matter in itself. Thus Scripture says: "That which was far off and exceedingly deep; who can find it out?" [Ecclesiastes 7:24]. And it is said: "But wisdom, where shall it be found?" [Job 28:12]. Now it is not fitting in teaching to begin with what is most difficult and obscure for the understanding. One of the parables generally known in our community is that likening knowledge[84] to water. Now the Sages, peace be on them, explained several notions by means of this parable; one of them being that he who knows how to swim [*ya'ūm*] brings up pearls from the bottom of the sea, whereas he who does not know, drowns [*gharaq*]. For this reason, no one should expose himself to the risks of swimming except he who has been trained in learning to swim.[85]

The connection between water and wisdom noted already in Proverbs 18:4 struck deep roots in philosophical interpretation.[86] Maimonides' interpreters and translators are unanimous in understanding his statement in the above passage, "one of the parables generally known in our community," as referring to talmudic literature, and tried to locate the aggadic statement connecting water and Torah. Maimonides seems to have related indirectly

---

82 Eran, "'Artifice,'" 118.
83 Moshe Idel, "*Sitre 'Arayot* in Maimonides' Thought," in *Maimonides and Philosophy*, ed. Shlomo Pines and Yirmiyahu Yovel (Dordrecht: Nijhoff, 1986), 79-91.
84 *al-'ilm* (Munk and Yoel, 49, ln. 8).
85 *Guide* I:34, 72-73.
86 See, for example, Dov Schwartz, *The Religious Philosophy of Samuel Ibn Zarza* (Ph.D. diss.: Bar-Ilan University, 1989), 209-210 [Heb].

to the well-known parable that opens Saadia Gaon's *Beliefs and Opinions* ("I saw, furthermore, men who were sunk [*gharaqū*], as it were, in seas of doubt and overwhelmed by waves of confusion and there was no diver to bring them up from the depths nor a swimmer who might take hold of their hands and carry them ashore").[87] Both Saadia and Maimonides used the word "drowning" [*gharaq*] to refer to those in doubt. Each of them, however, related to a different type of doubt: Saadia referred to those who lack the arguments needed to prove their belief and are consequently perplexed. Maimonides intended those who are incapable of contending with metaphysical knowledge and consequently suffer harm. Similar to Kalām, Saadia focused mainly on the outward interreligious polemic (Islam) or the inward one (Karaism), whereas Maimonides referred to the study of the sciences and to metaphysics. Nonetheless, Maimonides used the metaphor of the ability to swim (and alternatively, of drowning) in a style common in the Jewish thought that had preceded him. In any event, he makes no mention of the sexual imagery of water, which has roots in talmudic literature.[88] If, however, we follow the gradual development of the sexual motif in the chapter, we will be able at its end to go back to the beginning and wonder whether it had already been intimated in the metaphor of the water.

The second cause derives from the potential structure of material intellect. Maimonides writes as follows:

> The second cause is the insufficiency of the minds of all men at their beginnings. For man is not granted his ultimate perfection at the outset; for perfection exists in him only potentially, and in his beginnings he lacks this act. Accordingly it is said: "And man is born a wild ass" [Job 11:12]. Nor is it necessarily obligatory in the case of every individual who is endowed with some thing in potency, that this thing should become actual. Sometimes it

---

87 Saadia Gaon, *Beliefs and Opinions*, Introduction, 7. The Arabic is from *Sefer ha-Nivhar be-Emunot u-be-Deot*, ed. Yosef Qafih (Jerusalem: Sura Institute, 1970), 5 (Arabic and Hebrew).

88 See, for example, Elliot R. Wolfson, *Circle in the Square: Studies in the Use of Gender in Kabbalistic Symbolism* (Albany, NY: SUNY Press, 1995), 12; Daniel Abrams, *The Female Body of God in Kabbalistic Literature* (Jerusalem: Magnes, 2005), 55-56 [Heb]. Liebes ascribed no sexual meanings to the water motif in the narrative of the four who entered *pardes*. See Liebes, *The Sin of Elisha*, 133-144. Liebes, however, wrote to me that such an interpretation does seem possible to him. This interpretation seems particularly plausible if we take into account that the Mishnah also lists *sitrei 'arayot* with the esoteric topics. Note that the linkage of the *pardes* to sexual relations with foreign women appears later, in the writings of R. Menahem Recanati. See Moshe Idel, *R. Menahem Recanati: The Kabbalist*, vol. 1 (Jerusalem: Schocken, 1998), 161-162 [Heb].

remains in its defective state either because of certain obstacles or because of paucity of training in what transforms that potentiality into actuality. ... For the obstacles to perfection [*al-mawāniᶜ 'an al-kamāl*] are very many, and the objects that distract from it abound. When should he be able to achieve the perfect preparation and the leisure required for training so that what subsists in a particular individual in potency should be transformed into actuality?[89]

It is tempting to compare the first and second causes for not beginning with metaphysics with the second and third causes of disagreement according to Alexander of Aphrodisias—the complexity of the object of apprehension and the limitations of the one apprehending.[90] In the third cause, however, Alexander intended the limitations of intelligence ("the ignorance of him who apprehends and his inability to grasp things that it is possible to apprehend"),[91] while Maimonides held that the intellect, by its very nature, is not limited. Potentially, anyone can reach even as far as R. Akiva who, as noted, successfully overcame the hurdle of metaphysics, even though the process of actualizing the potential is exposed to disturbances.

Again, unlike Alexander of Aphrodisias who, in his third cause of disagreement, focused on the level and ability of the intellect, Maimonides highlighted material hindrances and returned the discussion to the sensual and social plane. Discussing the image of the harlot in the Introduction to the *Guide*, Maimonides used a similar formulation to speak of the material obstacles to perfection.[92] In *Guide* I:54, Maimonides argued that the "abominations" of the Canaanite nations were "the obstacles impeding the achievement of the perfection [*taʻūq 'an al-kamāl*]."[93] And in *Guide* III:37, he identified the "abominations" with unnatural kinds of sexual intercourse.[94] Erotic intimations, then, are discernible in the Maimonidean

---

89 *Guide* I:34, 73. This argument as well, that wisdom requires time, appears in another context in Saadia's introduction to *The Book of Beliefs and Opinions*. Saadia discussed the need for revelation in light of the fact that the intellect is capable of reaching the truth, and stated that "the conclusions reached by means of the art of speculation could be attained only in the course of a certain measure of time" (*Beliefs and Opinions*, 31).
90 Eran, "Artifice," 124.
91 *Guide* I:31, 66-67.
92 "For all the hindrances keeping man from his ultimate perfection [*al-ʻuqūl al-mufāraqa*], every deficiency affecting him and every disobedience, come to him from his matter alone" (*Guide*, Introduction to the First Part, 13; Munk and Yoel, 9, ln. 1).
93 *Guide* I:54, 127; Munk and Yoel 86, ln. 16.
94 *Guide* III:57, 548.

terminology and in the rational commentaries referring to the material hindrances to intellectual perfection.

In the third cause, the discussion is wholly channeled to human nature, with sexual tension slowly shifting from a concealed allusion to a hesitant and cautious explicitness. I analyze the third cause first. This cause focuses on the fact that the study of metaphysics is based on the acquisition of the preliminary sciences (logic, the mathematical sciences, and physics). Human nature, by contrast, demands attainment of the goal without the effort on which it is contingent, "for man has in his nature a desire [*tashawwuq*] to seek the ends; and he often finds preliminaries tedious and refuses to engage in them."[95] The term "*shawq*" appears in the philosophical literature also in the context of the lover's desire for the object of his love.[96] By nature, humans tend to ascend immediately to the summit of knowledge.

Maimonides held that the longing to acquire comprehensive knowledge of God, the universe, and the soul is inherent in human nature per se, independent of the person's intellectual capability. This principle appears both in his *Commentary to the Mishnah* and in the *Guide*:

> The meaning of *ma'aseh merkavah* is divine wisdom [metaphysics], which is the discussion of all existence and of the existence of the Creator [*al-bāri'*], His knowledge and His attributes, the necessity of all objects being from Him, the angels, the soul, and the intellect that adheres to man, and what will be after death. Since these two sciences, the natural [physics] and the divine, are noble, and it is fitting for them to be so, [the sages] prohibited teaching them like the other mathematical sciences. And it is known that every man by his nature thirsts [*yashtāq*] for all the sciences, whether he is a fool or a sage.[97]
>
> Now if you would awaken a man—even though he were the dullest of all people—as one awakens a sleeping individual, and if you were to ask him whether he desired [*tashtāq*] at that moment to have knowledge of the heavenly spheres, namely, what their number is and what their configuration, and what is contained in them, and what the angels are, and how the world as a whole was created, and what its end is in view of the arrangement of its various parts with one another, and what the soul is, and how it is created in time in the body, and whether the human soul can be separated from the body, and, if it

---

95 *Guide* I:34, 73.
96 For example, in al-Ghazālī. See Abrahamov, *Divine Love*, 75. See above.
97 *Commentary to the Mishnah*, Hagigah 2:1. The original Judeo-Arabic appears in the Qafih ed., 377.

can, in what manner and through what instrument and with what distinction in view, and if you put the same question to him with regard to other subjects of research of this kind, he would undoubtedly answer you in the affirmative. He would have a natural desire to know these things as they are in truth; but he would wish this desire to be allayed, and the knowledge of all this to be achieved by means of one or two words that you would say to him.[98]

The following table compares the subjects of longing included in the third cause to the list that appears in Maimonides' *Commentary to the Mishnah*:

Topic	Commentary to the Mishnah	Guide of the Perplexed
Existence of God	X	
Divine knowledge	X	
Divine attributes	X	
Existence as a whole	X	
Angels[99]	X	X
Heaven (structure, form, and number of heavenly spheres)		X
Final cause of the world		X
Soul	X	X
Intellect	X	
Soul-body relationship		X
Immortality	X	X
Nature of immortality		X

When he wrote the *Commentary to the Mishnah*, Maimonides held that the topics that interest humans generally, including the multitude, extend from the deity downward. When he wrote the *Guide*, he lowered the bar of expectations from this longing. By then, he thought that the longing and imagination of the multitude extend downward from the angels except that, in terms of order, they had replaced heaven with angels and their interest focused on what seemed to them sensorially more distant.

---

98   *Guide* I:34, 73-74.
99   Interestingly, only in *Guide* I:37 does Maimonides use the phrase "separate intellects" (*al-cuqūl al-mufāraqa*, 86). That is, in the unit of Chapters 31 to 35 he remains at the "popular" level of the term separate intellects. For Maimonides, it is only after the reader has understood the need for preliminary sciences before engaging in the study of metaphysics that we can speak of the separate intellects. The discussion of the separate

Be that as it may, Maimonides actually articulated a theory about the psychology of curiosity stating that humans are endowed with a longing for knowledge of the cosmic structure (heaven, the movers—meaning the angels or separate intellects—and the soul), the beginnings (the creation of the world and the soul), and the final causes. Maimonides himself translated *shawq* as *ta'avah* (desire), quoting Scripture accordingly. He writes:

> Thus speaking of the desire [*shawq*] of someone desirous to achieve his ends, but making no effort to achieve knowledge of the preliminary studies leading up to these ends does nothing else but desire, he [Solomon] says: "The desire of the slothful killeth him; for his hands refuse to labor. He coveteth greedily all the day long; but the righteous giveth and spareth not" [Proverbs 21:25-26]. In these verses he says that the reason why the desire of the slothful kills him is to be found in the fact that he makes no effort and does not work with a view to that which would allay that desire; he has only an abundance of longing and nothing else, while he aspires to things for whose achievement he lacks the necessary instrument ['*ālā*]. It would be healthier for him if he renounced this desire. Consider now how the ending of the parable explains its beginning. For in his dictum, "But the righteous giveth and spareth not," the word "righteous" is not antithetical to "slothful" except according to the explanation we have propounded. For [Solomon] says that the just one among men is he who gives everything its due; he means thereby that he gives all his time to seeking knowledge and spares no portion of his time for anything else. He says, as it were: "But the righteous gives his days to wisdom and is not sparing of them"; which corresponds to his saying: "Give not thy strength unto women" [Proverbs 31:3]. Now the majority of the men of knowledge [*al-'ulamā'*], I mean those generally known as men of knowledge, labor under this disease— I mean that which consists in seeking to achieve the ends and in speaking about them without having engaged in the studies preliminary to them.[100]

The word *ta'avah* does not usually appear in Scripture in a sexual context. Whereas in Amoraic and Tannaitic literature the term is infused with a certain dimension of sexuality and expounded derogatorily,[101] its use in a sexual context became widespread in the Middle Ages. Maimonides called man's longing for knowledge *ta'avah*, and scattered a series of hints alluding to the sexual context:

---

    intellects as movers of the heavenly spheres belongs to the metaphysical topics. See Michael Frede, *Essays in Ancient Philosophy* (Oxford: Clarendon Press, 1987), 81-95.
100 *Guide* I:34, 76.
101 See, for example, M. Makkot 3:15; PT Makkot 3:12, 32b; BT Hagigah 11b; BT Makkot 23b.

(1) Maimonides compared one embarking in the study of metaphysics without the preliminary sciences to one who feels desire but has no "instrument," that is, a means for satisfying it, meaning he lacks the sciences that prepare one for the study of metaphysics. Note, in this context, the image that Maimonides uses in his introduction to Chapter 10 of Tractate Sanhedrin (known as *Perek Helek*), which he apparently drew from Avicenna or al-Ghazālī—the eunuch who has no knowledge of the pleasure of sexual intercourse because he has no disposition for it.[102]

(2) Maimonides interpreted the giving of the righteous mentioned in Proverbs ("But the righteous gives") as absolute devotion to scientific study. His explanation relies on the negative aspect of devotion to women ("Give not thy strength unto women"). Here the sexual connotation is explicit from the outset.

(3) Sara Klein-Braslavy clarified that Maimonides' interpretation of "Give not thy strength unto women" should be read as reflected in the image of the woman as matter, like the image of the harlot in *Guide* III:8.[103]

(4) The source of the verse is in Proverbs, and the reader of the *Guide* will probably recall the connection between King Solomon, its author, and sexual desire.

(5) At the end, Maimonides mentioned the "men of knowledge" who strove to reach the end without preparation. He used the term '*ulamā*'[104] that, for example, denotes Islamic jurists. The reader who "connects its chapters one with another"[105] may recall *Guide* II:40, where Maimonides states that sexual desire is characteristic of the false prophets who presume to bring Torah and law, in an apparent allusion to Muhammad.[106]

Maimonides, then, included a plethora of hints for understanding the mental mechanism of longing for science by way of sexuality. The mention

---

102 See below, p. 135.
103 Klein-Braslavy, *King Solomon*, 151-152. She further added that "in *Hilkhot De'ot* 4:19, Maimonides interprets this verse differently, viewing it as guidance for sexual behavior" (ibid., 152, n. 103).
104 Munk and Yoel, 52, ln. 1.
105 *Guide*, Introduction, 15.
106 See, for example, Jacob S. Levinger, *Maimonides as Philosopher and Codifier* (Jerusalem: Bialik Institute, 1990), 30 [Heb].

of the verse "Give not thy strength unto women" denotes the surfacing of sexuality, from the initial hints to allusions to it through an image.

In the fourth cause, sexuality becomes an explicit argument that can no longer be ignored. This cause focuses on the proper foundation, physical and moral, for the study of metaphysics—a congenial temperament and moral attributes. Maimonides argues in Chapter Eight of his Introduction to Tractate Avot that every moral attribute ensues from a natural disposition, which is a given. In the *Guide*, he exemplified three such dispositions:

> There are, moreover, many people who have received from their first natural disposition a complexion of temperament with which perfection is in no way compatible. Such is the case of one whose heart is naturally exceedingly hot; for he cannot refrain from anger, even if he subject his soul to very stringent training. This is also the case of one whose testicles have a hot and humid temperament and are of a strong constitution and in whom the seminal vessels abundantly generate semen. For it is unlikely that such a man, even if he subject his soul to the most severe training, should be chaste.[107] Similarly you can find among people rash and reckless folk whose movements, being very agitated and disordered, indicate a corruption of the complexion and a poor quality of the temperament, of which it is impossible to give an account.[108] Perfection can never be perceived in such people. And to make an effort for their benefit in this matter is pure ignorance on the part of him who makes the effort.[109]

The dispositions that Maimonides lists in this passage are anger, lust, and instability. Klein-Braslavy drew a distinction between the notion of disposition in the introduction to Avot and that in the *Guide*. In the former, Maimonides supported the possibility of overcoming the disposition but not of dismissing it, while in the *Guide* he included a deterministic tone: some dispositions cannot be overcome, and those possessing them cannot attain perfection.[110]

Note that the lustful are mentioned in the middle, between the angry and the unstable. Maimonides then noted that the rabbis did not teach this wisdom to the young "because of the effervescence of their natures and of their minds being occupied with the flame of growth." He also

---

107 In the original *yakūn 'afīfan* (Munk and Yoel, 52, ln. 13). Qafih translated this as *parush* (ascetic), and Schwarz as *tzanu'a* (modest). Perhaps *kovesh et yitzro* ("subdue his nature," M. Avot 4:1) is preferable.
108 That is, their temperamental flaw is so great that it cannot be imagined or specified.
109 *Guide* I:34, 77.
110 Klein-Braslavy, *King Solomon*, 86-89.

interpreted R. Eliezer's refusal to engage in *ma'aseh merkavah* "and up to now [I] find in myself the effervescence of nature and the recklessness of adolescence."[111] This fact is highly compatible with the flaw of individuals whose sexual temperament is dominant, a trait typical of the young.

Finally, the fifth cause is that "men are occupied with the necessities of the bodies." Maimonides stressed that the concern with physical needs intensifies "if, in addition, they are occupied with taking care of a wife and of children."[112] Unequivocally, he states:

> Things are so that if even a perfect man, as we have mentioned, were to occupy himself much with these necessary things and all the more if he were to occupy himself with unnecessary things, and if his desire [*shawquhu*] for them should grow strong, he would find that his theoretical desires had grown weak and had been submerged. And his demand for them would slacken and become intermittent and inattentive. He accordingly would not grasp things that otherwise would have been within his power to grasp; or else he would grasp them with a confused apprehension, a mixture of apprehension and failure to apprehend.[113]

Family life harms apprehension [*'idrāk*]. Maimonides, then, depicted the following process:

(1) Two given passions drive humans in tandem—the metaphysical desire for cosmic comprehensive knowledge, and the physical desire that is particularly evident in the sexual urge and the continuation of the species. These passions are innate in both the multitude and the perfect man and inherent in their nature.
(2) These two passions are constraining and mutually contradictory—the satisfaction of one comes at the expense of the other.
(3) The decisive majority of people, the multitude, satisfy the physical and sexual passion, but not the speculative one.
(4) Satisfaction is gradual—as one passion is satisfied, the other wanes too. The increasing dominance of physical needs while sustaining family life leads to the waning of the speculative passion, beginning with its "submergence," and culminating in "a confused apprehension."

Implicitly, Maimonides sets forth a dialectical version of family life. Family life is the solution for sexual tension, balancing the sexual urge by

---

111 *Guide* I:34, 77-79.
112 Ibid., 79.
113 Ibid.

channeling it to family life. Yet, it is precisely this balance, involving conjugal relations and the continuation of the species, that constrains the metaphysical drive. Relieving sexual tension thus intensifies the tension of the metaphysical passion.

According to the fifth cause for the opposition to starting one's study with metaphysics, then, the perfect man replaced sexual with metaphysical passion. This approach also explains the displays of asceticism in the *Guide* that is prominent, for example, in the chapters on prophecy. The prophet conveys types of intellectual perfection parallel to other perfections, and ascetic characteristics, therefore, become an inherent component of his character.[114] Maimonides wanted to emphasize that metaphysical passion is a built-in universal inclination in the soul. As he tended to do, Maimonides argued that rabbinic sayings had intended to grapple with and regulate this inclination. Just as he tended to claim that the power of the Torah is that it leads different individuals to perfection in the most effective manner,[115] so did he assert that Jewish sources balance the passion for metaphysics in the most effective way.

The Political Movement

The political motif develops alongside the sexual motif. Just like the sexual motif, the political motif is absent from the first two causes, despite slight indications of its concealed presence. How does Maimonides do this? When explaining these two causes, he included metaphors and texts attesting to the multitude, and the concern with the dispositions of the multitude and their channeling is political.

The drowning man image that appears in the first cause was discussed above. Maimonides harnessed Saadia's metaphor, which had originally related to religious doubt or indecision regarding the choice of religion,[116] to repudiate ignorance in all that concerns scientific knowledge.

In the second cause, Maimonides cites Scripture and a rabbinic source ("I saw the people who have attained a high rank, and they were few")[117] attesting to the ignorance of the multitude.

---

114 See Aviram Ravitzky, "The Doctrine of the Mean and Asceticism: On the Uniformity of Maimonides' Ethics," *Tarbiz* 79 (2011): 439-469 [Heb].
115 See, for example, "The Epistle to Yemen," in *Crisis and Leadership: Epistles of Maimonides*, trans. Abraham Halkin, with discussions by David Hartman (Philadelphia/ Jerusalem: Jewish Publication Society of America, 1985), part iv, 123-131.
116 Meaning Judaism v. Islam, Judaism v. Karaism. See *Beliefs and Opinions*, 7.
117 BT Sukkah 45b; Sanhedrin 97b; *Yalkut Shimoni*, Ezekiel, para. 384 (cited in *Guide* I:34, 73).

In the third cause, Maimonides mentions the need for sciences preliminary to the study of metaphysics. He writes:

> You know that these matters are mutually connected; there being nothing in what exists besides God, may He be exalted, and the totality of the things He has made. For this totality includes everything comprised in what exists except only Him. There is, moreover, no way to apprehend Him except it be through the things He has made. ... As for the matters pertaining to the astronomy of the spheres and to natural science, I do not consider that you should have any difficulty in grasping that those are matters necessary for the apprehension of the relation of the world to God's governance [*tadbīr*] as this relation is in truth and not according to imaginings.[118]

In *Guide* I:54, Maimonides links the doctrine of divine attributes to political leadership.[119] The principle in this chapter and in Chapter 34 is similar: knowledge of the creatures, the "things He has made," leads not only to the Creator but also to God's ways of ruling the world. These ways, meaning the natural order,[120] are a paradigm for the ideal political regime. Many scholars have already pointed to Alfārābī's thought as the source of this approach. In several of his books, Alfārābī opened with the cosmic leadership and then proceeded to the political one. Berman noted that "Alfārābī's view is that there are two levels in philosophy. The first is knowledge of God and nature. The second is to resemble God by founding the ideal state in accordance with the pattern of the natural world which emanated from God."[121] Berman further writes: "We clearly see that in Maimonides' way of thinking, the philosopher must be a statesman, since the prophet, the highest type of the human race, has within him the traits of the philosopher, the legislator, and the state ruler."[122] Consequently, one who wishes to study metaphysics must have knowledge of the harmonious natural order, which expresses divine providence. The concept of "artifice"—the education of the multitude as aiding the personal development of the intellectual—was added above.

The principle of recourse to politics in the process of personal perfection is already clearly formulated in the fourth cause, the "natural aptitudes."

---

118 *Guide* I:34, 74.
119 See Shalom Rosenberg, "'And Walk in His Ways,'" in *Israeli Philosophy*, ed. Moshe Hallamish and Asa Kasher (Tel Aviv: Papyrus, 1983), 72-91 [Heb].
120 See Nuriel, *Concealed and Revealed*, 86.
121 See Berman, "Ibn Bājjah and Maimonides," 19. See also idem, "Maimonides, the Disciple of Alfarabi," *Israel Oriental Society* 4 (1974): 154-178.
122 Berman, "Ibn Bājjah and Maimonides," 7.

There are two such aptitudes: moral perfection and political perfection. Maimonides requires from the student of metaphysics actual political perfection. He interprets the merits of one to whom the mysteries of the Torah are given according to the verse in Isaiah 3:3 ("a counsellor, wise in crafts, and endowed with understanding of whispering") and according to BT Hagigah 13a, as follows:

> Now these are matters that undoubtedly require a natural predisposition. Do you not know among various people one who is very feeble in point of opinion, though he be the most understanding of men? Another, on the other hand, may have an unerring opinion and an excellent way of conducting affairs in political matters; such a one is called "counsellor." However, someone of that sort might not understand an intelligible notion even though it were close to being one of the first intelligibles. He might be stupid and lacking in ingenious devices [ḥīla].[123]... Among men there is also found one who is naturally full of understanding and perspicacity and capable of giving concise and coherent expression to the most hidden notions. Such a one is called "endowed with understanding of whispering." However, someone of this sort does not necessarily occupy himself with, and achieve knowledge of, the sciences. The one who actually has achieved knowledge of the sciences is called "wise in crafts." Of him the Sages say: "When he speaks, they all become deaf." Consider how, by means of a text of a book, they laid down as conditions of the perfection of the individual, his being perfect in the varieties of political regimes[124] as well as in the speculative sciences and withal his possessing natural perspicacity [dhakāʾ ḥabʿ] and understanding and the gift of finely expressing himself in communicating notions in flashes. If all this is realized in someone, then "the mysteries of the Torah may be transmitted to him."[125]

Maimonides asserts that the ruler's supreme mission is to prevent the dissemination of the mysteries of the Torah to the multitude. The superior ruler is one who is knowledgeable in science since he is the only one able to assess the risks of it for the wide public. The meaning of political perfection, that is, the leadership ability required of a student of metaphysics, can be summed up in these qualities:

---

123 On artifice, see above.
124 In the original, *fī al-siyāsat al-madaniyya*. This is also the name of Alfārābī's book on political regimes, which begins with the cosmic structure, while its second part is devoted to politics.
125 *Guide* I:34, 78.

(1) "Counsellor." He addresses the multitude and advises them by recourse to rhetorical means that will reach their hearts. The plausible assumption is that the intention is to impart the "artifice."[126]
(2) "Endowed with understanding of whispering." Concealment from the multitude of what should be concealed ("hiding").[127]
(3) "Wise in crafts." The emergence of a Platonic ruler, who is a philosopher gifted with a talent for political leadership.[128] It needs to be clarified why the study of metaphysics is conditional on political perfection.

Three answers can be formulated based on Maimonides:

(1) The quality of study: the study of metaphysics requires addressing God's governance of the world, and superb politics conveys this leadership.
(2) The religious danger: the multitude may endanger the student of metaphysics by suspecting him of heresy. Political ability is therefore necessary.
(3) The educational value: educating the multitude is particularly valuable for acquiring various sorts of artifices.

Another cause may be added. The passion for metaphysics, as noted, could inflict grievous harm on the student. Self-control ensuing from moral perfection is meant to balance this passion. Possibly, a leadership position and responsibility for the public balance this passion and bring it under control, a presumption supported by Maimonides' return to discussing passion immediately after he formulated the need for political perfection. He writes:

> It is likewise said there: "Rabbi Yohanan said to Rabbi Elazar: Come, so that I should teach you the Account of the Chariot! [ma'aseh merkavah] Whereupon [Rabbi Elazar] said to him: I am not yet old";[129] he means: I am not yet aged and up to now find in myself the effervescence of nature and the recklessness of adolescence. See accordingly how they posed age as a condition superadded to the above-mentioned excellencies. How then could one plunge into these studies together with all the multitude, "the women, and the children?"[130]

---

126 See Klein-Braslavy, *King Solomon*, 92.
127 Ibid.
128 Ibid., 93–101.
129 BT Hagigah 13a. Maimonides interprets this as does Rashi *ad loc*.
130 *Guide* I:34, 78–79.

Thus did Maimonides conclude the fourth cause for refraining from beginning one's studies with metaphysics. This passage, as noted, returns the reader to the physical realm. This ending ties political skill to self-restraint.

Just as sexual tension is relieved in the fifth cause through family life ("taking care of a wife and children"), so is political tension. Productive interest in family life channels the multitude to concern with the general welfare. Maimonides had emphasized at the beginning of the third cause that the passion for metaphysics is the lot of humans as such, and the multitude, therefore, suffers from it as well. The concern with bodily needs is thus meant to keep the multitude away from the premature and risky pursuit of metaphysics.

Chapters 33 and 34, then, present two kinds of tensions:

(1) Sexual tension: the desire for metaphysics is almost as uncontrollable as the sexual urge. Only this cognition will make it possible to restrain this passion.
(2) Political tension: the ruler meant to control the multitude is torn between two opposing factors—the simple man thirsts for metaphysics, but it will unquestionably harm him. The ruler, therefore, must keep the multitude away from metaphysics.

Political Leadership and Dogma

Maimonides used Chapter 35 to balance the harsh picture he had painted in the preceding chapters of this unit. The earlier chapters showed that the passion for metaphysics, inherent in humans as such, is extremely dangerous. The multitude, therefore, is to be distanced from this desire. A misleading picture might emerge, however, stating that metaphysical truths regarding the divine and its relation to reality should not be imparted to the multitude at all. Maimonides, however, did not despair of educating the multitude and held that faith in Scripture's mythic dimensions is not the ultimate goal. He, therefore, addressed the dogmatic aspects of metaphysics, meant for the multitude. Furthermore, since the desire for metaphysics in the multitude (as in the intellectual) is so strong, it needs to be balanced and regulated. The multitude is thus to be provided with a number of basic truths that will assuage the fervent zeal for comprehensive knowledge. Dogma now assumes different forms. In Chapter 35, Maimonides presented several lists of principles or key fundamental assumptions, letting the active reader work out their mutual relationships. To these lists, Maimonides added one intended specifically for those to whom the mysteries of the Torah are revealed. The result is a dogmatic mosaic requiring explanation.

Lists for the Multitude

Maimonides earmarked three lists for the broad public and one for the intellectuals, to whom the secrets and mysteries of Torah are revealed. These lists contain fundamental assumptions about the divine and its relationship with the world, some of which can easily be formulated as an article of faith, and some as fundamental metaphysical truths. Following are the lists meant for the multitude:

(1) For just as it behooves to bring up children in the belief, and to proclaim it to the multitude, that God, may He be magnified and honored, is one and that none but He ought to be worshipped, ... that God is not a body; and that there is absolutely no likeness in any respect whatever between Him and the things created by Him. ... Now everything that can be ascribed to God, may He be exalted, differs in every respect from our attributes, so that no definition can comprehend the one thing and the other. Similarly, as I shall make clear, the term "existence" can only be applied equivocally to His existence and to that of things other than He.

(2) This measure of knowledge will suffice for children and the multitude to establish in their minds that there is a perfect being, who is neither a body nor a force in a body, and that He is the deity, that no sort of deficiency and therefore no affection whatever can attain Him.[131]

(3) On the other hand, the negation of the doctrine of the corporeality of God and the denial of His having a likeness to created things and of His being subject to affectations are matters that ought to be made clear and explained to everyone according to his capacity and ought to be inculcated in virtue of traditional authority upon children, women, stupid ones, and those of a defective natural disposition, just as they adopt the notion that God is one, that He is eternal, and that none but He should be worshipped. For there is no profession of unity unless the doctrine of God's corporeality is denied.[132]

---

131 The list appears in *Guide* I:35, 79-80.
132 Ibid., 81. *Cf.* Arthur Hyman, "Maimonides' Thirteen Principles," in *Jewish Medieval and Renaissance Studies*, ed. Alexander Altmann (Cambridge, MA: Harvard University

Maimonides included in his lists different conceptual elements and principles at various levels of abstraction. Since he is speaking of the multitude, he probably intended different types of audiences, as shown below.

The three lists are presented in the next table, where the differences between them are easily evident:

Dogma	First list	Second list	Third list
Supreme Being		X	
One	X		X
None but He should be worshiped	X		X
Non-corporeality	X	X	X
Not a force in the body		X	
Homonymy in divine attributes (including existence)	X		
No deficiencies		X	
No affections		X	
Eternity			X

An analysis of this table enables us to make up a list of political and educational rules that will guide the perfect man's approach to the metaphysical needs of the multitude:

(1) The negation of God's corporeality, an ironclad principle that rulers must impose in every community, recurs in all three lists.[133]
(2) The two dogmas that follow the negation of divine corporeality are the unity of God and God as the sole object of worship, which are mentioned in two lists.
(3) We may assume that the other beliefs are imparted by the ruler according to the public and the specific situation. For example: according to (1), the denial of divine corporeality is necessary, but the development of this conception, such as that God is not a force within the body either, is subject to the ruler's perception of the public facing him.[134]

Press, 1967), 134-36; Eli Gurfinkel, "Maimonides: Between Dogmatism and Liberalism," *Daat* 60 (2007): 24 [Heb].
133 See Harry A. Wolfson, "Maimonides on the Unity and Incorporeality of God," *Jewish Quarterly Review* 56 (1965-1966): 129.
134 This principle seemingly settles the question raised by R. Shem Tov Falaquera, who challenged the inclusion of the principle of God's lack of affection in the list

(4) Eternity hints at creation since it denotes God's relation to the world, that is, that God preceded it.[135] These lists clearly indicate that Maimonides did not view this as a cardinal issue, but one to be decided by the ruler.

The negation of corporeality denotes the difference between Maimonides' Muslim sources and his own approach. These political-philosophical sources would have the multitude accepting biblical and Quranic writings literally, so as to fulfill religious commandments out of fear of divine retribution. Maimonides, by contrast, held that the multitude can be educated to negate corporeality, that is, to go beyond the Scriptures' literal meaning. He advocated, as noted, an educational approach that does not ignore the multitude's needs. Concerning corporeality, he maintained that the simple person transcends the anthropomorphic images of the sources. Despite the risks entailed by metaphysical truths, the ideal ruler provides a modicum of such truths to the multitude, given its passion for metaphysics. Implicit in the way of the ruler imparting the negation of corporeality, for example, is a movement of restraint, hiddenness, and concealment, yet also a movement of some openness, attentive to, and fulfilling the simple person's needs. The basic truths play a cathartic role in the education of the multitude, while also serving as a means of control by the ideal ruler.

A List for the Intellectual

In the lists of the principles given to the multitude, Maimonides included the esoteric matters fit only for the perfect individual. The list of these esoteric matters is actually a microcosm of the *Guide* as a whole. Maimonides writes:

> As for the discussion concerning attributes and the way they should be negated with regard to Him; and as for the meaning of the attributes that

---

of dogmas: "His words require further study, for we must say that the removal of the image is clear from several of the books of the prophets. But the denial of affection from Him, may He be blessed, is not fit to be revealed to the multitudes, because they lack the ability to grasp this and, rather than adding to knowledge, will only add to confusion, for they will only apprehend something perceptible or imagined. Removing affection from Him will only be grasped by one who has reached the level of contemplation." According to Falaquera, the reference is to a specific public that the ruler decides is better prepared to receive these truths than the ordinary multitude.

135 See Menachem M. Kellner, *Dogma in Medieval Jewish Thought: From Maimonides to Abravanel* (Oxford: Oxford University Press, 1986), 50-51.

may be ascribed to Him, as well as the discussion concerning His creation of that which He created, the character of His governance of the world, the "how" of His providence with respect to what is other than He, the notion of His will, His apprehension, and His knowledge of all that He knows; and likewise as for the notion of prophecy and the "how" of its various degrees, and the notion of His names, though they are many, being indicative of one and the same thing—it should be considered that all these are obscure matters. In fact, they are truly "the mysteries of the Torah."[136]

The list of issues that Maimonides describes in this passage encompasses the main topics of the *Guide*. If we consider their order, we will find in them not only allusions to these topics but also to the structure of the entire work, in an unconventional fashion:

(1) Divine attributes (Part I).
(2) Creation (Part II).
(3) Divine government, providence, and divine knowledge (Part III).[137]
(4) Prophecy (Part II).
(5) Divine names (Part I).[138]

The chiastic structure of the "mysteries of the Torah" according to the *Guide*'s parts is I-II-III-II-I and can hardly be assumed to be random. Maimonides obviously wanted to challenge the discerning reader by clarifying that these are "the matters that ought not to be spoken of except in 'chapter headings,' as we have mentioned."[139] Thus, on the one hand, he presented some of these issues out of order and, on the other, set them forth in a deliberate chiastic structure, clearly showing that the *Guide* was written with the aim of exploring the "mysteries of the Torah."[140]

---

136 *Guide* I:35, 80.
137 Entering the question of the *Guide*'s general structure exceeds my scope here. Presumably, the issue of divine knowledge discussed in *Guide* III:19-21, is included in the attributes and should have been discussed in Part I. Maimonides obviously thought differently.
138 *Cf.* Rawidowitz, "Structure," 61.
139 *Guide* I:35, 80-81.
140 See, for example, *Guide*, Part III, Introduction. On the connection between the mysteries of the Torah and metaphysics in this Chapter, see Arthur Hyman, "Interpreting Maimonides," in *Maimonides: A Collection of Critical Essays*, ed. Joseph A. Buijs (Notre Dame, ID: University of Notre Dame Press, 1988), 20.

It is evident from this list that the "mysteries of the Torah" comprise more than metaphysics, and Maimonides delved into theological questions as well. It is equally evident, however, that metaphysics is the basis for the mysteries of the Torah. Maimonides' list begins with the divine attributes and ends with the names of God, all patently metaphysical matters (the latter expressing metaphysics' hermeneutical implications). Chapter 35, then, concludes the discussion on the study of metaphysics by determining that metaphysics is the foundation of the "mysteries of the Torah." Maimonides appears to have drawn an analogy here: just as the sciences are a preparation for the study of metaphysics, so, too, metaphysics is a preparation for the "mysteries of the Torah." The analogy extends to the realm of politics as well: just as the multitude must be kept away from metaphysics then, even more so, they must be kept away from the "mysteries of the Torah." The elitism characteristic of Maimonidean rationalism is expressed precisely in what is common to the multitude and the perfect man—the passion for metaphysics. The perfect man, however, is expected to overcome this urge, learn cautiously, and then proceed to acquire the "mysteries of Torah." By contrast, members of the multitude must channel the passion for metaphysics to beliefs defined as "artifice," according to the lists that Maimonides presented in Chapter 35.

Summary

The style of Maimonidean thought concerning study and education will now be examined in an attempt to draw conclusions from the preceding discussion. Maimonides could largely be said to have formulated his views while engaged in a concealed dialogue with his predecessors, especially Saadia, representing the geonim who, in Maimonides' view, had been influenced by Kalām (*Guide* I:71). The polemical dialogue, however, is only one literary theme that merges with the dominant flow of motifs such as Eros and politics.

The Context

Understanding the passion for metaphysics and its standing enables further insight into this unit of chapters and its setting. A latent motif directing Maimonides' discussions in the *Guide* is a somewhat critical perception of the speculative (that is, non-halakhic) rabbinic approach. In Maimonides' view, the rabbinic approach coalesced with that of Kalām, which had influenced the geonim. In the letter accompanying the *Guide*, as noted, the quest for the metaphysical was tied to the path of Kalām. Maimonides attests that the student sought to study the "divine matters" concurrently with Kalām, meaning that the student was inclined to view rabbinic theological interpretation as useful to the understanding of metaphysical problems. In this respect, the *Guide* was written in order to distinguish the rabbinic theological approach from the philosophical one.

The critique of the rabbis assumed historiographic garb in *Guide* I:71, where Maimonides traced the roots of Kalām influence on Jewish thought. His critique then moves on to an exposition of Kalām principles that, as noted, had influenced pre-Maimonidean rabbinic thought. The *Guide* (II:1) then proceeds to proofs based on the eternity of the world, which lead to the definitive refutation of the rabbinic conception that had made creation a key idea, to some extent turning the belief in it into a principle of faith that conditions membership in the community of believers. In some measure, the unit of Chapters I:31 to I:35 is a preliminary to the open polemic with Kalām at the end of Part I of the *Guide*. The concealed polemic had already begun in the discussion of the attributes when, indirectly, Maimonides rejected the Kalām formulations of the doctrine of the attributes.

This unit of chapters is a preparation for two aspects of the anti-Kalām and anti-rabbinic controversy:

(1) The study of the sciences that Maimonides demands as a preliminary for metaphysics categorically rejects the Kalām theological approach to the study of metaphysics.
(2) The concealed confrontations with Saadia that Maimonides spread throughout this unit convey that these chapters are a preparation for contending with the Kalām approach.

The Kalām that, in many ways, expresses rabbinic theological thought, occupied the *Guide*. Maimonides sought to understand the psychological motivations of the Kalām scholars. He seemingly hinted to the reader that the passion for metaphysics had come to serve the interests of theologians, who channeled the urge for knowledge into an urge for the verification of religion.

None of this can explain why Maimonides embedded this unit in the midst of the lexicographical chapters. Scholars examining the order of the chapters in the *Guide* have already considered this question. The polemical element, however, clarifies the standing of this unit as preparation for both the chapters on the divine attributes—epitomizing the metaphysical discussion—and for the chapters contending with Kalām.

The order of the *Guide* invites another observation. I argued above that Maimonides constructed the *Guide* as an inverse pyramid regarding the quality of the issues he explored. He opened with the summit of metaphysics, the doctrine of the divine attributes, and slowly descended to other areas. Maimonides did stress that the *Guide* is not meant to teach science (end of *Guide* II:2), but he similarly argued against beginning the discussion with metaphysics. In one respect, this is paradoxical: Maimonides cautions against starting with metaphysics but himself began his book with it—the negation of God's corporeality and a discussion of the divine attributes. We learned, however, that this discussion has political aspects. Maimonides also emphasized in Chapter 34 that the multitude is to be shown the danger of beginning with metaphysics. He thereby unequivocally demonstrated that the *Guide* is not intended for the multitude, perhaps explaining the setting of this unit of chapters. At the heart of the discussion that opens the *Guide*, Maimonides clarified that his book is not a model of a work for the multitude since he himself does not follow its recommendations. This book, contrary to its messages, surrendered to the passion for metaphysics, and ordinary persons will consequently dismiss it on grounds of inconsistency. The wise, however, will understand that Maimonides charts different paths for the perfect man and for the multitude.

The Passion

Love of God is constitutive of Maimonidean thought, an issue that many have already addressed.[141] In this respect, he did not differ from leading thinkers in other religions. In this unit of chapters, Maimonides used *shawq* to denote the human longing for knowledge of the metaphysical realms, which culminate in the divine. For Maimonides, this longing is an innate feature, just like sexual desire. Abrahamov showed that *shawq* appears in al-Ghazālī's writings as an expression of the human longing for God, which is rooted in love and knowledge.[142] Josef Stern and David Blumenthal

---

141 See, for example, Kreisel, "Judah Halevi's Influence"; Daniel J. Lasker, "Love of God and Knowledge of God in Maimonides' Philosophy," in *Écriture et réécritures des textes philosophiques médiévaux: Volume d'hommage offert à Colette Sirat*, ed. Jacqueline Hamesse and Olga Weijers (Turnhout: Brepols, 2006), 329-345.

142 Abrahamov, *Divine Love*, 75-76.

disagree on the meaning of *shawq*. For Stern, the longing is purely epistemological—we strive for the limits of metaphysical knowledge.[143] By contrast, Blumenthal claimed that this desire transcends the epistemological limit: we seek an experience of love and an awareness of God's presence.[144] He further argued that another expression of passion, *'ishq*, denotes the second level of the spiritual experience.[145]

Be that as it may, what emerges is that Maimonides pointed out two stages of passion (and actually a process of attaining perfection), characterizing each one with a different concept of love. The first stage characterizes humanity in general and refers to the passion (*shawq*) for metaphysics. Maimonides himself, as noted, rendered *shawq* as *ta'avah* (desire), in one of the instances wherein he translated his own writings into Hebrew. If the one acquiring knowledge overcomes the *shawq*, learns the sciences in the proper order, does not require demonstration for what cannot be demonstrated and does not deny something whose contradiction has not been proven, he reaches the second stage—*'ishq*— contemplation and desire for God. Maimonides depicted passion undergoing a sublimation process, from coarse eroticism to refined love and from the urge to cross boundaries to the experience of focusing on the abstract divinity and on the longing for communion with it. The two stages of the process are the leitmotif of the entire *Guide*. They represent the meeting of the two extremes—Eros and rational conjunction. In the *Code*, by contrast, Maimonides preferred to mention only the supreme stage. Commentators and scholars frequently cite the well-known halakhah on love of God:

> When a man reflects on these things, studies all these created beings, from the angels and spheres down to human beings and so on, and realises the Divine Wisdom manifested in them all, his love for God will increase, his soul will thirst, his very flesh will yearn, to love God. He will be filled with fear and trembling, as he becomes conscious of his own lowly condition, poverty and insignificance, and compares himself with any of the great and holy bodies; still more when he compares himself with any one of the pure forms that are incorporeal and have never had association with corporeal

---

[143] See Josef Stern, "Maimonides' Demonstrations: Principles and Practices," *Medieval Philosophy and Theology* 10 (2001), 79-80.
[144] David R. Blumenthal, *Philosophic Mysticism: Studies in Rational Religion* (Ramat Gan: Bar-Ilan University Press, 2006), 34-36.
[145] Ibid., 132-136. See also Moshe Idel, *Maïmonide et la mystique juive*, trans. Charles Mopsik (Paris: Cerf, 1991).

substance. He will then realise that he is a vessel full of shame, dishonour and reproach, empty and deficient.[146]

Maimonides, then, omitted from the *Code* the metaphysical impulse typical of humans as such because he saw no need to mention in his halakhic formulation the beginning of the process—the first stage, which parallels Eros. Yet, the supreme stage of love of God, which is also depicted in the concluding chapters of the *Guide*, does merit halakhic formulation because it is both a halakhic and a philosophical final cause.

Rationalist Faith

Many scholars have commented on the nature of Maimonidean rationalism. Rationalism is usually measured by ends and aims: rational communion or (according to the agnostic criticism) its absence; the immortality of the intellect, and the like. It is also measured in relation to the sciences and their acquisition as a religious value. Others view the crux of Maimonidean rationalism in the encounter between Aristotelian and Neoplatonic scientific conceptions with Scripture and Aggadah, meaning the rationalist interpretation of the sources. This unit of chapters diverts the focus of Maimonidean rationalism toward the psychological beginning. Everything is overshadowed by the psychological determination that the will to know the beginning and the cosmic is inherent in human nature. Maimonides emphasized that ordinary individuals also seek universal knowledge, the source of being, the structure of the psyche, and so forth. Moreover, the quest for knowledge is instinctive and characteristic of humans as such.

The sexual motif latent in the unit's discourse as a whole conveys the passion for knowledge. Maimonides' use of sexuality was a priori intended to highlight the negation and the harm. Its very use, however, teaches that the passion for knowledge is almost as uncontrollable as the sexual act and, on these very grounds, entails enormous risks. Maimonides views the sexual urge as the lowest of human positions and the "sense of touch" as a terrible shame. But it is precisely this urge that enables the description of the fundamental passion for metaphysics—the quest for the most sublime type of knowledge pointing to a quasi-circularity that brings together the highest and lowest points.

---

146 *The Code of Maimonides (Mishneh Torah), The Book of Knowledge*, trans. Moses Hyamson (Jerusalem: Boys Town, 1962), "Laws of the Foundations of the Torah," 4:12, 39b. See BT Berakhot 17a; Yoma 87b.

Into this discussion, Maimonides wove not only the aim of knowledge but also the political goal. The ruler of the exemplary state must restrain the metaphysical drive and turn it into a cathartic element, making this the central task in the ruler's being. From the perspective of Andalusian philosophy and history of ideas, this unit of chapters seemingly denotes an almost Copernican revolution in the Jewish society's rationalist scale of values. From Maimonides' perspective, however, this was not a revolution, and these trends had already been hinted at in his *Commentary to the Mishnah*.

Henceforth, the key to the understanding of the human structure lies in the acquisition of knowledge. To reiterate: the darkest urges in the definition of humans are the sexual drive and the urge for knowledge. Maimonides tied together the two extremes between which humans fluctuate. At the beginning of the Introduction to Tractate Avot, he noted that the soul is one and its faculties many. Psychological unity now points to a new dimension: the animative dimension of procreation meets the rational dimension of knowledge acquisition. Maimonides' approach can be defined as "a belief in rationality." He formulated a theory about the passion for knowledge, anchored it in human psychology, and pointed to its full culmination in the supreme stages of knowledge.

Another intellectual phenomenon that had already begun in Maimonides' time will highlight the power of his rationalist belief. In the literature of Ashkenaz pietists, the sexual drive is harnessed to describe the human relationship with God. These pietists sensed that sexuality is the proper way of portraying the uncontrollable passion for God and, therefore, often resorted to such images. As his life was coming to an end, Maimonides may have heard about the circle of R. Judah he-Hasid, the prominent figure among these pietists. Maimonides replaced the divine as the object of sexual passion with metaphysical learning that, by its very nature, includes comprehensive knowledge. Controlling the passion for knowledge is thus also the proper way of drawing close to metaphysics. When this passion meets the passion for communion with the divine, or at least with the separate intellect, it becomes a genuine obsession, as evident from the concluding chapters of The *Guide of the Perplexed*.

Appendix A

A Note on the Commentary of Yehudah Even Shmuel (Kaufmann) on the Unit of Chapters I:31 to I:35

In the introduction to the first volume of his extensive commentary on the *Guide of the Perplexed*, Yehudah Even Shmuel (Kaufmann) devoted a separate essay to the order of the first forty-nine chapters of the *Guide*, a topic of concern before and after his time.[147] I intend to show that Even Shmuel mixed new and old in this essay, and interpreted Maimonides in accordance with terminological, and perhaps also substantive, criteria adopted in critical philosophy during the Enlightenment.

Even Shmuel classified the unit of the *Guide* I:31-35 under the headings "The world outside experience as rationally apprehended" (30-34) and "The *Weltgeist* [absolute spirit]" (35). As the first heading makes evident, Even Shmuel was partial to a Kantian style. For Kant, the term "experience" (*erfahrung*) denotes the objects resulting from the application of the epistemic framework (space, time, and the categories) to the senses.[148] Transcendental idealism deals with the relation between experience and what is beyond it, that is, the thing itself.

Even Shmuel intended such an interpretation for metaphysics, meaning that it is concerned with immaterial substances. For him, then, "experience" is merely the material world or matter in general. On the placement of Chapter 31, Even Shmuel wrote as follows:

> Intellective apprehension, although spiritual, is not unlimited. Indeed, its limits are not in space but in the scope and depth of this knowledge.

---

147 See Rawidowitz, "Structure"; Masha Turner, "The Structure of the Lexicographic Chapters in the 'Moreh Nevukhim,'" *HUCA* 62 (1991), Hebrew section, 29-42. The unit of Chapters considered here is not discussed in this article.

148 See, for example, Nathan Rotenstreich, *Experience and Its Sytematization* (Hague: Nijhoff, 1965).

> An examination of its possibilities shows that it can apprehend the phenomena of the experiential world. As for things outside of this world, the immaterial [ruhaniyyim] creations, it can create for it a regulative concept [musag mekhaven], and regarding the Weltgeist [absolute spirit], it has a way of apprehending its existence if indeed it absolutely cannot create the concept of its essence. Intellective apprehension, then, is limited by the existence levels of what it apprehends, but there is no level of existence it will fail to apprehend altogether—if not in its essence at least in its existence. Were you to inquire concerning the source of this confidence that, with all its limitations, assumes that intellective apprehension nonetheless has regulative knowledge of things found beyond the world of experience, the answer would be—examine the human emotion of curiosity and you will see that humans never long to know the things that are beyond their realm of apprehension. And given that tremendous passion draws a person to know the essence of Geist, and given that you can never find a generation when people will not devote the best of their faculties to answer this question, we learn that humans have the ability to attain regulative apprehension on these matters. And if, again, you were to ask—why are there so many solutions and is yet another one still lacking? Why do all people and all schools disagree on this, in every generation? Let your answer be: only the method is to blame for the dispute. When people shift from inquiry into the field of experience to inquiry into what is beyond experience, they must waive the method of proof by logical demonstrations and must seek a new method according to concepts that are completely new. And here, all will seek a method of their own, and solutions necessarily become individual and subjective. And examining the solutions we will find that, ultimately, they too, are taken from the world of experience, since people find it hard to overcome their habits.[149]

As is already evident from the title, Even Shmuel used a distinctly Kantian terminology. In this passage, he used the term "phenomena of the experiential world," which, for Kant, are opposed to noumena (the thing in itself). Even Shmuel often mentions the "regulative concept." Metaphysics deals with *Geist*, a term widely present in post-Kantian thought. Obviously, there are essential differences between Maimonides' approach and the Kantian and post-Kantian interpretation, beyond matters of time and style. The most striking difference is that Even Shmuel emphasized that passion is entirely framed by the human capacity of apprehension ("there is no level of existence

---

[149] *Moreh Nebukim: Guide for the Perplexed*, edited with vocalized and emended text with a new and full commentary based upon the results of literary and philosophic research by Dr. Yehudah Even Shmuel, Part One (1) (Tel Aviv: Shvil, 1935), lxvi-lxvii [Heb].

it will fail to apprehend altogether"), alluding to the forms of sensibility, that is, space and time. Maimonides, by contrast, meant the negative attributes, which are not amenable to human knowledge, at least according to Maimonides' open references to this question. Negative knowledge is not within the borders or the observations of cognition. Passion too is for what lies beyond cognition.

When Even Shmuel wrote that Maimonides presumably sought "to shift from inquiry into the field of experience to inquiry into what is beyond experience" and that, for this purpose, one "must seek a new method," he formulated an approach that was characteristic, for example, of religious Zionist thought, stating the noumena denotes the divine,[150] and that a new mental technique must be devised in order to reach it. Even Shmuel was a disciple of R. Hayyim Tchernowitz (Rav Tsair), who was active in the Mizrachi, even though he himself did not belong to the movement. Maimonides was aware of analogical modes of thought in the doctrine of the divine attributes,[151] but he did not search for a new logical approach besides Aristotelian logic. The various concealment techniques that present the *Guide* as a clearly esoteric work do not allude to a new type of logic either.

Even Shmuel adapted a Kantian terminology that, eventually, also permeated the line of thought that he presented in Maimonides' name. When explaining the order of the other chapters in the unit, Even Shmuel also included Kantian terms such as "antinomies."[152] This terminology recurs in other discussions in the essay, but especially in this section. Indeed, rather than attesting to Maimonides' approach, these terms convey the conceptual orientation of Even Shmuel himself. In his view, the chapters in this unit are no more than one layer in the general course endorsed in Part I of the *Guide*— breaking the shackles of day-to-day language as a preparation for the conception of God as absolute perfection.[153] Even Shmuel states that we must relate to the transcendent being in a different way from the one we relate to the experienced.[154] The aim of the *Guide*, then, is to liberate us from restricted, dogmatic thought. The Romantic spirit that infuses Even Shmuel's discussions also influenced his determination of the unit's structure, and its spirit is formulated in terms borrowed from modern thought.

---

150 Dov Schwartz, *Faith at the Crossroads: A Theological Profile of Religious Zionism*, trans. Batya Stein (Leiden: Brill, 2002).
151 See Schwartz, *Contradiction and Concealment*, 71.
152 *Guide*, ed. Even Shmuel, lxvii.
153 Ibid., li.
154 Ibid., xl.

Appendix B

On the Theory of the Intellect in Maimonides' Thought (on note 36)

Maimonides' theory of the intellect, as noted, remains cryptic, and issues that had been in dispute are not resolved in his writings.[155] At the end of Chapter 32, moreover, Maimonides tried to dissuade the careful reader from drawing conclusions relying on this chapter concerning "the truth of the essence of the intellect." Maimonides, then, intentionally evaded discussion of questions on the intellect.

Implicit in *Guide* I:68 is an additional comment in this style, dealing with the active intellect—an important component of the theory of intellect. This chapter deals with the unity of intellection (*sekhel*—"the intellect"; *maskil*—"the intellectually cognizing subject," and *muskal*—"the intellectually cognized object") in God. Maimonides noted that the active intellect depends on external factors and, therefore, intellection is at times not actualized in it:

> It is accordingly also clear that the numerical unity of the intellect, the intellectually cognizing object, and the intellectually cognized object, does not hold good with reference to the Creator only, but also with reference to every intellect. Thus in us too, the intellectually cognizing subject, the intellect, and the intellectually cognized object, are one and the same thing wherever we have an intellect in actu. We, however, pass intellectually from potentiality to actuality only from time to time. And the separate intellect too, I mean the active intellect, sometimes gets an impediment that hinders its act—even if this impediment does not proceed from this intellect's essence, but is extraneous to it—being a certain motion happening to it by accident.
>
> We do not intend at present to explain this, our intention being to affirm that which pertains solely to Him, may He be exalted, and which is specific to Him is His being constantly an intellect in actu and that there is no impediment either proceeding from His essence or from another that might hinder

---

155 See below, p. 129-130.

His apprehending. Accordingly it follows necessarily because of this that He is always and constantly an intellectually cognizing subject, an intellect, and an intellectually cognized object. Thus His essence is the intellectually cognizing subject, the intellectually cognized object, and the intellect, as is also necessarily the case with regard to every intellect in actu.[156]

Maimonides asserted that he does not intend to relate to the ways in which the active intellect works, but rather to distinguish between it and God, in which intellection is one in actu.

An additional stylistic aspect of Maimonidean concealment is implicit in this chapter. Maimonides noted that the *Guide* was written "with great exactness and exceeding precision," and therefore, "the diction of this Treatise has not been chosen at haphazard."[157] Thus, in I:68, he described the cognitive process, that is, the abstraction of form and its unification with the apprehending intellect, with many and wearing repetitions.

Maimonides presented the unity of intellection at three levels of existence: the human intellect, the active intellect, and God. He indicated that the unity of intellection is valid for all three levels, and the distinction between them is that, for God, there is no impediment to actualizing this unity, while such an impediment could be present in the other two levels.

A glance at the list immediately reveals the missing link—the separate intellects, except for the active intellect. Ostensibly, there is no impediment to their activity either. Given that nothing keeps the separate intellects from apprehending, nothing distinguishes them from God and some approaches, as is well known, identified God with the first separate intellect. In the *Guide* (II:11-12), Maimonides advocated a stance that distinguishes God from the separate intellects.[158] Possibly, his extended argument on human cognition was meant to divert the discussion from the separate intellects, and thereby avoid the need to contend with the difficulty mentioned. Alternatively, Maimonides may have adopted, *ab initio*, the notion that God is one of the separate intellects, even though this view would contradict explicit statements in the *Guide*. In any event, his discussions of intellect and cognition are characterized by esotericism, either stressed or implicit.

---

156 *Guide* I:68, 165-66. Scholars have dealt with various aspects of this discussion. See, for example, Alexander Even-Chen, "Maimonides' Theory of Positive Attributes," *Daat* 63 (2008), 31, 34 [Heb].
157 *Guide*, "Introduction with Respect to This Treatise," 15.
158 See Chapter 2 below.

Chapter 2

The Separate Intellects

Rationalist commentators and modern scholars have so far viewed Maimonidean philosophy as engaged in a critical discourse with Aristotelian scientific thought. In this chapter, I will argue that a re-evaluation of Maimonides' typical patterns of speculative thought will show that, in several essential areas of *The Guide of the Perplexed*, he departed from scientific Aristotelian thought and chose an independent course.

Analogical Thought

Maimonides' style of argumentation in general, and in *The Guide of the Perplexed* in particular, has been discussed in a variety of scholarly forums.[1] Maimonidean scholars agreed that Maimonides endorsed the Aristotelian preference for the syllogism over other modes of logical argument, but his attitude toward dialectical reasoning remained a controversial topic. I hold that neither Maimonides' explicit declaration in the Introduction to the *Guide* as to the principles of argumentation in physics and metaphysics nor his parable of lightning have received appropriate attention. Maimonides raised two arguments concerning physics and metaphysics:

(1) *Method.* "It is impossible to give a clear exposition when teaching some of their principles as they are."[2] Certain elements in these sciences require special formulation, and the prophets, therefore, stated the principles of physics and metaphysics in parables and riddles. Analogy is a methodological approach that fits the

---

[1] See the important article by Arthur Hyman, "Demonstrative, Dialectical and Sophistic Arguments in the Philosophy of Moses Maimonides," in *Moses Maimonides and His Time*, ed. Eric L. Ormsby (Washington, DC: Catholic University of America Press, 1989), 35-51.

[2] *Guide*, Introduction to the First Part, 7.

definition on various matters, which does not require direct description ("clear exposition.").[3]
(2) *Frequency.* The truths of physics and metaphysics, rather than continuously, are revealed fragmentarily. Maimonides relied on the parable of lightning to clarify this principle. Lightning strikes may flash frequently or infrequently, their reflections visible perhaps only to a spectator who is in darkness. Whereas Moses' apprehension conveys the high frequency, the multitudes do not even see the reflection and are in total darkness.

Maimonides hinted that habits of thought (*al-'ādāt*) often preclude attaining truth on issues of physics and metaphysics. These habits will be explained as deductive thought as opposed to, for example, analogical thought. Many of Maimonides' commentators did not emphasize the achievements of analogical thought, and Maimonides' adherence to a logical-Aristotelian scale of values became the accepted convention. This chapter will show, however, that analogical reasoning plays a major role in the arguments of the *Guide*, making for a new understanding of his esoteric style. In order to clarify the meaning of the analogical argument in Maimonides' thought, I intend to focus attention on a typically metaphysical issue—the separate intellects.

Separate Intellects

Chapters 2 to 12 in Part II of *The Guide of the Perplexed* constitute a single unit, dealing with the problem of the separate intellects[4] and the structure of the spheres (soul and intellect). Maimonides adopts the peripatetic system: intellects are construed, first and foremost, as the movers of the spheres. The movement of the spheres is caused by the apprehension of the sphere's intellect, which strives to resemble the separate intellect, and by the movement of the soul as the source of the permanent desire for regular eternal

---

3   The religious view concerning areas that cannot be described directly led to the significant role of analogy in the history of theology. See, for example, E. L. Mascall, "The Doctrine of Analogy," in *Religious Language and the Problem of Religious Knowledge*, ed. Ronald E. Santoni (Bloomington, ID: Indiana University Press, 1968), 156-181.
4   For the origin of the term "separate" see, for example, H. J. Blumenthal, "Neoplatonic Elements in the *de Anima* Commentaries," in *Aristotle Transformed: The Ancient Commentators and Their Influence*, ed. Richard Sorabji (Ithaca, NY: Cornell University Press, 1990), 318. On this matter in general, see also Herbert A. Davidson, *Alfarabi, Avicenna and Averroes on Intellect: Their Cosmologies, Theories of the Active Intellect, and Theories of Human Intellect* (New York: Oxford University Press, 1992).

movement—the resemblance. The active intellect, which is the last in the series of separate intellects, is not included in this framework since it does not move a sphere. Instead, it functions as the formal principle of material objects in the world and as the source of the human intellect. Maimonides identifies prophetic esotericism, defined by the sages in M. Hagigah 2:1 as *ma'aseh bereshit* ["the Account of the Beginning"] and *ma'aseh merkavah* ["the Account of the Chariot"] with, respectively, physics and metaphysics in Aristotelian science. The issue of the separate intellects in the *Guide*, which brings together *ma'aseh bereshit* and *ma'aseh merkavah*, has been discussed from different perspectives.[5] This unit of chapters precedes the extensive discussion of creation in Part II of the Guide.

In the first part of this chapter, I deal with literary and methodological aspects of the unit constituted by the initial chapters of Part II in the *Guide*, where the stamp of Maimonides' unique style, fraught with tensions and contradictions, is clearly evident. In the second part, I deal with various aspects of this unit's late medieval interpretations.

Exoteric and Esoteric Elements in Maimonides

In the first part of this chapter, I make three claims about Maimonidean esotericism as evident in *Guide* II:2-12:

(1) *Purpose*. Maimonides declares that, rather than philosophical, his purpose in writing the *Guide* is religious: to understand the texts of revelation. The biblical chapters and the rabbinic sources dealing with esoteric matters require interpretation and clarification. This declaration, which opens the specific discussion on metaphysics (the spheres and the separate intellects), merits examination. In the spirit of the medieval esoteric commentaries, I will show that Maimonides' purpose in writing this work was twofold: science for its own sake (esoteric), and science as a theological tool for religious purposes (exoteric).

(2) *Order*. Clarifying this matter could lead to the solution of another problem. The location of this unit of chapters (II:2-12) right before the chapters of the *Guide* that discuss creation calls for an

---

5 See Z. [H.] Blumberg, "The Separate Intelligences in Maimonides' Philosophy," *Tarbiz* 40 (1971): 216-225 [Heb].

explanation. I will argue that Maimonides had more methodological than substantial reasons for locating these chapters here.

(3) *Authority*. Maimonides considers rabbinic authority concerning the sciences and concludes that scientific truth is not subject to non-scientific authority. Allusions in his discussions of the separate intellects are even more radical, distinguishing between the teachings of the prophets, which contain scientific views that are prudent and accurate, and those of the sages, which are not scientifically sound. Between the lines, Maimonides even tries to provide a suitable historical-apologetic explanation for this seemingly puzzling situation. Addressing the rabbis' standing here is warranted because this discussion deals with mystical tradition (*ma'aseh bereshit* and *ma'aseh merkavah*).

This part will end with a comment on the implications of this unit for Maimonides' conception of creation *ex nihilo*. I intend to show that an understanding of Maimonides' argumentation, and in particular his analogical reasoning, is the key to understanding the style and content of this unit in particular and of the *Guide* in general.

Metaphysics and Creation (1): Questions

Why does Maimonides deal with the separate intellects right before the chapters on creation? Scholars considering the order of the chapters in the *Guide* have emphasized the contextual association of Chapters 2 to 12 with the later account of creation.[6] Maimonides seemingly sought to clarify the issue of emanation as the source of the spheres and the terrestrial world before his polemical engagement with the proofs of creation. According to this thesis, the world emanates from the deity in a series of stages (hypostases), a process whereby God is the cause of creation. Explicating in the *Guide* the essence and nature of creation should thus precede, according

---

6 See Simon Rawidowicz, "The Structure of 'The Guide of the Perplexed,'" in *Hebrew Studies in Jewish Thought*, vol. 1, ed. Benjamin C. I. Ravid (Jerusalem: Rubin Mass, 1969), 271-273 [Heb]; Howard Kreisel, "Moses Maimonides," in *History of Jewish Philosophy*, ed. Daniel H. Frank and Oliver Leaman (London: Routledge, 1997), 254-256; William Dunphy, "Maimonides' Not-So-Secret Position on Creation," in *Moses Maimonides and His Time*, ed. Eric L. Ormsby (Washington, DC: Catholic University of America Press, 1989), 155-161. Studies dealing with the possibility of conjunction with the active intellect and metaphysical knowledge, which also rely largely on the theory of intellects, will not be cited here.

to simple logic, the proofs of creation's actual existence. But this is not the meaning of Maimonides' statement on the separate intellects:

> Now I think it fit that I should complete the exposition of the opinions of the philosophers, that I should explain their proofs concerning the existence of separate intellects, and that I should explain the concordance of this opinion with the foundations of our Law—I refer to what the Law teaches concerning the existence of angels. I accordingly shall complete this purpose. After that I shall go back, as I have promised, to arguing with a view to proving that the world has come into existence in time. For our strongest proofs for this are valid[7] and can be made clear only after one knows that the separate intellects exist and after one knows how proofs for the existence may be adduced.[8]

Maimonides claims that explaining the meaning of the separate intellects is imperative for validating and understanding the proofs of creation. In other words, creation cannot be demonstrated without dealing with the separate intellects. All the proofs that Maimonides cites are rooted in physics and astronomy (though it is well known that he doubted the fitness of astronomical theories to physics),[9] but not in metaphysics (in the sense of a theory dealing with the separate intellects).[10] There is no need for a theory of intellects to consider proofs of creation. Quite the contrary—Maimonides detached the theory from the discussion of creation when he based his argument concerning the different motions of the spheres and their velocities on the matter of the spheres rather than on their movers—the separate intellects:

> But who is the one who particularized the differences that are found in the spheres and the stars unless it be God, may He be exalted? If, however, someone says that the separate intellects did it, he gains nothing by saying this. The explanation of this is as follows: The intellects are not bodies, which they would have to be in order to have a local position in relation to the sphere.[11]

This statement appears at the conclusion of Maimonides' argument on the diversity of celestial motion rather than in the course of it. Since the

---

7   See Schwarz, 268, n. 9.
8   *Guide*, II:2, 252-253.
9   See Y. Tzvi Langerman, "The True Perplexity: The Guide of the Perplexed, Part II, Chapter 24," in *Perspectives on Maimonides*, ed. Joel L. Kraemer (Oxford: Oxford University Press, 1991), 159-174.
10 See Harry Austryn Wolfson, "The Classification of Science in Medieval Jewish Philosophy," in *HUC Jubilee Volume 1875-1925*, ed. David Philipson et. al. (Cincinnati, OH: Hebrew Union College, 1925), 263-315.
11 *Guide* II:19, 311.

separate intellects are not subject to the laws of motion, they have no place in a detailed discussion of creation and the issue of the intellects is thus not essential to the argument. The separate intellects have two functions: they move the spheres, as already noted by Aristotle, and they play an important role in existence, a function that Neoplatonic literature associated with emanation. Thus, not only does Maimonides not use the separate intellects in his arguments for creation but he also ignores, almost completely, their role as movers. The argument from the diversity of celestial movement relies on the theory of the separate intellects given that, without the homogeneity of the intellects, the argument would fail. The intellects cannot be a source of different movements. This is a negative argument: the diversity of movement cannot be inferred from the intellects and, in the chapters dealing with the attributes, Maimonides had already noted that negative knowledge is also knowledge (I:59). Nevertheless, it hardly seems probable that Maimonides would have devoted an entire unit of chapters to this particular claim.[12]

Furthermore, Maimonides argues in II:3, citing Alexander of Aphrodisias, that the theory of the separate intellects is based on "simple assertions for which no demonstration has been made, yet they are, of all the opinions put forward on this subject, those that are exposed to the smallest number of doubts and those that are the most suitable for being put into a coherent order."[13] In chapter 22, Maimonides even challenges the validity of the theories of the separate intellects and of emanation as formulated by the peripatetic philosophers. Could a merely plausible theory, whose absolute validity remains doubtful, be essential for proofs of creation? Maimonides nevertheless insists that the issue of the intellects is important for the *process* of proving the truth of creation. Indeed, not all the proofs adduced for creation are apodictic, as Maimonides himself admits, but they are at least partly based on sciences that do contain apodictic proofs, such as physics. Hence, the declaration in II:2 about the need for separate intellects in the understanding and demonstration of

---

[12] It might equally well be argued that knowledge of the separate intellects is needed to understand the refutation of the inference from existence to coming into being (II:17). The movement of the spheres is the origin of the processes that take place in the materials of the terrestrial world, and the object of this movement is the separate intellects. See Gad Freudenthal, "Maimonides' Stance on Astrology in Context: Cosmology, Physics, Medicine and Providence," in *Moses Maimonides: Physician, Scientist, and Philosopher*, ed. Fred Rosner and Samuel S. Kottek (Northvale, NJ: Ktav, 1993), 78. Again, it hardly seems possible that Maimonides would devote a whole literary unit to this argument, which relies indirectly on the intellects.

[13] *Guide* II:3, 254. See also *Guide*, "Translator's Introduction: The Philosophic Sources of The Guide of the Perplexed," lxviii.

creation is puzzling. These perplexities prepare the readers for the tension awaiting them in the preface that Maimonides included in this chapter. I discuss below how this tension helps to understand the allusions about the link between the separate intellects and the problem of creation.

The Purpose of *The Guide of the Perplexed*

Maimonides explains in the preface to Chapter 2 that his purpose in writing the *Guide* was not science for science's sake and that he had never intended to discuss topics in physics and metaphysics per se. "Know that my purpose in this Treatise of mine was not to compose something on natural science, or to make an epitome of notions pertaining to the divine science."[14] His purpose was theological, that is, to elucidate the meaning of the biblical and prophetic texts. Leo Strauss argued that the *Guide* was a work of Kalām, a thesis that has been recurrently contested.[15] Strauss' statement is indeed questionable. Both in his *Commentary to the Mishnah* and in the *Guide*, Maimonides reiterates that, according to the Bible, perfection is bound up with a knowledge of the sciences. In his view, the prophets themselves advocate "the perfection of the soul,"[16] that is, a knowledge of existents, and that is also the meaning of their teachings. Since the prophets' message is a call to acquire a knowledge of science for its own sake, we could infer that this is the object of the *Guide* too.[17] But rather than consider Maimonides' general purpose, which has been widely disputed, I will concentrate on the ambiguous and convoluted exposition in the Preface to Part II:

> Now you know already from the introduction of this my Treatise that it hinges on the explanation of what can be understood in the "Account of

---

14 *Guide* II:2, 253.
15 Since we are dealing with the preface to the creation chapters, an allusion in them to the nature of the book merits note. Maimonides states in *Guide* II:16: "I have already set forth for your benefit the methods of the Mutakallimūn in establishing the newness of the world, and I have drawn your attention to the points with regard to which they may be attacked" (293). Now, the proofs adduced by the Mutakallimūn were indeed described in I:74, but nowhere does Maimonides refute them. Moreover, in II:16 he promises to show that the doctrine of the eternity of the world favored by his opponents is even more questionable than the doctrine of creation, which also lacks apodictic evidence. This approach, exposing the opponents' weaknesses even when they also point to difficulties in one's own arguments is typical of the Kalām. Perhaps Maimonides was hinting, as suggested by Strauss, that he too was using Kalām techniques.
16 *Guide* III:27, 511.
17 See also Steven Harvey, "Maimonides in the Sultan's Palace," in *Perspectives on Maimonides*, ed. Joel L. Kraemer (Oxford: Oxford University Press, 1991), 56–57.

the Beginning" and the "Account of the Chariot" and the clearing-up of the difficulties attaching to prophecy and to the knowledge of the deity. Accordingly in whatever chapter you find me discoursing with a view to explaining a matter already demonstrated in natural science, or a matter demonstrated in divine science, or an opinion that has been shown to be the one fittest to be believed in,[18] or a matter attaching to what has been explained in the mathematical sciences[19]—know that that particular matter necessarily must be a key to the understanding of something to be found in the books of prophecy, I mean to say of some of their parables and secrets. The reason why I mentioned, explained, and elucidated that matter would be found in the knowledge it procures us of the "Account of the Chariot" or of the "Account of the Beginning" or would be found in an explanation that it furnishes of some root regarding the notion of prophecy or would be found in the explanation of some root regarding the belief in a true opinion belonging to the beliefs of Law.[20]

In this passage, Maimonides twice lists four issues that form the subject-matter of the *Guide*. A comparison of the beginning of the passage with its middle and end, however, reveals a discrepancy between the two lists in the third and fourth items:

(1) The "Account of the Beginning" (*ma'aseh bereshit*)
(2) The "Account of the Chariot" (*ma'aseh merkavah*)
(3)
    (a) "Difficulties attaching to prophecy"
    (b) "Some root regarding the notion of prophecy"
(4)
    (a) "Knowledge of the deity"
    (b) "A true opinion belonging to the beliefs of Law"

What is the reason for this discrepancy? In the works of key Muslim thinkers such as Alfārābī, Avicenna, and Averroes, the issue of the divine attributes is considered a philosophical question addressed with philosophical tools. One example is the attribute of divine knowledge that Averroes

---

18 Probably meaning knowledge transmitted through a reliable tradition.
19 Arabic: *fi al-tacālīm*. The hierarchy, then, is metaphysics, physics, plausible beliefs, and mathematical sciences. Pines and Schwarz translate here "mathematics," perhaps under the influence of Ibn Tibbon's rendition, *limmudim*, on the assumption that this was essentially a translation of the term *al-riyāḍī*.
20 *Guide* II:2, 253–254.

considers at length in his commentary on the *Metaphysica*.[21] Maimonides could perhaps be hinting that the *Guide* was written to elucidate philosophical matters as well, such as knowledge of the divine attributes, and that he was blurring this by substituting "knowledge of the deity" in the first list (4a) with "a true ... belief of the Law" in the second (4b). This would also explain the difference between (3a) and (3b): the *Guide* was written not only to resolve doubts, that is, to interpret the words of the prophets, but also to engage in independent discussions about the principles mentioned by the prophets.

Maimonides clearly asserts that the *Guide* was (also) meant to explain *ma'aseh bereshit* and *ma'aseh merkavah*, areas that he identifies, as evident from the Introduction to the book, with physics and metaphysics.[22] The disjunctive formulation (… or … or …) at the end of the quoted passage also intimates that physics and metaphysics are part of the Guide's purpose as independent areas. Maimonides seems to be claiming in this passage that the first two (scientific) matters were intended to explain the last two (theological) ones. But this claim is itself problematic. Prophetic matters include "mysteries of the Torah" that, as stated, are identified with *ma'aseh bereshit* and *ma'aseh merkavah*. The exposition of physics and metaphysics is, therefore, an end in itself and not only an aid to understanding prophecy, as claimed in the above passage. Given that the *Guide* deals with science for its own sake, its scientific innovations should be evaluated on their own merits and beginning with the logical formulations in which they are articulated, which is my concern below. The purpose of the *Guide* is thus a challenge to any reader seeking the inner substance of the text.

Metaphysics and Creation (2): Answers

The solution to this problem lies in the importance of scientific methodology. Already in the Introduction to the *Guide*, Maimonides explains that

---

21 M. E. Marmura, "Some Aspects of Avicenna's Theory of God's Knowledge of Particulars," *Journal of the American Oriental Society* 82 (1962): 299-312; Dov Schwartz, "Divine Immanence in Medieval Jewish Philosophy," *Journal of Jewish Thought and Philosophy* 3 (1994): 249–278.

22 We could infer from Maimonides' text that the terms *ma'aseh bereshit* and *ma'aseh merkavah* are not pure philosophy—physics and metaphysics as presented in the works of the philosophers—but the contents of the prophetic books (Sara Klein-Braslavy, *King Solomon and Philosophical Esotericism in the Thought of Maimonides* [Jerusalem: Magnes, 1996], 41–42 [Heb]). I hold it could be argued that Maimonides did not distinguish the meaning of prophecy from the philosophers' physics, for example in his insistence that physics is entirely true (II:22).

the method applied to questions of physics and metaphysics is essential for understanding the book. This method includes intuitive and analogical approaches to many matters. The parable of the lightning also contributes to the unsystematic nature of these sciences. The terms *ma'aseh bereshit* and *ma'aseh merkavah* thus have two dimensions: one of substance (the theory of the separate intellects, the spheres, and the laws of physics) and one methodological (analogy). Maimonides implies that the mysteries of the prophets include not only matters of substance but also modes of thought. In fact, that is the nature of physics and metaphysics:

> Know that with regard to natural matters as well, it is impossible to give a clear exposition when teaching some of their principles as they are. For you know the saying of [the sages]... : "The Account of the Beginning ought not to be taught in the presence of two men" [BT Hagigah 11b]. Now if someone explained all those matters in a book, he in effect would be *teaching* them to thousands of men. Hence these matters too occur in parables in the books of prophecy. The sages..., following the trail of these books, likewise have spoken of them in riddles and parables, for there is a close connection between these matters and the divine science, and they too are secrets of that divine science.[23]

The study of metaphysics is, on the one hand, important in itself. On the other, its methodology helps to understand the teachings and thought of the prophets ("parables and riddles" as defined by Maimonides in the Introduction to the *Guide*), and also to solve problems attaching to their thought, for the prophets spoke in analogies and parables. Hence, Maimonides is speaking here of both science for its own sake and science as an aid to understanding the prophets' thought, thereby explaining the difference between the two formulations of the *Guide*'s four purposes. Maimonides' account of metaphysics and physics has a philosophical, content-oriented dimension, as conveyed in the theoretical account of divine knowledge (4a), and a methodological dimension of analogical thought, which dictates the formulation of the beliefs of the Torah (4b).

The analogical dimension of the sciences enables us to answer the question posed at the opening of this chapter. To understand the purpose of this unit of chapters (II:2-12), which deals with the separate intellects as a tool for grasping the account of creation and the relevant proofs, we must realize that the theory of separate intellects is based on analogical reasoning. In a passage that is relatively obscure but, to my mind, crucial

---

23 *Guide* I:1, 7.

in Maimonides' systematic, up-to-date ("the opinion of the later philosophers") presentation of the theory of the intellects, he writes:

> In this way the giver of a form is indubitably a separate form, and that which brings intellect into existence is an intellect, namely, the active intellect. Thus the relation of the active intellect to the elements and that which is composed of them is similar to the relation obtaining between every separate intellect particularly related to a sphere and that sphere. Furthermore, the relation of the intellect in actu existing in us, which derives from an overflow of the active intellect and through which we apprehend the active intellect,[24] is similar to that of the intellect of every sphere that exists in the latter, deriving its being in it from the overflow of a separate intellect—an intellect through which the sphere apprehends the separate intellect, makes a mental representation of the latter, desires to become like it, and in consequence moves.[25]

This passage is quite mystifying. The active intellect does not move any sphere and has nothing to do with the topics discussed in the chapters making up this unit. Why, then, did Maimonides bring it into play? According to Strauss's rules for identifying esoteric elements, this is an indication that the issue at hand is significant for the meaning of the literary unit as a whole. In this passage, Maimonides was alluding to two systems of proportional relationships:

$$(I) \quad \frac{\text{separate intellect}}{\text{sphere}} = \frac{\text{active intellect}}{\text{compound elements and objects in the material world}}$$

$$(II) \quad \frac{\text{active intellect}}{\text{intellect } in\ actu} = \frac{\text{separate intellect}}{\text{intellect of the sphere}}$$

Understanding the activity of the active intellect, therefore, becomes possible through an understanding of the separate intellects and by way of analogy. This is a clear-cut example of the mutual analogical relationship between physics (in this case the theory of the intellects, with its affinity to the laws of physics and to their emergence) and metaphysics. The analogical-proportional dimension of metaphysics is also reflected in

---

24 Schwarz adds in brackets: "to the active intellect."
25 *Guide* II:4, 258. Schwarz adds in brackets at the end of this passage, "to the same separate intellect." For the various scholarly discussions of this particular passage, see Schwarz's note to his translation, 273, n. 30.

the discussion of the theory of attributes.[26] In his discussion of divine knowledge (*Guide* III:19-21), Maimonides uses the parable of the artisan as an expression of the analogical method, a discussion illustrating the existence of the substance and methodology dimensions and the need to combine them.

The active intellect is important in arguments concerning creation as evident, for example, in *Guide* II:18. The question of matter's desire to assume a form is also significant in the argument from the diversity of spherical motions (II:19). Since physics and metaphysics are interdependent, at least methodologically, the theory of separate intellects must be a prerequisite in any discussion of the laws governing the material world. The theory of the intellects is therefore important for an understanding of arguments and modes of argumentation concerning creation.

Let us now return to the purpose of the *Guide*. Maimonides' declaration that the purpose of his work was theological concerned the methodological aspect of *ma'aseh bereshit* and *ma'aseh merkavah*, that is, the analogy. The analogical method applied in the sciences is an important tool for the interpretation of prophecies. Maimonides' declaration does not refer to the scientific contents that the *Guide* deals with per se, as he himself suggests immediately after. Concerning these contents, the study of physics and metaphysics is central to the work's purpose. By contrast, analogy plays a role not only in science but also in exegesis. The contents of physics and metaphysics are an end in itself; the methods are designed to uncover these truths in the prophetic teachings. Analogies and metaphors play an important part in biblical exegesis already in Chapters 5 and 6. In Chapter 5, for example, Maimonides considers the verse, "The heavens declare the glory of God" (Psalms 19:2) and asserts that, as speaking and telling are indications of intellectual perception (*taṣawwur* = concept) on a human plane, in the biblical account of the spheres too, speaking and telling must be understood as implying that they possess some intellectual perception. Analogy, then, is a major tool in both scientific thinking (physics and metaphysics) and in understanding what the prophets said about these matters.

The Prophets and the Sages

Maimonides was aware of scientific developments and of the mutual relationship between them and the Jewish world. We could, therefore, expect to find a

---

[26] See *Guide* I:58; Dov Schwartz, *Contradiction and Concealment in Medieval Jewish Thought* (Ramat-Gan: Bar-Ilan University Press, 2002), 71 [Heb].

linear development of the scientific outlook from the prophets to the sages. Yet, Maimonides seemingly embedded hints in this unit of chapters pointing to the superiority of the prophets' scientific knowledge over that of the sages.[27]

Chapters 5 and 6, as noted, were intended to expose the scientific conceptions reflected in prophetic and talmudic literature. The relevant biblical and midrashic sources, however, are not presented in a balanced manner. Chapter 5 cites sources of both types supporting the view that the spheres are "living and rational." Psalms 19:2 suggests that the spheres are rational as if the prophets skipped the spheres' animative qualities and referred immediately to their intellectual and apprehensive powers. The midrashim, however, begin with the statement that "those above are alive"[28] and are not "dead [bodies] like the elements"; for the sages, as it were, the fact that the spheres possess a living soul was something new.

In Chapter 6, Maimonides cites Scriptural proofs of the separate intellects' existence but only one rabbinic midrash, which he openly criticizes: "Marvel at their saying 'contemplating [the host above],' for Plato uses literally the same expression, saying that God looks at the world of the intellects and that in consequence that which exists overflows from Him."[29] In other words, the sages adopted the theory of separate intellects through Plato's theory of ideas, which Maimonides considers to be mistaken. Shem Tov Falaquera added a further hint when he notes, in an allusion to Maimonides' critique: "That is his wont in all midrashim, to interpret them in a near-rational manner."[30] In Chapter 6, Maimonides also considers the different meanings of the term "angel." The other midrashim mentioned in this chapter are concerned solely with psychology and biology, that is, with the meaning of the term "angel" as a natural force acting in various ways in the world of generation and corruption. Once more, Maimonides hints that the sages possessed considerable knowledge of the terrestrial but not of the celestial world.

Chapters 8 and 9 contrast the scientific errors of the sages with the accurate knowledge of the prophets. Chapter 8 presents the sages as

---

27 Maimonides' attitude to the sages has been frequently discussed; my object here is confined to the context of separate intellects and spheres. See, for example, Menachem Kellner, *Maimonides on the "Decline of the Generations" and the Nature of Rabbinic Authority* (Albany, NY: SUNY Press, 1996).
28 *Genesis Rabba* 2:1 (Theodor-Albeck edn., 15).
29 *Guide* II:6, 263.
30 Shem Tov ibn Falaquera, *Moreh ha-Moreh*, ed. Yair Shiffman (Jerusalem: World Union of Jewish Studies, 2001), 245, ln. 91 [Heb].

supporting the Pythagorean doctrine that, as the spheres move, they emit sounds. Maimonides established as an undeniable fact that the sages are mistaken on scientific matters, and even cited evidence of their own admission of error on astronomical questions (TB Pesahim 94b). By contrast, Chapter 9 may be construed as an implicit tribute to the prophets' scientific greatness. The chapter is mainly concerned with "saving" the theory of four spheres having stars or planets. What was the threat to this belief? The ancients held that the spheres of Mercury and Venus were above the sun, but Ptolemy rejected this belief and claimed that the sun is at the center of the planets and Venus is below it, challenging the four-sided model. Maimonides responded by claiming that Andalusian astronomers, who were "very proficient in the mathematical sciences," had reestablished the ancients' model that, moreover, had not been entirely refuted.

This model enables to count four spheres with stars [or planets]—a number that Maimonides considers "a very important basis for a notion that has occurred to me." Classical commentators and modern scholars agree that Maimonides was thereby alluding to the four beasts in *ma'aseh merkavah*.[31] The chapter opens with the sages' assertion that there are "two firmaments" (BT Hagigah 12b), which are interpreted as a general division of the spheres into two: the all-encompassing sphere and the spheres in which there are stars. Thus, the prophet Ezekiel alluded in his vision of the chariot to the precise number of spheres, whereas the sages were content with merely a general statement. Moreover, whereas the sages held faulty views in the realms of metaphysics (the ideas) and astronomy (the sounds of the spheres), the prophets' views were true. The principle of R. Moshe Narboni in his commentary to the *Guide*—claiming that Maimonides held that the prophets and the sages had simply articulated the scientific views prevalent in their times even though they may seem archaic to us—is not affected by my suggestion. My claim is that, according to Maimonides, the prophets, in their wisdom, selected metaphysical and scientific views that would survive the test of time, whereas the sages failed in this task.

In Chapter 10, Maimonides leaves the independent discussion on intellects and spheres to consider their influence on the laws of nature. Discussing the terrestrial meaning of "angel," that is, the four elements, he cites the following midrash:

> They said in *Midrash Rabbi Tanhuma*: "How many steps were in the ladder? Four"—which refers to the dictum: "And behold a ladder set up on the earth"

---

31 *Guide* III:2, 417. This is also the view in the commentaries of Moshe Narboni, Ephodi, and Shem Tov. On the scholarly studies, see Schwarz, 285, n. 12.

[Genesis 28:12]. And in all the Midrashim it is mentioned and repeated that there are four camps of angels. However, in some manuscripts I have seen the text: "How many steps were in the ladder? Seven." But all the manuscripts and all the Midrashim agree that the angels of God whom [Jacob] saw ascending and descending were only four and not any other number— two ascending and two descending—and that the four gathered together upon one step of the ladder, all four being in one row—namely, the two who ascend and the two who descend. They even learned from this that the breadth of the ladder seen in the vision of prophecy was equal to the dimension of the world plus one third. For the breadth of one angel in the vision of prophecy is equal to the dimension of one third of the world according to the dictum: "And his body was like *tarshish*" [Daniel 10:6]. Accordingly, the breadth of the four is equal to that of the world plus one third. In his parables, Zechariah—when describing that "there come four chariots ... these are the four airs of the heavens which go forth after presenting themselves before the Lord of all the earth" [Zechariah 6:5]... You shall hear an indication regarding this. As for their dictum that an angel is equal in breadth to a third of the world—namely, their dictum in *Bereshit Rabbah* which reads textually: "That the angel is the third part of the world" [Genesis Rabbah 68, 12; Theodor and Albeck, 787]—it is very clear. And we have explained it in our great compilation on the legalistic study of the Law [Laws of the Foundation of the Torah 2:3]. For all created things are divided into three parts: the separate intellects, which are the angels; the second, the bodies of the spheres; the third, first matter—I mean the bodies subject to constant change, which are beneath the sphere. In this way will he who wants to understand the prophetic riddles understand them. And he will awaken from the sleep of negligence, be saved from the sea of ignorance, and rise up toward the high ones.[32]

Maimonides alludes here to the four elements—two of them light and moving naturally upward ("ascending"), and two of them heavy and moving naturally downward ("descending").[33] The attribution of this knowledge of natural laws to the sages is not absolute either, and Maimonides actually pointed to other formulations ("seven"). Nevertheless, it is generally clear

---

32 *Guide* II:10, 272-273.
33 For other associations of the number four with the regularity of the material world see Sara Klein-Braslavy, "Maimonides' Commentary on Jacob's Dream of the Ladder" in *Moshe Schwarcz Memorial Volume* [= *Bar-Ilan Annual* 22–23], ed. Moshe Hallamish (Ramat-Gan: Bar-Ilan University Press, 1987), 336.

from this passage that, in his view, the sages were familiar with the laws of the material world. What does require explication is Maimonides' use of the "one third" and "the world plus one third" metaphor.

At first, the Midrash states that the breadth of the ladder was "the world plus one third." The measure "third" [*shelish*] reflects the size of each element's specific sphere relative to the spheres of the sublunary elements.[34] Maimonides probably means that the three spheres of the sublunary elements (earth, water, and air) are in the visible world, whereas the elemental fire, which is tangent to the lunar sphere, is neither seen nor sensed and is therefore construed as "one third" outside the world. Later, Maimonides returns to the "third" measure, now as one of the three parts of the created world—separate intellects, spheres, and the world of matter. The following picture thus emerges:

	Separate intellects		
	Spheres		
Earth	Water	Air	Fire

This is the interpretation of the Midrash, given by the sages. By contrast, the prophets, whose view begins with the words "For all created things ..." explained the matter differently. For them, what is outside the world is God, as follows:

God
Separate Intellects
Spheres
Elements

Maimonides clearly separates the two interpretations—the prophetic and the rabbinic—in the midrash on the *tarshish* and in "Zechariah's parables." He may be intimating to the understanding reader that the two interpretations of "angel" and "third" are equivalent. The implication is that the sages, in their exegesis of the dream of the ladder, apprehended only the physical world. After all, Maimonides has already declared that "even the elements are in their turn called 'angels.'"[35] The sages, then, did not consider the spheres in themselves and definitely not the separate intellects, which

---

34 See "Laws of the Foundation of the Torah" 3:10. The expressions "sphere of fire," "sphere of air," and so forth are common in medieval literature even before Maimonides. See, for example, *The Kuzari* 5:2; Ibn Ezra's commentary on Daniel 7:14, and others.
35 *Guide* II:6, 262.

constitute the two remaining "thirds." They do so contrary to the prophetic vision that deals with the spheres themselves, as Maimonides explained in the preceding chapter and as he would further elucidate at length at the beginning of Part III of the *Guide* (the "living creatures" in the vision of the chariot). The sages confined their attention to one third of the world only, the world of generation and corruption whose forces and components were also called "angels." Generally, note that Maimonides did not find this identification of the "third" with a material element ("a body formed of burning fire") adequate, and ascribes this view to "those who deem themselves the sages of Israel."[36] Even when the sages did address the active intellect or the spheres, it was always in the context of the physical, lower world.

It seems quite clear that Maimonides consistently sought to intimate to the understanding reader that the prophets and the sages differed in their scientific apprehension of the separate intellects and the spheres. The prophetic visions contain no mistakes because the prophets knew how to differentiate questionable scientific conceptions that would ultimately evolve and change from those that would remain constant over time. The prophets too were acquainted only with the scientific notions prevalent in their own times, and their ability to predict the future did not grant them knowledge of more progressive scientific theories.[37] In this respect, prophets and sages were no different. Moreover, some of the prophets, such as Ezekiel, did commit scientific errors.[38] It was the prophets' intellectual caution, however, that granted them an advantage over the sages. Hence, the prophets' scientific views were lucid and enduring unlike those of the sages who, at times, tended to adopt scientific ideas that later proved wrong. The sages' errors were particularly evident when they had already stated their views in the areas of metaphysics (Platonic ideas) and astronomy (the sounds of the spheres). The reason for their adoption of erroneous views is conveyed in the passage below:

> We have already explained that all these views do not contradict anything said by our prophets and the sustainers of our Law. For our community is a community that is full of knowledge and is perfect, as He, may He be exalted, has made clear through the intermediary of the Master who made us perfect, saying, "Surely,

---

36 *Guide* II:6, 263. *Cf.* Klein-Braslavy, "Maimonides' Commentary," 335–336, n. 14.
37 A hint to this can be found in *Guide* II:11, 274, where Maimonides enunciates the principle of economy in scientific theory ("it is preferable for us to rely on the arrangement postulating the lesser number of motions"). By contrast, the biblical verse he cites actually shows the opposite: "'Is there any number of His armies?' [Job 23:5]—he means because of their multiplicity."
38 See Kellner, *Maimonides on the "Decline of the Generations,"* 59.

this great community is a wise and understanding people" [Deuteronomy 4:6]. However, when the ignorant from among the ignorant communities ruined our good qualities, destroyed our words of wisdom and our compilations, and caused our men of knowledge to perish, so that we again became ignorant (*jāhiliyya*).[39]

Maimonides surely does not mean that there is no contradiction between the true "views" and "anything said by ... the sustainers of our Law," for he himself had already pointed out at least two mistaken rabbinic views. The biblical verse cited in Moses' name also refers solely to the prophets. The subsequent explanation clarifies the distinction between the prophets and the sages: the sages lived in troubled times, plagued by persecutions so that their wisdom was adversely affected and a gap opened up between them and the prophets' generations that had preceded them. The prophets, therefore, possessed the true, correct philosophy, which was passed on to the Gentile nations when they conquered the Land of Israel. This passage is not only a legitimation of the pursuit of philosophy but also a historical-apologetic explanation of why Aristotle rather than the sages held the correct views on metaphysical and astronomical issues.

Yet, the systematic reason for Maimonides' latent distinction between the prophets and the sages in this unit of chapters is that the prophets relied on analogical reasoning and approached the metaphysical secrets according to the criteria laid down by Maimonides in the Introduction to the *Guide*. He shows here the influence of Neoplatonic hermeneutics, which posits a division into three stages:

(1) Image (*eikon*) and likeness (*homoia*). The concern here is with direct reflection, as in the case of a picture and its subject.
(2) Symbol (*symbolon*). This stage expresses the object through one of its parts or characteristics, such as representing Jerusalem through the Old City.
(3) Analogy. The juxtaposition of the plain or outward meaning of the text with its inner, profound meaning.[40]

Thus, according to Maimonides, a "correct" analogy results from the use of images and symbols. By relying on analogical thought, the prophets

---

39 *Guide* II:11, 276.
40 See John Dillon, "Image, Symbol and Analogy: Three Basic Concepts of Neoplatonic Allegorical Exegesis," in *The Significance of Neoplatonism*, ed. R. Baine Harris (Norfolk, VA: Old Dominion University, 1976), 247–262.

created images, symbols, and analogies that led them to real achievements in the metaphysical field. The sages, who were interpreters rather than creators, at times misunderstood the prophets' intention. Analogical reasoning is thus the key to an understanding of the chapters on the separate intellects from the standpoint of prophetic and rabbinic authority as well.

Again: Emanation and Creation

Chapter 11 formulates the thesis that the world of existents is based on emanation (*fayḍ*) and, in the course of the chapter, Maimonides explains the order of the emanation—from God to the material world.[41] The last chapter of the literary unit considered here elucidates the action of emanation, which depends neither on distance nor on time but only on preparation.[42] Such action is hard to reconcile with the concept of creation *ex nihilo* since emanation taking effect is contingent on the preparation of the matter in question. The concept of creation *ex nihilo* ("after having been nonexistent") appears in Chapters 2 to 12—in Chapter 2 as an alternative to the concept of the eternity of the world. But henceforth it vanishes,[43] to reappear at the beginning of the unit of chapters on creation (II:13), where Maimonides explains the three views on the world as created or as eternal. The Torah holds that "the world as a whole ... was brought into existence by God after having been purely and absolutely nonexistent." In Chapter 12, however, Maimonides uses the term *'adam*, "nonexistence," in the sense of the existing matter's lack of preparation. The discussion on the action of the separate intellects and the spheres, therefore, rests on the concept of eternity, that is, of given, pre-existent matter. Only later, in the unit of chapters devoted to creation, does Maimonides articulate the concept of creation *ex nihilo*.

Up to this point, I have explained the location of the *Guide* II:2-12 unit as clarifying the methodology required for the understanding of natural and intellectual activity. Understanding the action of the active intellect, which is essential for Maimonidean natural science, relies on analogy and

---

41 The relationship between emanation and creation has been debated at length, as detailed in Schwarz's notes on II:12. I am only interested here in the unit in II: 2-12 and its implications. See also David B. Burrell, "Creation or Emanation: Two Paradigms of Reason," in *God and Creation: An Ecumenical Symposium*, ed. David B. Burrell and Bernard McGinn (Notre Dame, ID: University of Notre Dame Press, 1990), 27–37.

42 See Y. Tzvi Langerman, "Maimonides' Repudiation of Astrology," *Maimonidean Studies* 2 (1991), 132–133.

43 This concept is mentioned only at the ends of chapters (6, 11), as a reference to the discussion in Chapter 13 and later.

vice-versa—the activity of the separate intellects and the spheres becomes understandable as a result of such an analogy. This is only one example of the analogical method's importance. Another aspect of this unit's location emerges here. The beginning of Part II of the *Guide* is devoted to the issue of creation, with Maimonides expressing support for the doctrine of creation *ex nihilo*, as he does in the unit's opening chapter. The explanation of the action of the intellects and the spheres, however, relies on the concept of eternity, which is the target of Maimonides' polemics. The location of these chapters, therefore, may be explained in a negative sense as well: Maimonides expounds at length on the concept of eternity in order to acquaint the reader with the foundations of the view that he wishes to confront. The Peripatetics were persuaded to adopt the doctrine of eternity not only because of the laws of motion but also because of metaphysics, meaning the emanating action of the separate intellects and the spheres.[44] Maimonides chose a frontal confrontation with the laws of physics while expressing doubts about the functional structure of the intellects and the spheres (II:22). The location of this unit of chapters, then, is explicated not only on methodological grounds (analogical thought) but also on substantial ones. The special character of this unit thus attests to Maimonides' esoteric style and to the unique structure of *The Guide of the Perplexed*.

Medieval Commentaries on *The Guide of the Perplexed*

This section explores the approaches of medieval commentators to the problems raised in the preceding analysis and to other issues touching on the *Guide* II:2-12. The writings and commentaries of Moshe Narboni and Mordekhai Komtiyano will be at the focus of my discussion. Narboni has received considerable attention in the scholarly literature on medieval Jewish thought. Komtiyano was a figure of exceptional stature in the Byzantine-Jewish thought of the late Middle Ages. His style is often measured and concise and his work includes several genuinely scientific works in logic, astronomy, and so forth.[45] Komtiyano wrote a running

---

44 See Richard Sorabji, *Time, Creation and the Continuum: Theories in Antiquity and the Early Middle Ages* (Ithaca, NY: Cornell University Press, 1983). For the combination of these arguments see, e.g., Richard C. Dales, *Medieval Discussions of the Eternity of the World* (Leiden: Brill, 1990), 58.

45 See Jean-Christophe Attias, *Le commentaire biblique: Mordekhai Komtino ou l'herméneutique du dialogue* (Paris: Cerf, 1991); Dov Schwartz, "Rationalism and Astral Magic in Jewish Thought in Late Medieval Byzantium," *Aleph* 3 (2003):165–211.

commentary on the *Guide* where he pondered the location of the unit of chapters discussed here. I deal below with some issues in his commentary and with treatises by Provençal and Spanish exegetes who influenced him.

The Location of the Unit (II:2-12)

In Chapter 2, Maimonides explains the location of these chapters:

> Now I think it fit that I should complete the exposition of the opinions of the philosophers, that I should explain their proofs concerning the existence of separate intellects. ... After that I shall go back, as I have promised, to arguing with a view to proving that the world has come into existence in time.

He himself considered Chapters 2 to 12 an independent literary unit, beyond the discussion of creation. Profiat Duran and Shem Tov b. Joseph ibn Shem Tov, therefore, stated that the unit deals with *ma'aseh merkavah*[46] and that it is fundamentally a "prolegomena to *ma'aseh merkavah*, which deals with emanation."[47] That is, before dealing with creation, which is the process of emanation that gave rise to the material world, Maimonides described the separate intellects and the spheres as the source of the emanation. Mordekhai Komtiyano's view was different and, regarding Chapter 3, he writes as follows:

> After the preceding chapters, from which he extracted the three supreme prerequisites[48] in relation to the belief in the eternity [of the world], he introduced this chapter, an exposition from which he will proceed to explain the production [of the world] in time that is in dispute between us and the philosophers, as he mentioned previously. And this is also a supreme prerequisite for religious people, for the belief in the eternity [of the world] would demolish the entire Torah.[49]

Komtiyano, then, held that the discussion of creation begins in chapter 3 and not in chapter 13, where Maimonides lists the views on "the eternity of

---

46 *Sefer Moreh Nevukhim im Mefarshim* [Guide of the Perplexed with Commentators], vol. 2 (Jerusalem: offset, 1960), 17b [Heb].
47 Ibid., citing Shem Tov, 29b.
48 The existence, uniqueness, and non-corporeality of God.
49 Komtiyano's commentary on *The Guide of the Perplexed*, Ms. Cambridge, Trinity College 126, 71v. See Dov Schwartz and Esti Eisenmann, *Commentary on Guide of the Perplexed: The Commentary of R. Mordekhai ben Eliezer Komtiyano on Maimonides' Guide of the Perplexed* (Ramat-Gan: Bar-Ilan University Press, 2016). See also Dov Schwartz, "Creation in Late Medieval Byzantine Jewry: A Few Aspects," *Pe'amim* 97 (Autumn 2003): 63–80 [Heb].

the world or its production in time." Komtiyano's view is interesting both in light of Maimonides' explicit affirmation that he was placing the issue of the intellects and the spheres before that of creation and in view of the fact, mentioned above, that creation *ex nihilo* is not mentioned until Chapter 13. Clearly, Komtiyano thought that the proofs of God's existence, uniqueness, and non-corporeality, as well as of God moving the spheres, were concentrated in the two opening chapters of Part II of the *Guide* and that, henceforth, Maimonides dealt directly with the creation.

Analogy

The preceding analysis drew attention to the significant role of analogy in the *Guide* and to the role of the active intellect as an auxiliary tool in understanding the position of the separate intellects. Some commentators, such as Shem Tov b. Joseph ibn Shem Tov, explain Maimonides' text as is, while others take a more critical stance. Among the critical ones is Moshe Narboni who, in chapter 14 of his commentary on Averroes' *Epistle on the Possibility of Conjunction*, deals at length with Maimonides' discussion of the proportions in *Guide* II:4.[50] Narboni compares Maimonides' approach with that of Averroes on the topic. Averroes would have agreed to the first proportion (the separate intellect is to the sphere as the active intellect is to the elements). Regarding the second proportion, however, Maimonides and Averroes differ. Maimonides argues that the soul of the sphere, the intellect of the sphere, and the separate intellect that moves the sphere are three distinct entities. Averroes, however, (and Narboni in his wake) rejects the very existence of the intellect of the sphere as "the form of the celestial body,"[51] that is, as the form of the sphere. In Narboni's view, "The soul and the intellect [of the sphere] and the separate intellect are substantially one but conceptually three, contrary to what the late Master believed, that it is a composite."[52] The distinction between the three animative and intellectual agents moving the sphere is functional, but not ontological. Narboni, therefore, concludes regarding Maimonides' second proportion (which distinguished the intellect of the sphere from the

---

50 See below, p. 83.
51 Kalman P. Bland, ed., *The Epistle on the Possibility of Conjunction with the Active Intellect by Ibn Rushd with the Commentary of Moses Narboni* (New York: Jewish Theological Seminary of America, 1982), 96.
52 Moshe Narboni, *Commentary on The Guide of the Perplexed*, ed. J. Goldenthal (Wien, 1832), 27b [Heb].

separate intellect) that "the relation [posited by Maimonides] is not true in existence, for they are things that have absolutely no existence, and nature does not act in vain."[53] Narboni's approach (following Averroes) thus makes it possible to combine Maimonides' two proportions into one:[54]

$$\frac{\text{active intellect}}{\text{human intellect (second preparation)}[55]} = \frac{\text{active intellect}}{\text{elements and composites in the material world}} = \frac{\text{separate intellect}}{\text{sphere}}$$

But this proportion is not perfect. Narboni comments that, while the separate intellect is the only form of the sphere, elements and composites have a material form on the one hand and, on the other, a form "in the sense of absolute existence,"[56] which is the active intellect. Narboni, then, addresses the issue of Maimonides' proportions and criticizes them in light of Averroes's theory of the intellect. His discussion is philosophical-technical rather than literary-methodological. Neither in his commentary on the *Guide* nor in that on Averroes's *Epistle of the Possibility of Conjunction* does Narboni consider the proportions a reflection of Maimonides' general system. He thereby remained loyal to medieval conventions, refraining from dealing with the meaning of the divergence from the logical inference, even after Maimonides' explicit declaration.

God as the Mover of the Sphere

Much has been said about Maimonides' self-contradiction both in the *Guide* and in the *Mishneh Torah* (in "Laws of the Foundation of the Torah") on the

---

53   See, for example, *De Caelo* 271a33; *Epistle on the Possibility of Conjunction*, 96.
54   Ibid.
55   Narboni states that "the relation of the active intellect insofar as it conjoins with us—it being a form in us—is the relation of the Separate [Intellect] with the sphere in one respect, I mean, in certain ways, but different in certain ways, as is clear from what has already preceded" (ibid., 98). According to the *Epistle on the Possibility of Conjunction*, the active intellect conjoins with humans after the material preparation of the intellect has disintegrated in the highest stage of intellection and is replaced by a second preparation, which makes conjunction possible. On this matter, see Herbert A. Davidson, "Averroes and the Material Intellect," *AJS Review* 9 (1984): 174–184; Dov Schwartz, *The Philosophy of a Fourteenth-Century Jewish Neoplatonic Circle* (Jerusalem: Bialik Institute, 1997)179 [Heb]; Gitit Holzman, *The Theory of the Intellect and Soul and the Thought of R. Moshe Narboni, Based on His Commentaries on the Writings of Ibn Rushd, Ibn Tufayil, Ibn Bajja and Al-Ghazali* (Ph. D. dissertation: The Hebrew University of Jerusalem, 1997), 86–87 and *passim* [Heb].
56   Narboni, *Epistle on the Possibility of Conjunction*, Bland ed., 130, ln. 277.

question of God being the mover of the highest sphere.[57] In some passages, Maimonides claims that God moves the sphere. In *Guide* II:4, however, he states that "it cannot be true that the intellect that moves the highest sphere should be identical with the necessary of existence."[58] Komtiyano's view is that God clearly does move the sphere:

> What is clear from Aristotle's principles is that the mover of the first sphere is the Creator, blessed be He. Moreover, the Master explained this in Chapter 70 of the first part,[59] and that is the truth, for there is no separate [intellect] that is not a mover, for nature does not act in vain. But the Master's argument rejecting this view and saying that, if that were the case, it would have something in common with the other movers, is the opinion of the commentators on Aristotle's books. Now this doubt may be resolved, for the movement of the Prime Mover is universal and voluntary, while the movement of the other movers is partial and necessary, and they can have nothing at all in common.[60]

Even if God does move the sphere, he is still clearly distinct from the intellects because: (1) The intellects move only part of the system of spheres whereas the movement of the highest sphere causes that of the entire system. (2) The intellects move necessarily while God moves voluntarily. Komtiyano thus rejects the Neoplatonic approach endorsed by Maimonides in these chapters.

"The World Plus One Third"

Many commenting on the more esoteric aspects of Maimonides' thought have been at a loss to understand his ambiguous explanation of the puzzling midrash. I have tried to propose a solution that combines his two interpretations of the "third," on the assumption that he had downplayed his view of the sages' approach to scientific matters. R. Joseph ibn Kaspi explains "that sometimes these four angels will meet in one line across the ladder; thus, it seemed to [Jacob] that the width was one world and a third."[61] What he means is that the steps along the length of the ladder are three: the world of the intellects, the world of the spheres, and the

---

57 Schwarz, 274, n. 34.
58 *Guide* II:4, 258–259.
59 "Similarly, the deity… is the mover of the highest heaven, by whose motion everything that is in motion with this heaven is moved" (*Guide* I:70, 172).
60 Mordekhai Komtiyano, *Commentary on The Guide of the Perplexed*, Ms. Cambridge, 72r–v.
61 Joseph Kaspi, *Ammudei kesef u-maskiyyot kesef*, ed. S. Werbluner (Frankfurt am Main, 1848), 96.

sublunar world. In his vision, Jacob saw the lower step, that of the sublunar world, divided into four, meaning that the width of the lower step is split into four—the four elements or the four sides of the world (the four directions). Since "the size of the one angel is one third of the world, as will be explained below," Jacob believed that the width of the lower world is "one world and a third." The second step, that of the spheres, Kaspi adds, also splits into four—the four spheres described in chapter 9. Seemingly, then, Kaspi is intimating that, according to the midrash, Jacob believed that the width of the lower world exceeds its length by one third, which is scientifically wrong.

What was seemingly clear to Kaspi, as he indicates, was not so for Narboni:

> Now these four that came together on one step [of the ladder] were the four directions, and the four directions of the heavens are precisely the four angels that came together on one step, and they constitute only one third, which is a third of the world; so how could that be one world and a third?!

Indirectly, Narboni rejects the interpretation of Jacob's vision as referring to the excessive width occupied by the elements, since the width of the sublunar world cannot exceed that of the world of the spheres. Narboni explains simply that since each element is called an "angel," and the midrash added that "an angel is one third of the world," it follows at first glance that the width of the lower world is indeed one world plus a third. On further examination, however, the width of the four elements is revealed as only one third of the world ("the four of them are but that angel, who is one third of the world, and he is the third, lowest, part of the parts of the created beings").

Narboni's commentary was available to Komtiyano when he wrote his own. Referring to the passage in the *Guide*, Komtiyano cites Narboni and professes himself dissatisfied with it:

> This is the explanation offered by the best of commentators, but I say that this explanation is inconsistent both with the midrash and with the context, if explained in this fashion. I will now explain what I have been able to understand after much study. Know that caused existence is divided into three parts, and these are the parts of existence mentioned everywhere [= matter and form], and existence corresponding to privation. But you will find a further, fourth part, and that is what is alluded to in the midrash stating that there are four camps of angels.[62] And it is not wrong to include everything

---

62 See Schwarz, 288, n. 28.

under the noun "angels," seeing that the noun "angel" is an equivocal word, and the formulation of [the midrash] was guided by the majority usage [of the noun "angel"]. By "ladder" [the midrash] is alluding to the totality of existence corresponding to privation, and since the three parts constitute existence, and the fourth part is above it, [the midrash] sets it apart [from them] after including it, saying "[God was] standing over him." The midrash also understands the *bet* of *ba-sullam* ["on the ladder"] as extending the meaning or again follows the majority usage. The angels of God ascending and descending are four in number: The two <descending ones>[63] are man and the rest, and the two ascending ones are the celestial bodies, both the eternal and the corrupted, and all of caused existence, that is, the world whose parts are three in number. And when you contemplate the linkage of the totality of existence with the [First] Cause which fashions it and does everything, you will find that everything [measures] one world and a third, and that is the width of the ladder. And the Master did not have to bring this because of the steps of the ladder, of which there were four, for he had already stated in some versions "seven"; but it was only because of those ascending and descending.[64]

Komtiyano found a simple solution: the noun "angel" has several meanings, among them "privation." Jacob's ladder, then, symbolizes not only the levels of being, but also modes of being: existence (intellects, spheres, and the lower world) and privation. An "angel" in the sense of intellects, spheres and the material world is "one third of the world," and an "angel" in the sense of privation is the third in "one world and a third." Komtiyano must obviously postulate a correspondence between existence and privation for "privation" to possess, as it were, absolute existence, as his interpretation requires. But given Maimonides' basic philosophical and scientific assumption that "nonexistence" is not a species or mode of existence, Komtiyano's interpretation, despite his efforts, seems highly problematic to say the least.

Conclusion

The interpretations of Jacob's dream and the discussion of "one world and a third" reflect the difference between modern scholarship and various trends found in the medieval exegesis of *The Guide of the Perplexed*. Medieval commentators constituted rabbinic midrashim on knowledge of the four spheres and the rabbinic interpretation of the concern with the

---

63 The manuscript reads here "who speaks with" (*ha-medabber 'im*) (?).
64 Komtiyano, *Commentary on The Guide of the Perplexed*, Ms. Cambridge, 74v–75r.

separate intellects as part of the three parts of existence.[65] By contrast, modern esoteric research stresses the difference between prophecy and rabbinic midrashim. In the modern view, the dominant motive for the concealment of esoteric lore is political, whereas medieval commentators seek to conceal the sciences because of their abstruseness and high level of sophistication.[66]

My emphasis has also been on the methodological aspect, that is, the use of analogies, as part of the reasons for the esotericism. Analogical thought was not held in high regard in Aristotelian scientific circles, being considered an inferior method of proof. Maimonides, however, acknowledging his use of analogical methodology, declared in the Introduction to the *Guide* that metaphysical truths were inherently unprovable. He still concealed, however, his extensive reliance on analogies and the essential role they play in the understanding of the *Guide*. The unit of chapters in the *Guide* II:2-12 thus reflects an approach fitting the works' general character: the new insights of the *Guide* are not necessarily a product of the scientific-deductive thinking appropriate to the ordinary philosophical-religious treatises of the late Middle Ages. Maimonides holds that metaphysical achievements would be attained in other ways. Many early and modern commentators have failed to take note of this Maimonidean declaration and have not implemented his explicit instruction, which this chapter has sought to highlight.

---

65 See, for example, the commentary of Shem Tov b. Joseph (26r). Shem Tov himself adopts an esoteric approach in his interpretation of the chapters of the *Guide*. See Schwartz, *Contradiction and Concealment*, 196–217.

66 On the distinction between medieval and modern scholarship, see Aviezer Ravitzky, "The Secrets of *The Guide to the Perplexed*: Between the Thirteenth and the Twentieth Centuries," in *Studies in Maimonides*, ed. Isadore Twersky (Cambridge, MA: Harvard University Press, 1990), 159–207.

Appendix

On Analogy and the Attributes

Analogical arguments, as noted, are very common in the *Guide*. This appendix analyzes one example of key importance for understanding Maimonides' thought in the *Guide*, dealing with the theory of divine attributes.

In the relevant chapters of the *Guide*, Maimonides raises the problematic issue of how to draw distinctions among the wise after the theory of divine attributes has been rejected. If no positive attribute can be associated with the deity, how can a distinction be made between the wisest of all men (such as "Moses our Master and Solomon") and an ordinary individual? In *Guide* I:59-60, the two chapters most relevant to this issue, Maimonides relies on a demonstrative argument to state that the wise man negates the attributes.[67] These two chapters are placed immediately after a series of almost desperate attempts to distinguish God from all other existents, which can be described in positive terms. The difficulty is obvious: we cannot distinguish *a* (God) from *b* if *a* is indescribable and indefinable. Since the attributes, and the one of existence above all, are associated with God and with objects in a "purely equivocal" manner (II:56), we have no way of presenting a difference between them and the discussion becomes pointless. To overcome this difficulty, Maimonides proposes two conceptual schemes that afford an insight into the distinction between God and other existents:

(1) *Distinction between essence and existence*, postulating that God's essence and existence are identical, contrary to all other existents (I:57). If we accept Faizur Rahman's interpretation of the accidentality of existence in Avicenna, and Alexander Altmann's interpretation of this matter in Maimonides, we apparently cannot assume a world of essences, some or all of which become existent. In their view, the distinction is between an object that has a cause for its

---

67 See Hyman, "Demonstrative, Dialectical and Sophistic Arguments." On demonstration in the context of the theory of attributes, see p. 43.

existence and one that does not.[68] In that case, this approach does not prove particularly helpful in presenting a clear distinction between the deity and other existents.

(2) *Analogy.* A partial description, such as presenting humans as animals (given that humans are defined as intelligent animals and, therefore, "animal" is part of the definition of humans), is in some degree analogous to the negative attributes. Maimonides is probably alluding to such an analogy:

$$\frac{\text{animal}}{\text{human}} = \frac{\text{negative attributes}}{\text{God}}$$

In Maimonides' view, this analogy leads to "a certain particularization,"[69] but he admits the deficiency of such an analogy between attributes of affirmation and attributes of negation. The analogy becomes more accurate insofar as its members are more narrowly defined or closer together (as an inference from primates to human beings). Thus, negative attributes constitute "guidance"[70] toward the greatest possible apprehension.

Having suggested two ways of overcoming the total non-apprehension of God so as to distinguish the deity from the attributes of the existents, Maimonides then tries to apply them to distinguish the knowledge of perfect-wise persons from superficial or deficient knowledge. Ostensibly, the split between essence and existence on the one hand and analogy on the other enable a gradation of apprehension, even when its object cannot be construed in positive terms. Briefly: the wise person understands the profound meaning of the term "existence" and is acquainted with the elements of the analogy, and, in that respect, differs from the ignorant one. Chapters 57 and 58 are thus an introduction to Chapter 59, where Maimonides proposes the distinction between the apprehension of the wise and that of the ignorant. Analogy, then, plays a major role in Maimonides' theory of attributes.

---

68 Fazlur Rahman, "Essence and Existence in Avicenna," *Medieval and Renaissance Studies* 4 (1958): 1-16; Alexander Altmann, "Essence and Existence in Maimonides," *Studies in Religious Philosophy and Mysticism* (Ithaca, NY: Cornell University Press, 1969),

69 "For instance, if you would see a man at some distance and if you would ask: What is this thing that is seen? and were told: This is a living being—this affirmation would indubitably be an attribute predicated of the thing seen, though it does not particularize the latter, distinguishing it from everything else. However, a certain particularization is achieved through it; namely, it may be learnt from it that the thing seen is not a body belonging to the species of plants or to that of the minerals" (*Guide* I:58, 134).

70 Arabic *irshād* (Munk and Joel, 92, ln. 11).

Chapter 3

Astral Magic and the Law

Maimonides' style in the *Mishneh Torah* has been a concern in both rabbinic and scholarly literature, at times as a controversial topic. Over the centuries that followed, exegetes have been engaged in extensive discussions about this work. Relying mainly on literary and halakhic-comparative claims, Jacob Levinger pointed out that the style of the *Mishneh Torah* merits reexamination.[1] José Faur strongly objected to these claims, stating that the *Mishneh Torah* should be understood according to the school of the geonim and of R. Joseph ibn Migash, without recourse to literary criteria unsuited to it.[2] Isadore Twersky presented a comprehensive approach that tends to integrate a number of perspectives on it—hermeneutic, literary, philosophical, and aesthetic—and ascribed a rigorous order to its chapters and laws.[3] Hayim Soloveitchik returned to deal with the style and the classification of the *Mishneh Torah*.[4] All these approaches reopened the discussion on Maimonides' vast halakhic enterprise that had taken place at the end of the nineteenth and the early twentieth centuries (involving, among many others, Adolf Schwartz, Yehiel Guttmann, and Hayyim Tchernowitz [Rav Tsair]). The unique style of the *Mishneh Torah* is thus still a topic of discussion alive for both commentators and scholars.

One issue they addressed are the Laws Concerning Idolatry and Maimonides' view of magic in general, which is not surprising given Maimonides' courageous stance on this matter, as shown below. I wish to make a modest contribution to the acknowledgment of the *Mishneh*

---

1 Jacob Levinger, *Maimonides' Techniques of Codification: A Study in the Method of Mishneh Torah* (Jerusalem: Magnes, 1965) [Heb].
2 José Faur, *Studies on Maimonides' Code (The Book of Knowledge)* (Jerusalem: Mosad Harav Kook, 1978) [Heb].
3 Isadore Twersky, *Introduction to the Code of Maimonides (Mishneh Torah)* (New Haven, CO: Yale University Press, 1980).
4 Haym Soloveitchik, "*Mishneh Torah*: Polemic and Art," in *Maimonides after 800 Years: Essays on Maimonides and His Influence*, ed. Jay M. Harris (Cambridge, MA: Harvard University Center for Jewish Studies, 2007), 339-355.

Torah's uniqueness by remarking briefly on the order of two of the Laws Concerning Idolatry, which appears to offer some clues to the process of the *Mishneh Torah*'s writing.

Background

For his conception of magic and the cult of images, Maimonides relied on a naïve perception of the concrete reality. He attested that he had read, examined, and inspected many sources on idolatry in search for final answers on halakhic rulings or the reasons for the commandments. The evidence available to Maimonides showed that the Sabian religion—founded on idolatry and on hermetic trends that included astral magic—was widespread in Harran during the ninth and tenth centuries.[5] Maimonides relied on sources such as *The Book of Nabatean Agriculture* by Ibn Waḥshīyya to obtain details as precise as possible on the character` of this idolatrous cult.[6] He pointed to Harran as a focus for the preservation of idolatry over centuries and approached the views prevailing in this center as representing a continuous ritual of idolatrous worship from antiquity until his times making the Sabians, as it were, a paradigm of biblical idolaters. This anachronistic view also shaped Maimonides' hermeneutical, halakhic, and conceptual teachings in his *Commentary to the Mishnah*, in the *Mishneh Torah*, and in *The Guide of the Perplexed*.

Maimonides' conceptual and halakhic view of idolatry and magic has been discussed at length. His halakhic attitude toward witchcraft, as is well known, was clearly negative, and his conceptual view of it can be summed up as a denial of its reality and effect, an approach that compelled him to present the sorcerer as a juggler and a swindler (a "trickster"). Maimonides, however, did acknowledge non-Aristotelian scientific paradigms, and pharmacology is a good example. The many references to magic in his halakhic and philosophical ideas suggest complexity and diversity.

---

5 This approach is systematically presented in Part III of the *Guide*, but appears in other Maimonidean writings as well. See, for example, Sarah Stroumsa, "The Sabians of Harran and the Sabians of Maimonides: On Maimonides' Theory of the History of Religions," *Sefunot*, New Series 7 (1999): 277-295 [Heb]; idem, "'Ravings': Maimonides' Concept of Pseudo-Science," *Aleph* 1 (2001): 141-163.

6 See, for example, Daniil Avramovitch Khwolson, *Die Ssabier und der Ssabismus*, vol. 2 (St. Petersburg: Kaiserlichen Akademie der Wissenschaften, 1856); idem, *Über die Überreste der altbabylonischen Literatur in arabischen Übersetzungen: Mémoires des Savants étrangers*, vol. 8 (St. Petersbourg: Kaiserlichen Akademie der Wissenschaften 1859); Jan Hjarpe, *Analyse critique des traditions arabes sur les sabéens harraniens* (Uppsala: Skriv, 1972); Michel Tardieu, "Sabiens Coraniques et 'Sabiens' de Harran," *Journal Asiatique* 274 (1986): 1-44.

In what follows, I will point to a specific issue to show how the philosophical foundations of Maimonides' thought shaped his halakhic doctrine and enable its understanding as a coherent and developing process. Specifically, I present a structural and substantial puzzlement about the *Mishneh Torah*, and its resolution according to Maimonides' view of magic.

Puzzlement

The last two laws in Chapter 3 of the Laws Concerning Idolatry are puzzling regarding both their contents and their order. Maimonides' famous translator, exegete, and advocate, R. Yosef Qafih, had already noted at the beginning and at the end of his discussion on them that these laws "are unclear to many"[7] and that "interpretations have proliferated on this obscure issue."[8] Following are the laws:

> 10. It is forbidden to make figures for purposes of ornaments,[9] even if they are not idolatrous, as it is said, "Ye shall not make with Me gods of gold and silver"[10] (Exodus 20:23); that is to say, figures of gold and silver which only serve as ornaments; so that those likely to err shall not err and imagine that these figures serve idolatrous purposes. The prohibition of making ornamental figures only applies to representation of the human form. Hence, a figure of a human being must not be made in wood, clay or stone; provided that the figure is in high relief like sculptures and figures in palaces and the like places; and whoever makes such is punished with stripes. But if a figure is in bas-relief or painted, such as pictures on boards and tablets, or woven in tapestry—it is permitted.
>
> 11. If a signet ring has a human figure on it, and the figure is in high-relief, it is forbidden to wear the ring, but it may be used as a seal. If the figure is in bas-relief, the ring may be worn but may not be used for sealing, because the impression it would make would be in high-relief. It is also forbidden to make figures of the sun, moon, stars, constellations, or angels,[11] for it is said,

---

7   *Sefer Mishneh Torah*, first edition according to Yemen MSS with a comprehensive commentary by Yosef b. David Qafih (Kiriyat Ono: Machon Mishnat ha-Rambam, 1984), 399 [Heb] (henceforth *Mishneh Torah*, Qafih ed.).
8   ibid., 403.
9   This formulation appears in *Mishneh Tora*, Qafih ed., and also below. On the aesthetic dimension of this prohibition, see Menachem Kellner, ed., *The Pursuit of the Ideal: Jewish Writings of Steven Schwarzschild* (Albany, NY: SUNY Press, 1990), 110-112.
10 In several MSS, the "gods of gold and silver" phrase is missing.
11 See Menachem Kellner, *Maimonides' Confrontation with Mysticism* (Oxford: Littman Library of Jewish Civilization, 2006), 265-285. Marc Shapiro views this as an expression

"Ye shall not make with Me" (Exodus 20:20); that is, 'ye shall not make figures representing My ministers that minister before Me on high';[12] and such figures may not be made even on tablets. Figures of quadrupeds and of other animals—with the exception of Man,—and of trees and plants, etc., may be made, even if the figures are in relief.[13]

I will briefly present several difficulties in the understanding of these two laws, which have already been widely explored in the rabbinic literature, beginning with Maimonides' contemporaries. I will then introduce the foundations of the Maimonidean view on magic and on idolatry, using them to show that there was no room for these difficulties to begin with.

Ostensibly, the distinction between the two laws is clear: since Law 9 had dealt with the prohibition on making figures to be used in idolatrous worship, Laws 10 and 11 deal with the prohibition on making such figures for ornamental purposes. In other words, the alternatives before Maimonides were either worship or ornamentation and, as R. Menachem Meiri defined in his novellae, "for ornamentation, that is, not intended for worship."[14] But this distinction raises several difficulties, which commentators had already noted:

(1) The prohibition on making figures in the middle of Law 11 is entirely superfluous since Maimonides had already noted many times, explicitly and by inference, that making figures that could be used for idolatrous purposes even if they are not worshiped, is forbidden.[15]
(2) Law 10 opens by categorically stating that making figures for ornamentation purposes is forbidden, but immediately after it

---

of the multitudes' belief in angels as actual beings. See Marc B. Shapiro, *Studies in Maimonides and His Interpreters* (Scranton: University of Scranton Press, 2008), 146. I present a different approach below.
12 BT Avodah Zarah 43a, and a parallel version in BT Rosh Hashanah 24b.
13 Maimonides, *Mishneh Torah: The Book of Knowledge*, trans. Moses Hyamson (Jerusalem: Boys Town, 1962). Note that the talisman, that is, the figure meant to attract the powers of the stars, was usually made on a tablet or a board. The distinction was apparently one between an engraving and a high-relief.
14 Menachem Meiri, *Beith ha-Behirah al Masekhet Avodah Zara*, ed. Abraham Sofer (Jerusalem, 1964), 153 [Heb].
15 For example: "If one acquires an idol for himself, he is punished with stripes, even though he did not make it with his own hand and did not worship it, as it is said, 'Thou shalt not make unto thee a graven image nor any manner of likeness' (Exodus 20:4)"(Laws Concerning Idolatry 3:9). In Chapter 1, Maimonides recurrently notes that idolatrous worship resorts to figures.

becomes clear that what is forbidden is only the making of human figures. The opening of this law is thus puzzling.

(3) The laws rely on a series of statements by Abaye in BT Avodah Zarah 43a-b:
   (a) The Torah only forbids making figures of God's serving ministers.
   (b) The Torah only forbids making a figure of the four faces together.
   (c) You shall not make Me [a human face].[16]
   (d) The Torah only prohibits making figures of the ministers in the higher firmament.
   (e) [Ministers] in the lowest firmament are also [forbidden in the Torah].

The tosafists, as well as R. Nissim Girondi (Ran) and other exegetes commenting *ad locum*, clarified that Abaye is not retreating here from one statement to the next, and Rav Qafih's premise was that Maimonides did not accept their view.[17] But even without accepting their view, it is still clear that making specific astronomical figures for ornamental purposes is forbidden. Why, then, forbid only the making of human figures as Maimonides did in Law 10?

(4) In Law 11, Maimonides draws a distinction between a human figure, which is forbidden only when made in high relief, and the figures of stars, which are forbidden both in high-relief and engraved. In a gloss on this ruling, R. Abraham of Posquières [Rabad] wrote, "and I do not know why, and how he learns this."

In order to show that there is no room for any of these queries, I will briefly present two elements of Maimonides' view of magic.

Basic Assumptions

Talmudic and midrashic literature had already established a connection between idolatry and magic,[18] and the two are indeed linked in Maimonides' teachings.[19] For example, in *The Guide of the Perplexed* III:37, he discusses

---

16 See Ephraim E. Urbach, "The Laws Concerning Idolatry and the Archeological and Historical Reality in the Second and Third Centuries," in *The World of the Sages: Collected Studies* (Jerusalem: Magnes Press, 1988) [Heb].
17 *Mishneh Torah*, Qafih ed., 401.
18 See, for example, Ephraim E. Urbach, *The Sages: Their Concepts and Beliefs*, trans. Israel Abrahams (Jerusalem: Magnes Press, 1975), 97-99.
19 Maimonides' approach to magic and astrology has been of interest to many scholars. See, for example, Lynn Thorndike, *A History of Magic and Experimental Science*, vol. 2 (New York:

them together. The clarification of the puzzling laws in the *Mishneh Torah* is thus anchored in the systematic development of Maimonides' view on magic in his various works. This approach assumes that, between ornamentation and worship, there is another use for the figures and effigies—the "scientific" or "learned" use, implemented, for example, in healing through the use of amulets that rely on the stars. Such use requires some measure of astrological and medical knowledge.

Maimonides' view of magic, as it developed in his various writings, is based on two assumptions:

(1) Both historically and methodologically, magic relies on astrology. Maimonides writes in *The Guide of the Perplexed*:

> In all magical operations it is indispensable that the stars should be observed. I mean, they deem that a certain plant should be assigned to the portion of a certain star; similarly they assign every animal and every mineral to a star. They likewise deem that the operations performed by the magicians are various species of worship offered to a certain star, which, being pleased with that operation or speech or fumigation, does for us what we wish.[20]

Columbia University Press, 1964), 205-213; H. S. Lewis, "Maimonides on Superstition," *Jewish Quarterly Review*, o.s. 17 (1905): 474-488; Leon Nemoy, "Maimonides' Opposition to Magic in Light of the Writings of Jacob al-Qirqisani," *Ha-Rofe ha-'Ivri* 27, 1-2 (1954): 102-109 [Heb]. See also Yitzhak Heinemann, *The Reasons for the Commandments in the Tradition* (Jerusalem: WZO, 1966), 91-92 [Heb]; Twersky, *Introduction to the Code of Maimonides*, 479-484; idem, "Halakhah and Science: Perspectives on the Epistemology of Maimonides," *Annual of Jewish Law* 14-15 (1988-89): 135-140 [Heb]; Bezalel Safran, "Maimonides' Attitude to Magic and to Related Types of Thinking," in *Porat Yosef: Studies Presented to Rabbi Dr. Joseph Safran*, ed. Bezalel Safran and Eliyahu Safran (Hoboken, NJ: Ktav, 1992); Yitzhak Tzvi Langermann, "Maimonides' Repudiation of Astrology," *Maimonidean Studies* 2 (1991): 123-158; Gad Freudenthal, "Maimonides' Stance on Astrology in Context: Cosmology, Physics, Medicine, and Providence," in *Moses Maimonides: Physician, Scientist and Philosopher*, ed. Fred Rosner and Samuel S. Kottek (Northvale, NJ: J. Aronson, 1993), 77-90; Dov Schwartz, *Studies on Astral Magic in Medieval Jewish Thought*, trans. David Louvish and Batya Stein (Leiden/Boston: Brill, 2005), ch. 2; idem, *Amulets, Properties, and Rationalism in Medieval Jewish Thought* (Ramat-Gan: Bar-Ilan University Press, 2004) [Heb].

20 *Guide* III:37, 542. This linking of all idolatrous practices to astrology is not easily reconciled with the rich talmudic material on this matter. See, for example, Saul Lieberman, *Hellenism in Jewish Palestine: Studies in the Literary Transmission of Beliefs and Manners of Palestine in the I Century B.C.E.-IV Century C.E.* (New York: The Jewish Theological Seminary, 1962), 128-138. On astral magic in medieval Jewish thought, see Dov Schwartz, "Astral Magic and Specific Properties (*Segullot*) in Medieval Jewish Thought: Non Aristotelian Science and Theology," in *Science in Medieval Jewish Cultures*, ed. Gad Freudenthal (New York: Cambridge University Press, 2011), 301-319.

Maimonides cites no evidence in support of this assumption. In his view, his claim is anchored in the concrete reality—meaning in Sabianism and, consequently, needs neither proof nor justification. This assumption entails several implications. For example, the use of *segullot* (meaning remedies whose influence cannot be explained according to the theory of humors) is allowed so long as they are not connected to astrology.[21]

> (2) Folk magic differs from "learned" or "professional" magic. "Learned" magic is usually equated with astral magic. According to such works as *Ghāyat al-Ḥakīm* (The Aim of the Sage), we know that astral magic practices could be found in Maimonides' cultural surroundings. Although Maimonides views both the folk and the "learned" variations as illusory and entirely ineffectual, he did set himself the challenge of contending with the "learned" option. In his *Commentary to the Mishnah*, Maimonides writes as follows on the types of magic:

One consists of those who are well versed in idolatrous practice—that is, the calculation of the sign that is in the ascendant at the time of the idolatrous act, and the bringing down of spirituality [*rūhaniyyāt*] by it,[22] and all the other delusions and foolish things that soil the intellect [*'aql*] and are imagined by those of this type. The second type consists of those who worship those man-made images as they have learned to do, without any knowledge [*'ilm*] of how they were made or for what purpose, except for the stories of their sages alone—and such are the majority of idolaters.[23]

---

21 *Guide*, III:37, 542. See Schwartz, *Studies on Astral Magic*, 42.
22 Maimonides' examples clearly attest that he contested astral magic.
23 Maimonides, *Commentary to the Mishnah*, ed. Yosef Qafih (Jerusalem: Mosad Harav Kook, 1967), Hullin 1:1, 173 [Heb]. *Cf*. Faur, *Studies on Maimonides' Code*, 228-229. In my *Studies on Astral Magic*, I showed this distinction in regard to *Guide* III:37. Faur pointed out that the worship of idols took place "at two levels—the cult of the masses and the cult of the scholars. The masses worshipped idols because they saw them as having power and influence over nature: to bless their crops, bring down rain, and remove harm from their homes. Against this type of cult, the claim was that worshipping idols is useless and ineffective. By contrast, the cult of the scholars reflects a recognition of the divinity and is based on theological principles that are harmful to the Jewish concept of the divinity. Against this type of cult, the claim was that idolatry was no longer forbidden" (Faur, *Studies on Maimonides' Code*, 237). Faur, then, sensed a distinction between kinds of magic, although he did not ascribe the "learned" kind to technical-scientific knowledge (astronomic and astrological) but to knowledge of the theological background, that is, the cult of spirituality or of effigies in Christianity. See, for example, Liana Saif, *The Arabic Influences on Early Modern Occult Philosophy* (Houndmills, Basingstoke, Hampshire: Palgrave Macmillan, 2015).

While the first type involves bringing down the spiritual powers of the stars at a time determined by the astral configuration, the second is restricted to worship of the image without any astrological motivation, as is typical of the unlearned masses. Indeed, only the first type is at all related to the intellect, which is therefore contaminated by involvement with it. The second type has no intellectual aspect. Hence, Maimonides states further on that this type is not true idolatry, for those who practice it "are [merely] maintaining the custom of their ancestors"; the intellectual and halakhic challenge is thus primarily to discount the former type. It follows that Maimonides' distinction between the two types of magic is deliberate and reasoned. In other words, there are good grounds for the thesis that Maimonides drew a distinction between magic based upon detailed, meticulous astrological calculations, on the one hand, and the popular magic of the ignorant masses, on the other; between "learned" magic and "primitive magic." While he was undoubtedly concerned to reject and refute both types, which the masses held in considerable respect, he saw his major intellectual and polemical challenge in contending with the former category of astral magic, which is based upon knowledge. Maimonides was going to develop this twofold pattern of magic in the *Guide*.

Although this value distinction between types of magic is not found in most of Maimonides' sources (such as *The Book of Nabatean Agriculture*), Maimonides adopted it and made it a pillar of his controversial approach.

Incidentally, note that the controversy that erupted at the end of the thirteenth century in a cultural climate entirely different from the one where Maimonides had operated, hinged on the "learned" type of magic. This Maimonidean distinction between types of magic struck roots in the West. Abba Mari attacked scholars who used forms to draw down spirituality from the stars ("the form of a lion for the kidneys" and so forth), but R. Shlomo b. Aderet (Rashba) refused to forbid acts of astral magic, *inter alia* because his teacher, Nachmanides, had used astrological amulets for healing purposes.[24]

Maimonides was aware that the Andalusian Jewish sages who had preceded him had recognized the efficacy of "learned" magic. R. Moshe Ibn Ezra, R. Judah Halevi, R. Abraham Ibn Ezra, and others both hinted and explicitly stated that this technique is real and effective.[25] Ibn Ezra related briefly to astral

---

24 Joseph Schatzmiller dealt with the connection between astral magic and university studies in Provence. See Schwartz, *Studies on Astral Magic*, ch. 5.

25 See, for example, Moshe Idel, "Hermeticism and Judaism," in *Hermeticism and the Renaissance: Intellectual History and the Occult in Early Modern Europe*, ed. Ingrid Merkel and Allen Debus (London and Toronto: Associated University Presses, 1988),

magic in his professional astrological writings as well. Maimonides, however, did not agree with them. Indeed, he was extremely critical of them and, in his commentary on Avodah Zarah, wrote as follows on the use of talismans:

> And even good and pious men of our Torah think that these things are true but that they are forbidden only because of [the prohibition of] the Torah. And they do not know that these are empty and false things, against which the Torah has warned us just as it has warned us against falsehood.[26]

For Maimonides, drawing down spirituality for healing or other purposes is not a feasible option, even though many Andalusian thinkers did support it. Maimonides may well have fought against Andalusian tradition, which ascribed theological and hermeneutical value to the making of figures for healing and for other "scientific" purposes. His aim was to expose the pointlessness and futility of "learned" astral magic.

Solving the Puzzlement

The various difficulties noted above in the two laws and in their structure can now be resolved as follows:

(1) *The relationship between the two laws*: Law 10 deals with the making of figures for ornamental purposes, whereas Law 11 deals with their making for "scientific" or "learned" purposes. Law 11, for example, forbids making a figure of a constellation for healing purposes.

(2) *The opening of Law 10*. Maimonides assumed as a given that forms are made to be used, above all, to bring down forces from the supernal world. He had already attested that he had applied himself to the study of idolatry and magic,[27] and had found that, historically and socially, the forms made and worshiped are, above

---

59-76; Shlomo Pines, "On the Term *Rūḥaniyyāt* and its Origin, and on Judah Halevi's Doctrine," *Tarbiz* 57 (1988): 511-540 [Heb]; Schwartz, *Studies on Astral Magic*, ch. 1

26 *Commentary to the Mishnah*, Avodah Zarah 4:7, 357. On Maimonides' respect for the Andalusian sages, see Dov Schwartz, "The Figure of Judah Halevi as Emerging from Maimonides' *Guide* I:71," *Daat* 61 (2007): 23-40 [Heb].

27 In the "Letter to the Rabbis of Montpelier on Astrology." See Alexander Marx, "The Correspondence between the Rabbis of Southern France and Maimonides about Astrology," *HUCA* 3 (1926), 351. For the Hebrew original of this letter, see Itzhak Shilat, ed. *The Letters and Essays of Moses Maimonides* (Jerusalem: n. p., 1995), 481. Maimonides' ruling in Laws of Idolatry 2:2, which forbids reading books on idolatry, is discussed in the literature.

all, the forms of stars. The opening of Law 10, then, takes for granted the making of forms symbolizing stars, and Maimonides adds that they should not be made for ornamental purposes. By contrast, making forms of earthly entities lacking any association with astrology is allowed. Maimonides, therefore, immediately expresses reservations and states that making a human form for ornamentation purposes, even though it is an earthly form unconnected to stars, is forbidden, relying on his approach that all idolatry is somehow related to the stars. Again, he holds that this is a self-evident historical fact and explanations would be superfluous. The prohibition on the making of heavenly forms is thus sweeping, and Law 10 should be read as follows:

> It is forbidden to make figures <usually made for healing or for a similar "scientific" purposes> for purposes of ornaments, even if they are not idolatrous <and idolatry is always related to the stars> ... so that those likely to err shall not err and imagine that these figures serve idolatrous purposes. <But non-supernal figures are allowed for ornamentation purposes>, and the prohibition of making ornamental figures <of the permitted ones> only applies to representation of the human form.

(3) *The correspondence with the talmudic source.* Maimonides obviously objected to the view of Ran and the tosafists that Abaye had not retreated from one to the next statement and, in that sense, he adhered to the literal meaning of the talmudic text. According to Maimonides, as noted, making supernal forms is definitely forbidden and there are no grounds for creating a hierarchy of them ("higher firmament" and "lower firmament").

Law 11 introduces an innovation: contrary to the seal, which can be made if it is not in high relief, the making of supernal figures is forbidden, be they in high relief or engraved in some board. One reason is that supernal elements are generally perceived as engraved because most of them are invisible. Maimonides clarified several times in the *Guide* that the angels are the separate intellects driving the spheres that, as we know, are made up of an invisible transparent material (the fifth element).[28] Making

---

28 R. Qafih noted this as a possibility: "Perhaps he holds that, because the ministering angels have no body, and because the sun, moon, stars and constellations do not appear in high relief, and even in the sphere they are not in high-relief but engraved within it, it makes no difference whether they are in high relief or engraved" *(Mishneh Torah,* Qafih

their forms for healing or for any other purpose, even when engraved, is therefore forbidden, because the supernal reality and the scientific milieu support this. Maimonides then begins with the seal in order to clarify that making any supernal forms is unequivocally prohibited.

Development

Maimonides' statements in Laws Concerning Idolatry 3:10-11, then, are structured and in perfect order. I conclude by addressing an additional aspect of these laws and the development of Maimonides' halakhic thought. M. Avodah Zarah 3:3 reads: "If one finds a vessel and on it a drawing of the sun or a drawing of the moon, or a drawing of a dragon, he should cast them into the Salt Sea." Writing on it in his *Commentary to the Mishnah*, Maimonides notes:

> "A drawing of the sun or a drawing of the moon" does not mean that one will find a circle and say, this is the sun, or a semicircle and say, this is the moon. Makers of "talismans" ascribe figures to the stars and say that the figure of Saturn is that of a very old black man, and the figure of Venus is that of a beautiful young girl decked in gold, and the figure of the sun is that of a crowned king sitting in a chariot, and so they ascribe to all the stars and constellations many figures, and they engage in a fierce dispute concerning these figures because they are falsehoods, and the falsehood about a thing tends to grow and spread. And when it says "a drawing of the sun or a drawing of the moon" it means, when he finds the figure ascribed to the sun and the figure ascribed to the moon, according to whatever view.[29]
>
> And the "dragon" is the figure of a man with fins and many scales on his back between his fins like fish scales, and this figure was highly respected among them because they used to ascribe it to a part of the sphere [*ʾajzāʾ al-falak*], and a man who is said to be knowledgeable on these matters told

---

ed., 402). The view that the heavenly world is engraved appears in other thirteenth-century and early fourteenth-century circles. See, for example, *Hiddushei Talmidei Rabbenu Yona al Masekhet Avodah Zarah*, ed. Zvi Hacohen Zashrakovsky (New York, 1956), 83 [Heb]. Menachem Meiri writes: "But concerning a constellation, we hold it does not matter whether it is engraved or in high relief since, in their place, they are not seen in high relief" (Meiri, *Beith ha-Behirah al Masekhet Avodah Zara*, 150-151). Talismans were the most precious of stones or metals. See Eli Davis and David A. Frenkel, *The Hebrew Amulet: Biblical-Medical-General* (Jerusalem: Institute for Jewish Studies, 1995) [Heb].

29 *Madhhab* in the original, which could also be rendered as "system" or "way."

me that this is the figure of the moon *teli*[30] and that it is made in such-and-such a manner, and at such-and-such a time, and has such-and-such an effect. And I asked him about the book where this is mentioned because I had never seen such a figure, and he claimed that his rabbi and teacher had told him about this figure among all the other secrets he had told him.[31]

Already in his *Commentary to the Mishnah*, then, Maimonides points to an urge to elucidate magic astral traditions. He certainly encountered a problem in this mishnah, where the first two examples (the sun, the moon) attest to figures related to the supernal world, whereas the third (a dragon) is seemingly different and not related to heaven. Clearly, then, Maimonides knew from the start that the "dragon" denoted a *teli*, but could not find in his surroundings amulets engraved with the figure or the symbol of a *teli*. He therefore inquired and found that such a tradition had indeed existed in the past.[32]

The *Commentary to the Mishnah* thus gives a reason for the distinction between a human figure and other earthly forms in Laws Concerning Idolatry 3:10, even though this interpretation deals with the finding of figures while the *Mishneh Torah* law deals with their making. The common denominator of all the astrological figures that Maimonides presented in his *Commentary to the Mishnah* is a human figure in different manifestations (an old man, a young girl, a king, and so forth).[33] The human figure

---

30 *Jawzahr* in the original, referring to the intersection of the sun's and the moon's orbits. On the source of the term, see Shlomo Pines, *Studies in the History of Jewish Thought*, ed. Warren Zev Harvey and Moshe Idel (Jerusalem: Magnes Press, 1997), 142. The *teli* and the solar and lunar eclipses taking place in its surroundings had astrological implications. See, for example, Abū Maʿšar, *The Abbreviation of the Introduction to Astrology*, ed. and trans. Charles Burnett, Keiji Yamamoto, and Michio Yano (Leiden and New York: Brill, 1994), 54, l. 17. See also Abraham Ibn Ezra's commentary on Numbers 1:19; Joel 3:4 (Ernst Simon, *Abraham Ibn Ezra's Two Commentaries on the Minor Prophets: An Annotated Critical Edition*, vol. 1 (Ramat-Gan: Bar-Ilan University Press, 1989), 164 [Heb]. It is interesting that Maimonides viewed the making of a *teli* figure as an innovation, although it was an ancient astrological topos.
31 *Commentary to the Mishnah*, Avodah Zarah 3:3 (Qafih edn. 350-351)
32 Maimonides does not negate the tradition that he had heard from "a man who is said to be knowledgeable on these matters" a suitable explanation of the "dragon." See ibid., Qafih's commentary *ad locum*, 351, n. 10.
33 On the human image in Greek-Muslim magic literature, see, for example, Moshe Idel, "An Astral-Magical Pneumatic Anthropoid," *Incognita* 2 (1991): 9-31; idem, *Golem: Jewish Magical and Mystical Traditions on the Artificial Anthropoid* (Albany, NY: SUNY Press, 1990), 86-88. The Hebrew translation of this volume was enlarged by the author and includes an appendix entitled "A Magic-Astral-Spiritual Golem," 258-270.

thus serves as a symbol of heavenly bodies. The mythological dragon is also described as a human figure that the two magic traditions cited by Maimonides place in the supernal realm. The human figure is thus part of the heavenly figures because astrologers used it in their amulets, and the *Mishneh Torah* therefore categorically forbids their making for ornamental purposes.

In the *Mishneh Torah* (Laws of Idolatry 7:8), Maimonides copied the text of the Mishnah almost literally:

> If one finds articles bearing the figure of the sun, moon, or dragon, whether they are gold or silver vessels or robes of scarlet embroidered with any such figure, or earrings or finger rings so engraved, they are forbidden to be used. Other articles with those figures are permitted, the presumption being that the figures are ornamental. Other figures than those enumerated, or any vessels, are presumed to be ornamental, and the vessels may be used.

Maimonides never mentioned the symbolic human figures he discusses in the *Commentary to the Mishnah*. Hence, it seems plausible that, by the time he came to write the *Mishneh Torah*, Maimonides had changed his mind and forbade amulets with engravings of heavenly bodies as well, even when made for ornamental purposes.[34]

Summary

My inquiry in this chapter related to the broader issue of the encounter between the visual, the aesthetic, the scientific or semi-scientific, and the halakhic. This clarification is one component of the reservations in the attitude toward the visual and the artistic.[35] From many perspectives, it is part of Maimonides' suspicious attitude toward art in general, and toward sculpture, painting, and music in particular.[36]

In the *Mishneh Torah*, Maimonides aimed for a comprehensive and systematic formulation of the prohibition on making figures and, therefore, he prohibited making them, be it for ornamental purposes or for a specific

---

34 R. Qafih tried to claim that Maimonides had not changed his mind and he only prohibited human forms (*Mishneh Torah*, Qafih ed., 469).
35 See Kalman P. Bland, *The Artless Jew: Medieval and Modern Affirmations and Denials of the Visual* (Princeton, NJ: Princeton University Press, 2001).
36 See, for example, Dov Schwartz, *Music in Jewish Thought* (Ramat-Gan: Bar-Ilan University Press, 2013) [Heb], Index, under Maimonides.

need (healing). Furthermore: when he later came to write the *Mishneh Torah*, he seemingly expanded the prohibition in two ways:

(1) Making figures: All human figures were categorically forbidden and not only those that idolaters tended to use, meaning human figures symbolizing heavenly bodies. Nevertheless, Maimonides refrained from imposing further restrictions and from forbidding engraved human figures as well. Rabad's gloss grapples with this specific difficulty.
(2) Finding figures: The prohibition applied not only to symbolic human figures but also to figures of heavenly bodies as such. The rulings on the finding of figures reflect the plausibility that they had previously been used for worship. The surrounding reality persuaded Maimonides to expand the prohibition of forbidden amulets to heavenly figures as well, which in the past he had tended to allow.

Maimonides' adoption of a stricter stance in the *Mishneh Torah* vis-à-vis the one he had endorsed in the *Commentary to the Mishnah* becomes clear in light of his claim in the "Letter on Astrology," stating there was hardly a single work concerning idolatry he had not read and understood.[37] In his youth, Maimonides probably became familiar with the amulets and effigies that had been common in his Spanish surroundings. The *Commentary to the Mishnah* and the *Mishneh Torah*, as we know, were written in the cultural transition from Spain to Egypt. Maimonides was curious and craved knowledge, particularly when matters touched on the war he had declared on idolatry. Upon his arrival in Egypt, he became acquainted with the astral magic means available in his new environment and possibly with further testimonies of Sabianism, broadening his knowledge of the actual reality. Delving into the idolatrous astral magic corpus seemingly led him to conclude that the prohibitions should be more sweeping than he had previously assumed.

Be that as it may, the order and the contents of the two laws in the *Mishneh Torah* can be seen as deliberately and rigorously structured.

---

37 See n. 29 above.

Chapter 4

Idolatry as Mediation

Astral magic was perceived in the Middle Ages as an area related to ancient astrology cults[1] and, among Jewish thinkers, Maimonides exposed this fact more than others. As noted in the previous chapter, he was strongly opposed to astrology and magic on both theological and scientific grounds, and the nature of his dissent has been discussed at length. Maimonides saw the witchcraft based on astrology as a fundamental and significant target of his general war against magic. His struggle was two-pronged. Ontologically, Maimonides denied the reality of astral magic, and on halakhic grounds, he absolutely forbade its use. Bringing down spirituality on amulets and images, which he considered an act based on knowledge, was presented as futile and as a basis for idolatry. Maimonides also dismissed the value of remedies based on astrology and banned their use. As part of his attempt to undermine astral magic and proscribe it as idolatry, Maimonides turned to the exposure of its idolatrous sources, pointing out the various modes of image worship and attempting to trace its ancient roots. In this chapter, I will point to sources potentially available to Maimonides on this count.

A Means that Became an End

Maimonides identified the Nabateans and the Sabians as remnants of ancient idolaters and presented the commandments of Judaism as attempts to grapple with the traditions of these nations.[2] In a letter on astrology to

---

1 See Steven Wasserstrom, "The Unwritten Chapter: Notes Towards a Social and Religious History of Genizah Magic," *Pe'amim* 85 (2000), 48-50 [Heb]. On the gap between the perception of magic in the Middle Ages and its existence in antiquity and on its image in antiquity, see Meir Bar Ilan, "Astrology and Magic in the Middle Ages," review of *Astral Magic in Medieval Jewish Thought*, by Dov Schwartz, *Kabbalah* 7 (2002): 361-384 [Heb].
2 On the idolatrous traditions in Maimonides' writings, see chapter 2 above. *Cf.* the Hebrew translation of 'Abd al-Jabbār's testimony in Dov Schwartz, *Amulets, Properties and Rationalism in Medieval Jewish Thought* (Ramat-Gan: Bar-Ilan University Press,

the scholars of Provence (Montpellier), he made the following well-known statement:

> Know, my masters, that I myself have investigated much into these matters; the first thing I studied is that science which is called judicial astrology [*gezerat ha-kokhavim*]—that is, [the science] by which man may know what will come to pass in the world or in this or that city or kingdom and what will happen to a particular individual all the days of his life. I also have read in all matters concerning all of idolatry, so that it seems to me that there does not remain in the world a composition on this subject, having been translated into Arabic from other languages, but that I have read it and understood its subject matter and have plumbed the depth of its thought.[3]

Maimonides was not dismissive of the object of his struggle and devoted time to the study of idolatrous sources. His assertion about the comprehensive sources of knowledge he had acquired on the various idolatrous cults, therefore, should be taken seriously. In *Guide* III:29, Maimonides lists a long series of hermetic-magical and pseudepigraphic works that served as fruitful sources for various forms of witchcraft he defined as idolatry. An examination of the cults that Maimonides describes in his writings indicates that image worship based on astrological principles—bringing down the spirituality of celestial bodies on idols, images, and talismans—is a significant concern in the *Commentary to the Mishnah*, the *Mishneh Torah*, and the *Guide*.[4]

The study of Maimonides' sources on image worship shows that his foremost concern was the world view that had emerged in the Harran center and, in particular, the tradition described in *The Book of Nabatean Agriculture* (Kitāb al-Filāḥat al-Nabāṭiyyah) by Ibn Waḥshīyya.[5] It is a

---

2004), 283-285. See also Michael Schwarz, "Maimonides and the Babu'ah," *Daat* 42 (1999): 5-6 [Heb].

3 "Maimonides' Letter on Astrology," in *Medieval Political Philosophy: A Sourcebook*, ed. Ralph Lerner and Muhsin Mahdi (Ithaca, NY: Cornell University Press, 1963), 229. See also Alexander Marx, "The Correspondence between the Rabbis of Southern France and Maimonides about Astrology," *HUCA* 3 (1926), § 8, 351; Itzhak Shilat, ed., *The Letters and Essays of Moses Maimonides*, vol. 2 (Jerusalem: n. p., 1995), 481.

4 See Dov Schwartz, *Studies in Astral Magic in Medieval Jewish Thought*, trans. David Louvish and Batya Stein (Leiden/ Boston: Brill, 2005), ch. 2.

5 Ibid., 33-37. On Ibn Wah.shīyya's thought, see, for example, Jaakko Hämeem-Anttila, "Ibn Wahshiyya and Magic,"*Anaquel de Estudios Árabes* 10 (1999): 39-48; Angelo Alves Carrara, "Geoponica and Nabatean Agriculture: A New Approach into Their Sources and Authorship," *Arabic Sciences and Philosophy* 16 (2006): 103-132; Janne Mattila, "Ibn Wahshiyya on the Soul: Neoplatonic Soul Doctrine and the Treatise on the Soul Contained in the Nabatean Agriculture," *Studia Orientalia* 101 (2007): 103-155.

reasonable assumption, however, that if Maimonides did bother to read rare works, as he attests, he most certainly studied standard theological texts containing heresiographic accounts of various forms of image worship. In this chapter, I will point to possible sources for Maimonides' approach on the motives of image worshippers.

In *Guide* I:36, Maimonides presents a historical and psychological-religious explanation for the emergence of image worship, its perception by people in general ("the multitude"), and the motives of its believers:

> Now you know that whoever performs *idolatrous worship* does not do it on the assumption that there is no deity except the idol. In fact, no human being of the past has ever imagined on any day, and no human being of the future will ever imagine, that the form he fashions either from cast metal or from stone and wood has created and governs the heavens and the earth. Rather it is worshiped in respect of its being an image of a thing that is an intermediary between ourselves and God. ... However, in spite of the fact that those infidels believe in the existence of the deity, their idolatrous worship entails their deserving destruction; for the reason that their infidelity bears upon a prerogative reserved to God alone, may He be exalted—I mean the prerogative of being worshiped and magnified. ... This is so ordained in order that God's existence may be firmly established in the belief of the multitude. Now the idolaters thought that this prerogative belonged to that which was other than God, and this led to the disappearance of the belief in His existence, may He be exalted, from among the multitude. For the multitude grasps only the actions of worship, not their meanings or the true reality of the Being worshiped through them. Consequently, the idolatrous worship of the infidels entails their deserving destruction; just as the text has it: "Thou shalt not save alive a soul" (Deuteronomy 20:16).[6]

---

6 *Guide* I:36, 83-84. *Cf.* Maimonides, *Mishneh Torah, The Book of Knowledge*, ed. Moses Hyamson (Jerusalem: Boys Town, 1962), Laws of Idolatry 1:1, 66a: "In the days of Enosh, the people fell into gross error, and the counsel of the wise men of the generation became foolish. Enosh himself was among those who erred. Their error was as follows: 'Since God,' they said, 'created these stars and spheres to guide the world, set them on high and allotted unto them honour, and since they are ministers who minister before Him, they deserve to be praised and glorified, and honour should be rendered them; and it is the will of God, blessed be He, that men should aggrandise and honour those whom He aggrandised and honoured—just as a king desires that respect should be shown to the officers who stand before Him, and thus honour is shown to the king.' When this idea arose in their minds, they began to erect temples to the stars, offered up sacrifices to them, praised and glorified them in speech, and prostrated themselves before them—their purpose, according to their perverse notions, being to obtain the Creator's favour. This was the root of idolatry, and this was what the idolaters, who

In this passage, Maimonides claims that image worshippers do not view the images as the objects of their cult but only as intermediaries and as means for worshipping God. According to Maimonides, idol worshippers never ascribed animative powers to the idol or the image, nor any powers derived from a living spirit. In their view, idols symbolize ("image") the celestial bodies, which themselves derive or emanate from God and operate as a result of or driven by divine decisions. The image worshipper thus uses idols as a means for the worship of God, while the multitude distorts this intention, believing that the worship of images is an end in itself. Image worshippers are perceived as an elitist group, upholding a theological or theurgic world view (that Maimonides views as flawed), while the public merely imitates this group. In the *Guide*, Maimonides indeed related in these terms to those bringing down spirituality on images. Image worship, then, although the elitist group performing it perceived it merely as mediation, is subsumed under the halakhic category of idolatry. Maimonides presented image worship as a means and not necessarily as an end in itself. These worshippers, then, are not ignorant fools, since they do not ascribe independent powers to the images.

Jewish Sources

What inspired this Maimonidean interpretation of image worship? There were presumably two types of sources at Maimonides' disposal, Jewish and Muslim. Particularly prominent among the former is Judah Halevi, on the assumption that Maimonides could have been acquainted with *The Kuzari*.[7] To some extent, this view is supported by Abraham Ibn Ezra, Halevi's younger colleague, possibly pointing to an Andalusian tradition.

---

knew its fundamentals, said. They did not however maintain that there was no God except the particular star which was the object of their worship)." Maimonides suggests various approaches to this issue in his writings, but I will not expand on these differences here. See also Hayyim Gevaryahu, "Maimonides' Concept of Paganism," in *Sefer Karl*, ed. Asher Weiser and Ben Zion Luria (Jerusalem: Kiriyat Sefer, 1960), 351-363; David Hartman, "Philosophy and Halakhah as Alternative Challengers to Idolatry in Maimonides," in *Shlomo Pines Jubilee Volume on the Occasion of His Eightieth Birthday*, vol. 1, ed. Moshe Idel, Warren Zev Harvey, and Eliezer Schweid (Jerusalem: Hebrew University, 1990), 319-333 [Heb]; Moshe Halbertal and Avishai Margalit, *Idolatry*, trans. Naomi Goldblum (Cambridge, MA: Harvard University Press, 1992), 42-44.

7 On this possibility, see Maimonides, *The Guide of the Perplexed*, ed. Yehuda Even Shmuel (Kaufmann), vol. 1 (Tel Aviv: Shvil, 1935), xvii-xviii [Heb]; *Guide*, "Translator's Introduction: The Philosophic Sources of The Guide of the Perplexed," cxxxiii; Howard Kreisel, "Judah Halevi's Influence on Maimonides: A Preliminary Appraisal," *Maimonidean Studies* 2 (1991): 95-121.

Judah Halevi presented a sociological-religious claim, extremely plausible in the cultural climate of the Middle Ages, stating that all humankind longs to receive "divine traces"(*al-athar al-'ilāhī*).[8] Every living being wishes to receive a revelation from God and the distinction between a believer and an unbeliever hinges of the individual's readiness to receive such traces. Believers prepare themselves in the manner ordered by God at revelation, that is, through the commandments, whereas unbelievers, infidels, choose preparations dictated by their rational considerations.[9] According to Halevi, image worshippers hold that attaining those "divine traces" depends on bringing down spirituality onto talismans. On those endorsing this course, he writes:

> Whosoever strives by speculation and deduction to prepare the conditions for the reception of this inspiration,[10] or by divining, as is found in the writings of astrologers,[11] trying to call down supernatural beings, or manufacturing talismans,[12] such a man is an unbeliever. He may bring offerings and burn incense in the name of speculation and conjecture, whilst he is in reality ignorant of that which he should do, how much, in which way, by what means, in which place, by whom, in which manner, and many other details, the enumeration of which would lead too far.[13]

Image worshippers, then, recognize God's divinity and in fact desire to approach God through the idols. They do not err concerning their faith as such but concerning its realization, that is, in their acceptance of the talisman and the idol as mediators, and in their neglect of God's specific commandments in the Sinai epiphany. Halevi explained in similar terms the worship of the golden calf.[14] In making the golden calf, the people of Israel

---

8   Judah Halevi, *The Kuzari*, trans. Hartwig Hirschfeld (New York: Schocken, 1964), 1:77, 56 (henceforth *Kuzari*). In the Arabic original—*Kitāb al-Radd wa-'l-Dalīl fī'l-Din al-Dhalīl*, ed. D. Z. Baneth and H. Ben-Shammai (Jerusalem, 1977) (henceforth Baneth and Ben-Shammai)—p. 20, ln 8.
9   For an analysis of this issue from other perspectives, see Dov Schwartz, *Contradiction and Concealment in Medieval Jewish Thought* (Ramat-Gan: Bar-Ilan University Press, 2002), 54-55 [Heb].
10 Even Shmuel: "those impressions."
11 In the original, *al-munajjimīn*.
12 In the original, *istinzal al-rūḥaniyyāt wa'amal al-ṭalāsim*. See also Shlomo Pines, "On the Term *Rūḥaniyyāt* and its Origin, and on Judah Halevi's Doctrine," *Tarbiz* 57 (1988): 511-540 (especially 524-530) [Heb]. Pines stresses the difference between Halevi and Maimonides on this issue. Nevertheless, both share the basic notion of bringing down spirituality in order to mediate between humans and God, possibly attesting to a common source.
13 *Kuzari* 1:79, 56-57.
14 *Kuzari* 1:97, 67.

were merely seeking to draw closer to God, and the golden calf was to serve as an intermediary to bring down spirituality to the people. Halevi's defense of the people of Israel was based on a perception of the calf as a mediating agent rather than as an object of worship. Furthermore, according to an exegetical tradition suggested by Ibn Ezra, the calf was chosen because it was in the sign of Taurus or because of a planetary conjunction in the constellation of Taurus.[15] The intention in making the calf, then, was to attract the spirituality of the planets according to this constellation.

Already in Judah Halevi's work, then, we find the view that image worshippers do not worship the planet itself as the source of emanation; rather, they see in the image or the planet means of approaching God and receiving the divine emanation. This view could have been a source for Maimonides' analysis of image worshippers' motives. The perception of image worship as mediation had already become a tradition in pre-Maimonidean sources and appears in Ibn Ezra's commentary on the Torah.[16]

---

15 Abraham Ibn Ezra, in his long commentary to Exodus 32:1, writes: "And the astrologers have stated that the major conjunction for the first two [planets] took place in the constellation of Taurus." See Abraham Ibn Ezra, *Perushei ha-Torah le-Rabbenu Abraham ibn Ezra*, vol. 2, ed. Asher Weiser (Jerusalem: Mosad Harav Kook, 1977), 206 [Heb]. In his short commentary on this book, he writes: "Whoever understands the secret of the celestial science knows the meaning of the shape of the calf." See Abraham Ibn Ezra, *Be'ur Ibn Ezra le-Sefer Shemot [ha-Perush ha-Katsar]*, ed. Judah Leib Fleischer (Vienna: n. p., 1926), 301 [Heb]. The mid-fourteenth century commentary of Shlomo Franco on this passage of Ibn Ezra is interesting in this context: "One who understands the celestial pictures will understand why the shape of a calf ['*egel*]—it is because it is in the shape of the sign of Taurus, as they said, "Thus they exchanged their glory for the likeness of an ox" (Psalms 106:20), and R. Papus said the ox above (*Mekhilta de-Rashbi, va-Yehi be-Shalakh*, 6), and perhaps it is derived from the word circle ['*igul*], and there are many like them in the pictures, as well as the calves made by Yerobo'am ben Nevat, and all are for the purpose of obtaining celestial powers" (Oxford-Bodleian Ms. 1258, 73b). Although Ibn Ezra does not refer here to Judah Halevi, it is known that the two were acquainted and exchanged views and ideas, as follows from many references in Ibn Ezra's Bible commentaries. See Naphtali Ben-Menahem, "Rabbi Judah Halevi and Rabbi Abraham Ibn Ezra," in *Ibn Ezra Topics* (Jerusalem: Mosad Harav Kook, 1978), 224-240 [Heb]. See also Schwartz, *Studies in Astral Magic*, ch. 1; Shlomo Sela, *Astrology and Biblical Exegesis in the Thought of Abraham Ibn Ezra* (Ramat-Gan: Bar-Ilan University Press, 1999) [Heb]; idem, *Abraham Ibn Ezra and the Rise of Medieval Hebrew Science* (Leiden/Boston: Brill, 2003). Finally, note the possibility that Maimonides was influenced by the writings of Ibn Ezra. See Isadore Twersky, "Did R. Abraham ibn Ezra Influence Maimonides?," in *Abraham ibn Ezra: Studies in the Writings of a Twelfth-Century Jewish Polimath,* Hebrew Section, ed. Isadore Twersky and Jay M. Harris (Cambridge, MA: Harvard University Center for Jewish Studies, 1993), 21-48.

16 Ibn Ezra, *Perushei ha-Torah le-Rabbenu Abraham ibn Ezra,* Weiser edn., Exodus 20:20. See also Schwartz, *Studies on Astral Magic*, 16.

Muslim Sources

In the Muslim world, before Maimonides, we find clear descriptions of image worship as mediation between humans and God. One important description of this kind appears in the writings of the famous Muslim theologian and heresiographer ʿAbd al-Jabbār (d. 1025). In his work *Kitāb al-Mughni fi ʾAbwāb al-Tawḥīd wal-ʿAdl*, ʿAbd al-Jabbār presents a broad description of different types of idolaters, including image worshippers.

ʿAbd al-Jabbār devotes an entire chapter to image worshippers, quoted in full below. The translation will be followed by a presentation of its main points and a discussion of their meaning. ʿAbd al-Jabbār describes image worship as follows:[17]

Account of the Adherents of Images and of the Arab's Methods in the Jāhiliyyah

> Al-Hasan ibn Musa reported in the name of Abu Maʿshar the astronomer that many Indians and Chinese believed that Allah is angels, that He is a body possessing form, like the most elevated forms,[18] and the angels are elevated bodies, and that He and the angels are concealed in the heavens. This induced them to make images in the form of the angels in order to worship them and offer them sacrifices, insofar as in their [the worshippers'] eyes, they [the images] resemble Allah and they believe they will be beneficial to them. They [the image worshippers] remained in this state until some of those whom they considered to be prophets[19] said: the spheres and the stars are closer in level to Allah, and they live, ratiocinate[20] and guide.[21] As a result, they [the worshippers] revered them and offered them sacrifices. And they remained in this state for a long time. When they saw that the stars

---

17 The translation into Hebrew by Eliezer Schlossberg and edited by both of us follows ʿAbd al-Jabbār al-Asādabādī, *Kitāb al-Mughni fi ʾabwāb al-Tawḥīd wal-ʿAdl*, Part 5, "The Non-Muslim Sects," ed. by Ṭāhā Ḥusayn and Ibrāhīm Madkūr (Cairo: Wizārat al-Thaqāfa wa-ʾl-Irshād al-Qawmī, al-Idāra al-ʿĀmma li-ʾl-Thaqāfa, 1961), 155-159.
18 Arabic *kaʾaḥsan al-ṣuwar* and, alternatively, "the best forms."
19 Arabic *baʿḍman kāna ʿindahum* and, alternatively. "until one whom they considered to be a prophet."
20 Arabic *nāṭiqah*.
21 Meaning that the planets influence the material world, as in the formation of compounds of elements, and they are therefore called "guides" (*mudabbirah*).

disappear by day and sometimes even by night, in clouds and the like, some of their leaders advised them to make images of them [of the stars], so that they might see them at all times. And they made images of them, seven in number of the stars, and each group of them revered a certain star through a [single] type of sacrifice. And they believed that, if they revered the images, the stars would grant them their desires. And they built a temple for each image and named that temple for the star. They remained in this state for a long time and continued to worship the images and bow down to them.

The people of Persia reported that King Jamshīd[22] was the first to revere fire, and he called upon people to revere it because it resembles the sun and the stars by virtue of its light.

Then some of the Arabs moved the images of al-Sha'm[23] to Mecca, and called upon people to revere them until Allah revealed Islam.

It was reported in the name of Abu 'Isā al-Warrāq that he said of the Arabs that they included different sects. Some of them recognized the Creator, the Beginning[24] and the Revival,[25] denied [the authority of] the prophets, worshiped the images out of their desire for the nearness of Allah, made pilgrimages to them, slaughtered sacrifices[26] to them, conducted ceremonies in their honor and observed the permitted and forbidden things.[27] Some of them recognized the Creator and denied the Revival and the Resurrection. Some of them denied the Creator and were inclined toward denial[28] and toward speaking of the eternity [of the universe]. These are the persons quoted in the Quran as having said: "There is nothing but our present life; we die, and we live, and nothing but Time destroys us."[29] And some of them were inclined to Judaism or to Christianity. And some of them[30] recognized the Creator, the Revival, and Reward and Punishment. And they are 'Abd

---

22 In other manuscripts, Hamir.
23 That is, Syria.
24 Arabic '*ibtidā*', meaning creation *ex nihilo*.
25 Arabic, '*i'ādah*, meaning resurrection of the dead.
26 Arabic *al-hadaya*, and alternatively, votive offerings.
27 That is, they heeded the prescriptions and proscriptions applying to the vicinity of a holy place, such as those observed in the vicinity of the Ka'abah.
28 Arabic WT4, generally denoting the denial of divine attributes. In this context, the word may refer specifically to the denial of Creation.
29 *Quran* XLV:23. Translations from the Quran here and henceforth cite Arthur J. Arberry, *The Koran Interpreted* (London: Oxford University Press, 1964), 518.
30 According to the emendation on p. 156, n. 2.

al-Muttalib ibn Hāshim,³¹ and Zayd ibn ʿAmr ibn Nufayl,³² and Qass ibn Saʿadah.³³ And reports attesting to that effect were told of them.

Allah, may He be exalted, reported of some of them that they denied the Revival and the Resurrection, saying, "Nay," but they said the like of what the ancients had said. They said, "What, when we are dead and become dust and bones, shall we indeed be raised up? We and our fathers have been promised this before."³⁴ And He also said of them, "What, when we are dead and become dust and bones, shall we indeed be raised up? What, and our fathers, the ancients?"³⁵

There were among them persons who worshiped the angels, contending that they were daughters of Allah, in order that they should intercede for them with Allah. Some of them contend that Allah has a son and they made him a god besides Him.

Some of them worship images in order to achieve the nearness of Allah, and He, may He be exalted and praised, has already told this of them, saying: "Those upon whom you call other than God are servants the likes of you,"³⁶ and saying: "And they serve, apart from God, what neither profits them nor hurts them."³⁷ And those who worshiped images were people who lived in India, al-Sind³⁸ and the like.

And Allah has already reported thus of the men of Noah, saying: "And [they] said, 'Do not leave your gods, and do not leave Waddʿ, nor Suwaʿ, Yūghūth, Yaʿuq, neither Naṣr. And they have led many astray.'"³⁹

Know that we have already discussed them, for we have already proved the denial of the statement about the eternity of bodies, and that there is no escape from proving that there is an eternal Creator⁴⁰ and Guide. And we have proved that a body cannot make a body, this refuting the words of those of them who speak of eternity and of the denial [of creation] and

---

31 Grandfather of Muhammad, who raised him after the death of his father ʿAbd Allah.
32 A leader of the Kurayish tribe during the Jāhiliyyah period (d. 606), cousin of Khalif ʿUmar ibn al-Khaṭṭāb.
33 Celebrated preacher of the Jāhiliyyah period (d. ca. 600). According to some traditions, he was a Christian from Najrān.
34 Quran XXIII:83-85 (348-349).
35 Quran XXXVII:16-17 (456); LVI:47-48 (561).
36 Quran VII:193 (167).
37 Quran XXV:57 (367).
38 A district in present-day Southern Pakistan.
39 Quran LXXI:22-23 (609). The five idols referred to in these verses were worshipped (according to Muhammad) by Noah's people.
40 Arabic ṣaniʿ. This argument is directed against image worshipers who believed in the eternity of the universe.

[claim] that the stars guide and create the bodies. And we have already proved that He, praise be to Him, cannot be a body possessing a form, this refuting their words that He has a form and that it is proper to compare images[41] and the like to him, which should therefore be worshiped as He is worshiped.

But worship is appropriate solely to Allah, may He be exalted, and it is not proper to worship anything else and it would not be beneficial [to do so], as we have said before. How do some say, therefore, that we worship images in order to seek Allah's nearness? And how shall it be correct to say that they [the images] bring one close to Allah, whereas they are [in the category of] things that cannot act and choose? It is true that they would bring whoever worships them close to Allah if they had free choice. But how could that be true that they [the images] bring their worshippers close to Allah, while that [worshipping them] is a sin? For to approach Allah through a sin is useless and does not have the meaning of nearness, for nearness to Him is seeking elevation and exaltation from Him through worship, and an act that is improper is not worthy of that, and it is not correct to say that it has the meaning of nearness. And this refutes their worship of an image to that end, just as it refutes their worship of an image because it is the Creator and God. Hence there is no difference between the abomination of worshipping an image in the first way and in the second way.

Should a person say, "In your view, is Divine Worship[42] at all possible in some way through the worship of images and bowing down to them?" Then we shall say to him, "In truth, their worship is forbidden. For we have already explained that worship is not beneficial unless [it is directed] toward One who bestows special favors, just as it is not worthy to give thanks to any but to Him who bestows favors; for worship is a kind of submission and humiliation before what is worshiped, through special acts. And we already know that this meaning is not correct relative to images. As to the possibility of [image] worship in such a way that some of the images or some of the bodies become like the *qiblah*,[43] that is not inconceivable, provided it be true, as it

---

41 Arabic *al-aṣnām*. Variant text—*al-ajsām* [the bodies], but the context favors the first version.
42 Arabic *taʿabbud*, which denotes devotion to worship of God, modes of worship. To denote image worship, ʿAbd al-Jabbār uses the word *ʿabādah*, as he does later in this sentence.
43 I.e., the direction of Mecca, faced in worship.

is in the case of worship, that we worship Allah through our prayers in the direction of the Ka'bah.

As to the worship of an image in order to bring us nearer to Allah, it is impossible that such be worship, because of our previous arguments. And this teaches us that the ancients who worshiped the image were in any event in error.[44]

The second way in which we have permitted worship through its agency is not worshipping an image or bowing down to it, but worshipping Allah, praise be to Him, and bowing down to Him and desiring His nearness. And whoever worships Allah in this way without obeying Him—he too is in error, for such worship is beneficial only when it involves utility and benevolence, and that cannot become known other than through obedience, and reason has no place in that.

That is the summary [of the discussion], and there is no need to speak further of the reasons for image worship among those who practiced it because exposing the reasons for errors committed by human beings in the past is of no avail.

The idolatry is described as typical of the pre-Muslim era (Jāhiliyyah). 'Abd al-Jabbār's description resembles that of other Muslim heresiographers, who presented idolatry as mediation and as an expression of monotheistic faith resorting to mediating tools (images).

Following are the main points in 'Abd al-Jabbār's discussion. At the opening of the chapter, he notes that two kinds of images were made—those of angels and those of stars or planets. Both these worlds, that of the angels and that of the celestial bodies, are superior to the material world and, therefore, angels and planets are close to Allah and even resemble him. According to the basic sympathetic principle of image worship, a symbol helps to draw the emanation from the symbolized source and functions as a substrate for the flux of the upper world. Image worshippers thus inferred that worshipping images was beneficial to them, a conclusion in agreement with the utilitarian characterization of magic.

After describing the motives for image worship, 'Abd al-Jabbār cites various traditions that he had collected about the practices and beliefs of image worshippers. In the manner typical of a Muslim heresiographer, later in the chapter he mixes several heretical beliefs—such as the worship of fire, of angels, and of the son of God—with image worship. 'Abd al-Jabbār randomly

---

44 That is, the ancients were mistaken, whether they worshipped the image as an intermediary or as an end in itself.

mentions the worship of images as intermediaries between humans and Allah among all the other cults he rejects, such as Judaism and Christianity.

At the end of the chapter, he resumes his description of the content and ideas of image worship as such, documenting the methods that image worshippers resorted to in their search for closeness to God through the mediation of an image. ʿAbd al-Jabbār then presents several detailed counter-arguments, as follows:

(1) Image worship is the outcome of a grave theological fallacy—the ascription of form to Allah, that is, the corporeality of God.
(2) Technically speaking, images cannot serve as intermediaries because they have neither personality nor free choice.
(3) The very desire to achieve a positive goal (closeness to Allah) by negative means (image worship) is self-contradictory.

These arguments indeed fit well the polemical style of the Muʿtazila, of which ʿAbd al-Jabbār was a major representative. It is well known that the Muʿtazilites appealed to the unchallengeable authority of reason (*ʿaql*) to demonstrate and justify their theological positions. In their view, God abides by the principles of reason, and his commands and prohibitions are therefore logical.[45]

At the end of the chapter, ʿAbd al-Jabbār ponders the possibility of worshipping images within a positive religious context but remains undecided. Although he firmly asserts that Allah should be worshiped directly, without intermediaries, he does not reject the possibility that image worship might find its place among Allah's precepts. Note that, according to Halevi, the cherubim are an example of image worship that God allowed.[46] Whereas Halevi had no hesitations in this regard, ʿAbd al-Jabbār tends to condemn image worship from the perspective of religious law (*fiqh*).

Potential Influence

What we have here, then, is a detailed account of the worship of images as intermediaries between humans and God, furnishing a rational reasonable

---

[45] See, for example, George F. Hourani, *Islamic Rationalism: The Ethics of ʿAbd al-Jabbār* (Oxford: Clarendon Press, 1971), 21. *Cf.* Michael Schwarz, "The Qāḍī ʿAbd al-Jabbār's Refutation of the Ashʿarite Doctrine of Acquisition (Kasb)," *Israel Oriental Studies* (1976) 6: 229-263; Binyamin Abrahamov, "ʿAbd al-Jabbār's Theory of Divine Assistance (*Luṭf*)," *Jerusalem Studies in Arabic and Islam* 16 (1993): 41-58; idem, "The Appointed time of Death (*Aǧal*) According to ʿAbd al-Ǧabbār," *Israel Oriental Studies* 13 (1993): 7-38.
[46] *Kuzari*, 1:97, 70.

explanation for this cult (deriving benefit from the resemblance of the image to the sources of the divine emanation) and for its theological merit (closeness to Allah achieved through the image's mediation). This source, together with possible magic and hermetic sources,[47] may have influenced Maimonides in the formation of his stance regarding image worship. Moreover, when Maimonides states the fifth principle of faith (*qa'idah*) that rejects the worship of intermediaries in the introduction to Chapter 10 of Tractate Sanhedrin (*Perek Helek*), he relies on the same reason as 'Abd al-Jabbār:

> For these are all fashioned in accordance with the works they are intended to perform. They have no judgment [*ḥukm*] or free-will [*'ikhtiyar*], but only a love for him (be he exalted!). Let us adopt no mediators to enable ourselves to draw near unto God, but let the thoughts be directed to him, and turned away from whatsoever is below him.[48]

Maimonides thus presented the second of 'Abd al-Jabbār's counterarguments: images possess no personality or free choice and, therefore, cannot serve as intermediaries. Note that, in many sources, Maimonides does not bother to present detailed and well-argued claims against idolatrous approaches and merely presented them broadly, believing that exposing them was enough to refute them. His aim is to warn against danger or to explain the purpose of the Torah's warnings rather than to confront idolatrous notions, which do not merit deep rational discussion. Contrary to astrology, which Maimonides definitely sought to deprive of its "scientific" aura while limiting its theological damage, he did not view magic practices as requiring serious discussion. Presenting them as folly should suffice. In this sense, this presentation of idolatrous beliefs resembles his detailing of Kalām principles in Part I of the *Guide*. Maimonides did not enter into a detailed controversy with the Muslim theologians and held that contrasting their doctrines with the correct scientific theories would suffice to undermine their foundations.[49]

---

47   See Schwartz, *Studies in Astral Magic*; Sarah Stroumsa, "The Sabians of Harran and the Sabians of Maimonides: On Maimonides' Theory of the History of Religions," *Sefunot*, New Series 7 (1999): 277-295 [Heb]; idem, "'Ravings': Maimonides' Concept of Pseudo-Science," *Aleph* 1 (2001): 141-163.

48   J. Abelson, "Maimonides on the Jewish Creed," *Jewish Quarterly Review* 19 (1906), 49-50. This is the English version of the introduction to Chapter 10 of Tractate Sanhedrin, known as *Perek Helek* (henceforth and throughout the book, Abelson, "Introduction").

49   See Dov Schwartz, *Faith and Reason: On Patterns of Discussion in Medieval Jewish Thought* (Tel Aviv: Broadcast University, 2001), 81 [Heb]. See also Michael Schwarz, "Who Were Maimonides' Mutakallimūn? Some Remarks on *Guide of the Perplexed*, Part I, Chapter 73," *Maimonidean Studies* 2 (1991): 159-209; 3 (1992/1993): 143-172.

The notion of idolatry (the Jāhiliyyah era) as mediating between humans and God appears also in the writings of other heresiographers, such as Muhammad al-Shahrastānī[50] and the thirteenth century thinker Ibn Abī al-ʿIzz Al-Dimashqī.[51] ʿAbd al-Jabbār's account, then, contributes to our understanding of the twelfth-century cultural and religious climate that led to the rejection of image worship in astral magic, a climate that Maimonides himself did much to create. In addition, one cannot discount the possibility that ʿAbd al-Jabbār's description of image worshippers served Maimonides as a direct or indirect source for understanding the religious and psychological motives that induce humans to worship images as intermediaries between themselves and God. Al-Shahrastānī and al-Jabbār on the one hand, and Judah Halevi and Ibn Ezra on the other allowed for the perception of idolatry as mediation, and Maimonides used this approach to expose not only the error of image worshippers but also their destructive influence on the faith of the wider public.

---

50 al-Shahrastānī, *Kitāb Al-Milal wa al-Nihal*, ed. Ṣidqī Jamīl al-ʿAṭṭār (Beirut, 1997), 245. Based on ʿAbd al-Azīz Muḥammad al-Wakīl's edition (Cairo, 1967),
51 ʿAli ibn ʿAli Ibn Abī al-ʿIzz, *Sharḥ al-ʿaqīda al-taḥāwiyya*, ed. ʿAbdallāh ibn ʿAbd al-Muḥsin al-Turki and Shuʿayb al-Arnaʾūṭ(Beirut, 1991), 29.

Chapter 5

Immortality and Imagination

The discussion of immortality in Maimonides' early writings affords some understanding into his use of sources. Directly or indirectly, Maimonides was aware of Avicenna's writing and, although he was suspicious of Avicenna's philosophical views, he did absorb many of his methods and approaches. One of them is the concept of immortality.

The Scope of the Discussion

At first sight, Avicenna's and Maimonides' accounts of the human soul in general and of the intellect in particular, would seem to have little in common. The difference is already obvious at the formal level. Avicenna delivers in his works a comprehensive account of the essence of the human soul and its immortality; he proves with painstaking thoroughness that the soul is a substance, not pre-existent, which originally emanated from the active intellect. As to the epistemological question of how the intellect acquires its knowledge, he argues that the acquisition of knowledge is not just a process confined to the abstraction of forms, but is also illuminative, sustained by the active intellect. Finally, he discusses at great length the different modes of immortality that the soul may attain, depending on its achievements in earthly life.[1] These discussions, presented mainly in such

---

1 See, for example, Fazlur Rahman, *Avicenna's Psychology* (London: Oxford University Press, 1952), 1-21; B. C. Law, "Avicenna and his Theory of the Soul," in *Avicenna Commemoration Volume* (Calcutta: Iran Society, 1956), 179-186; Harry Blumberg, "The Problem of Immortality in Avicenna, Maimonides and St. Thomas Aquinas," in *Harry Austryn Wolfson Jubilee Volume on the Occasion of His Seventy-Fifth Birthday*, ed. Saul Lieberman (Jerusalem: American Academy of Jewish Research, 1965), 165-185; Gérard Verbeke, "L'immortalité de l'âme dans le *De anima* d'Avicenne: Une synthèse de l'Aristotélisme et du néoplatonisme," *Pensamiento*, 25 (1969): 271-290; Herbert A. Davidson, "Alfarabi and Avicenna on the Active Intellect," *Viator* 3 (1972): 171-175. See also idem, *Alfarabi, Avicenna, and Averroes, on Intellect: Their Cosmologies, Theories of the Active Intellect, and Theories of Human Intellect* (Oxford: Oxford University Press,

works as *Kitāb al-Najāt, Kitāb al-Shīfā; al-Ishārāt wal-Tanbīhāt* as well as in *Maʿrifat al-Nafs* (which is attributed to Avicenna), cover broad areas and are sometimes clumsily worded. One can also detect inner contradictions, incoherence, and philosophical difficulties in some of Avicenna's views. Avicenna, however, conveyed his views on the human soul explicitly and extensively.[2] Not so Maimonides.

In *The Guide of the Perplexed*, he refers to the nature of the soul and the intellect only sporadically and unsystematically. In the introduction to his *Commentary on Avot* [*Shemonah Peraqim*], he devotes the first two chapters to the nature of the soul in general and the human soul in particular, without ever providing direct answers to such classic questions as the origin of the soul and whether it is a substance. Maimonides sometimes states that the intellectual faculty of the soul is really a form, and on one occasion he uses the term "disposition" (*istiʿdad*).[3] One should not, however, draw any conclusions from this as to whether, in Maimonides' view, the soul is a spiritual substance or of material origin, for the term "form" (*ṣūra*) implies neither that the soul is a "substance" nor that is it not.[4] Moreover, Maimonides' rare recourse to the term "disposition" does not clearly attest that Maimonides had endorsed the view of Alexander of Aphrodisias on this point.[5] By contrast, Maimonides left far more explicit formulations concerning the immortality of the soul. He deals with the problem directly, both in his *Commentary to the*

1992); Lenn E. Goodman, *Avicenna* (London and New York: Routledge, 1992), 123-183; Peter Adamson, "Correcting Plotinus: Soul's Relationship to Body in Avicenna's Commentary on the Theology of Aristotle," *Bulletin of the Institute of Classical Studies* 47 (2004): 59-75; Dimitri Gutas, "Avicenna: The Metaphysics of the Rational Soul," *The Muslim World* 102 (2012): 417-425.

2   See, for example, Davidson, "Alfarabi and Avicenna," 175.
3   For the term "form" in relation to the soul see *Shemonah Peraqim*, ch. 1; *Mishneh Torah*, Laws of Repentance 8:3; *Guide* I:41, and others. For the term "disposition" see *Guide*, I:70, and also Munk and Yoel, 119, ln. 28.
4   Aristotle had already defined form in terms of "substance." See, for example, W. K. C. Guthrie, *A History of Greek Philosophy*, vol. 6, *Aristotle: An Encounter* (Cambridge: Cambridge University Press, 1981), 215-220. Note that Avicenna too uses the term "form" for the soul. See Rahman, *Avicenna's Psychology*, 10-11. Alfred Ivry devoted three comprehensive papers to Maimonides' neoplatonic sources, but he says nothing of the nature and origin of the soul, as Maimonides' position on this question is obscure. On the question of the soul in a different neoplatonic context, see Alfred L. Ivry, "Neoplatonic Currents in Maimonides' Thought," in *Perspectives on Maimonides*, ed. Joel L. Kramer (Oxford: Oxford University Press, 1991), 118-119.
5   Again, Avicenna too uses the term "disposition" in relation to the soul, while he absolutely rejects Alexander's views. See Binyamin Abrahamov, "Ibn Sina's Influence on Al Ghazali's Non-Philosophical Works," *Abr-Nahrain* 29 (1991):8.

Mishnah (in the introduction to *Perek Helek*) and in the *Mishneh Torah*, Laws of Repentance, Chapter 8. These discussions enable us to trace Maimonides' sources properly, even though his view of immortality in the *Guide* is different.[6] Hence, I do not deal in detail with the *Guide* in this chapter and focus on the explicit accounts in Maimonides' other works.

As I will argue below, the influence of Avicenna's discussion of the question in *Kitāb al-Najāt* is clearly evident in the mentioned writings of Maimonides, both in the formal literary and in the substantive content sense. Maimonides, however, radically modifies one component of Avicenna's doctrine, and this modification enables him to avoid some of the pitfalls Avicenna had confronted. Following is thus a comparison between Avicenna's and Maimonides' views of immortality.

Immortality as Pleasure

Avicenna's starting point in his discussion of immortality in *Kitāb al-Najāt* is that, as a rule, one can describe the state of the soul after death as one of either happiness *(saʿāda)* or misery *(shaqāwa)*.[7] Situations of happiness and misery, in the material corporeal level, are known to us through day-to-day experience and, therefore, we desire physical happiness by our very nature. On the

---

6 The *Guide of the Perplexed* seems to support two contrary views. One view states that immortality may be achieved through the conjunction of the human and the active intellects, while the other states that the human mind cannot apprehend the separate intellects, so there can be no immortality. Scholars are divided in their interpretation of Maimonides' views. See, for example, Pines, "The Limitations of Human Knowledge," 82-102; Alexander Altmann, "Maimonides on the Intellect and the Scope of Metaphysics," in *Von der mittelalterlichen zur modernen Aufklaerung: Studien zur juedischen Geistesgeschichte* (Tüebingen: JCB Mohr, 1987), 60-129. *Cf.* also Warren Zev Harvey, *Crescas' Critique of the Theory of the Acquired Intellect* (Ph. D. dissertation, New York, NY: Columbia University, 1973—University Mic. no. 74-1488), 28-29, 40-45; Herbert A. Davidson, *The Philosophy of Abraham Shalom: A Fifteenth-Century Exposition and Defence of Maimonides* (Berkeley, CA: Universtiy of California Press, 1964), 79-80.

7 *Kitāb al-Najāt*, ed. Muḥyiddīn al-Din Ṣabrī al-Kurdī (Cairo: Saʿadat Press, 1938), 291. The definition of *saʿāda* is a general one, and in this respect Avicenna is no different from Aristotle and Alfārābī, who describe the perfection of bliss. As shown below, however, Avicenna is more precise and refers to this condition as *ladhdha*, that is, pleasure and delight. This term compels a psychological substrate, hence the series of problems that characterizes Avicenna's approach to immortality. *cf.* Amira Eran, "Al-Ghazali and Maimonides on the World to Come and Spiritual Pleasures," *Jewish Studies Quarterly* 8:2 (2001): 137-166.

other hand, we learn to yearn for spiritual abstract happiness through the works of the metaphysicians *(al-fḥukamā' al-ilāhiyyūn)*. Avicenna describes the happiness manifest in the soul's various faculties in terms of pleasure *(ladhdha)* and success *(khair)*. He, therefore, offers a lengthy analysis of the concept of pleasure. The pleasure that accompanies the condition of human happiness, he says, is not homogeneous; it shows a gradation, depending on the soul's various faculties and their qualities.[8] Indeed, the pleasure we experience from food and drink does not resemble that derived from remembering forgotten things, and neither of them is like the pleasure of power and authority. Avicenna then goes one step further: if pleasure can indeed be graded, surely it can be ascribed to the upper levels of reality, that is, to the separate intellects,[9] and even to God. Humans are obviously incapable of visualizing such supernal pleasure, but they can conjecture its existence by drawing an analogy *(qiyās)* with human pleasure.

Avicenna contrasted two types of pleasure, mean and exalted: the soul's pleasure in its various faculties (from the nutritive to the imaginative and the remembering power) on the one hand, and the pleasure of the separate intellects and even of God on the other. The mean pleasure is rooted in the internal and external senses whereas the exalted pleasure is purely intellectual. Between these two extremes of pleasure, says Avicenna, is the middle link: the "rational soul" *(al-nafs al-nāṭiqa)*.[10] This soul is essentially tied to the animal soul but is capable of realizing its intellectual powers and perceive truths such as "the form of reality" *(ṣurat al-kull*, lit. the All) and "the intelligible order of reality" *(al-nizām al-ma'qūl fī al-kull)*, which is found in the knowledge of God. Thus, one cannot compare the perfection of the soul's intellectual faculty to the perfections of other parts of the soul—the former is concerned with the eternal and the durable, whereas the latter

---

8 *Cf Aḥwāl al-nafs*, ed. Ahmad Fuād al-Ahwānī (Cairo: Īsā al-Bābī al-Ḥalabī, 1952), 127-140; 187-188. Davidson views the attribution of this work to Avicenna as dubious.

9 Avicenna calls them *al-mabādi' al-'ūlā al-muqarraba 'inda rabb al-'alimīn* ["the First Principles, which are close to the Sovereign of the Universe" (ibid., 292)]. The description of the separate intellects as close to God recurs in the works of al-Ghazālī and Averroes as well. See Harry Blumberg, "The Separate Intelligences in Maimonides' Philosophy," *Tarbiz* 40 (1971), 220 [Heb]. Avicenna considers the separate intellects "close to God," most probably also because he identifies them with the angels and the theological functions that they perform. See Seyyed Hossein Naṣr, *An Introduction to Islamic Cosmological Doctrines: Conceptions of Nature and Methods Used for Its Study by the Ikwān as Safā', al-Bīrūnī, and Ibn Sīnā* (Cambridge, MA: Harvard University Press, 1964), 238.

10 *Kitāb al-Najāt*, 293.

relates to the changeable and the corruptible.[11] The gulf between physical pleasure and spiritual/intellectual pleasure is as deep as that between the perfections, and Avicenna therefore poses a rhetorical question: "How can ... this spiritual pleasure *(ladhdha)* [that of apprehending truths] be compared to the other sensual, bestial, wrathful pleasure?"[12] These arguments clarify that intellectual pursuits are a source of pleasure.

As for immortality. Being defined as a spiritual substance, the soul is neither perishable nor corruptible. Hence, Avicenna does not bother to prove that the soul is in itself eternal and, instead, devotes a detailed discussion to prove that the nature of the body-soul connection does not lead the soul to extinction.[13] If the soul is indeed inherently eternal, regardless of what happens to it when in the body, in what way can its sojourn in the body affect its mode of immortality? Avicenna replies: Upon leaving the body, the soul will experience pleasure if it acquired knowledge in its earthly state because real pleasure, as noted, is tied to the acquisition of knowledge. Moreover, the soul's pleasure after death will be immeasurably greater, being unfettered by a material body. Alternatively, a soul that has not acquired knowledge will suffer after death, when exposed to what it had hitherto neglected. Avicenna likens the intellectual soul's condition after death to a person who is given delicious food and whose sense of taste has been deadened by drugs but, once the effect of the drugs has worn off, will experience an exquisite sensation. On the other hand, the ignorant soul resembles a person, sick with some debilitating disease, who has received tranquilizing drugs but, when the effect of the drugs has worn off, will again feel excruciating pain. Avicenna concludes: "This then is the happiness *(sa'āda)* and that the misery *(shaqāwa)* awaiting every soul in the afterlife."[14] Throughout the discussion, eternal happiness is

---

[11] According to Avicenna, most human beings agree on the superiority of the spiritual over the physical, as evidenced by their willingness to renounce certain forms of physical enjoyment because of shame, or to suffer deprivation in order to win some victory, and so forth. *Cf.* Al-Ghazālī, *Mīzān al-'amal*, ed. Suleimān Dunyā (Cairo: Dār al-Ma'ārif, 1964), 184. The sensations of shame and victory are called "intellectual modes" *(aḥwāl 'aqkiyya—Kitab al-Najat*, 294). See also *Al-ishārāt wal-Tanbihāt*, ed. Suleimān Dunyā, vol. 3 (Cairo: Dār al-Ma'ārif, 1960), 213.

[12] *Al-ḥissiyya wal-bahīmiyya wal-ghadhabīyya; Kitāb al-Najāt*, 294 ("wrathful" because wrath too may cause pleasure).

[13] See *Aḥwāl al-nafs*, 99-105; Rahman, *Avicenna's Psychology*, 58-63; Davidson, "Alfarabi and Avicenna," 171-172.

[14] *Kitāb al-Najāt*, 295. The notion of pleasure in immortality is central among Avicenna's commentators as well. See the commentary of Jūzjānī [?} on *Ḥayy ibn Yaqẓan*, §24, in Henry Corbin, *Avicenna and the Visionary Recital*, trans. Willard R. Trask (Princeton: Princeton University Press, 1960), 375.

identified with the pleasure *(ladhdha)* inherent in the impact of intellectual apprehension after death.

Consider now Maimonides' views on the subject. Maimonides agrees with Avicenna that the acquisition of knowledg is a pleasurable process,[15] and he even accepts the view that immortality is characterized by pleasure. The account of this subject in the introduction to *Perek Helek* in his *Commentary to the Mishnah* is clearly based on Avicenna's discussion in *Kitāb al-Najāt*. Avicenna's influence on Maimonides is evident, first and foremost, in the very definition of immortality in terms of pleasure, but also in the structure of the discourse that leads up to this conclusion. Maimonides' starting point is clearly hermeneutical. He sees the concept of the "world to come" as reflecting " immortality,"[16] and therefore discusses it in his commentary on the Mishnah statement, "All Israel have a part in the world to come."[17] Maimonides' pours Avicenna's notion of pleasure into the closure of the talmudic saying: "In the world to come there will be no eating and no drinking, no washing and no anointing and no marriage but only the righteous sitting with crowns on their heads enjoying the splendor of the *Shekhinah*."[18] More precisely, the

---

15 Maimonides, too, employs the term *ladhdha* to denote the delight of intellection. Two examples follow. The first is Positive Commandment 3: "We have thus made it clear to you that through this act of contemplation [*i'tibār*] you will attain a conception of God and reach that stage of joy [*ladhdha*] in which love of Him will follow of necessity." See Maimonides, *The Commandments: Sefer Ha-Mitzvoth*, vol. 1, transl. Charles B. Chavel (London & New York: Soncino, 1967), 4. The second is from *The Guide of the Perplexed*: "when a perfect man is stricken with years and approaches death … joy over this apprehension and a great love for the object of apprehension becomes stronger, until the soul [*nafs*] is separated from the body at that moment in this state of pleasure [*ladhdha*]" (*Guide* III:51, 627). *Cf.* Warren Z. Harvey, "Crescas versus Maimonides on Knowledge and Pleasure," in *A Straight Path: Studies in Medieval Philosophy and Culture—Essays in Honor of Arthur Hyman*, ed. Ruth Link-Salinger (Washington, DC: Catholic University of America Press, 1988), 119. Note the distinction here between "happiness" and "pleasure." The idea of the acquisition of knowledge as a source of spiritual and intellectual happiness can be traced back to Aristotelian philosophy and appears extensively in the works of Alfārābī and Ibn Bājja. Aristotle's commentators, however, already realized that this happiness lies beyond the psychological condition of delight. See, for example, Richard Norman, "Aristotle's Philosopher-God," in *Articles on Aristotle,* ed. Jonathan Barnes et. al., vol. 4 (London: Duckworth, 1979), 101. By contrast, Avicenna argued that happiness is not merely a spiritual-intellectual condition, but is also bound up with the distinctly psychological condition of *ladhdha* (as described by Aristotle, *Rhetoric* 1369b 33-35, and elsewhere).

16 On "immortality" in Maimonides' teachings see Arthur Hyman, "Maimonides' 'Thirteen Principles,'" in *Jewish Medieval and Renaissance Studies*, ed. Alexander Altmann (Cambridge, MA: Harvard University Press, 1967), 126 and n. 44.

17 M. Sanhedrin 10:1.

18 BT Berakhot 17a; Abelson, "Introduction," 39.

characteristic feature of the world to come is "enjoyment" or pleasure in the splendor of the Divine Presence, which Maimonides explains as meaning pleasure in intellectual achievement.

Like Avicenna, Maimonides too draws a sharp line between the physical pleasure derived from our internal and external senses on the one hand, and the pleasure in intellectual attainment and knowledge enjoyed by the supernal beings such as the various ranks of angels (*ṭabaqāt al-malā'ika*) on the other. And here, too, just like Avicenna, Maimonides infers that humans can reach this second kind of pleasure and apprehend spiritual knowledge "as do the higher bodies (*al-ajrām al-'alawiyya*) or more," which is the highest of all possible pleasures.[19] Immortality for Maimonides, then, is characterized by pleasure in the knowledge that the intellect has achieved during its earthly life. In addition, Maimonides' Hebrew style clearly suggests that the pleasure in question is equivalent to "joy."[20]

Avicenna's influence on Maimonides is also evident in other literary and philosophical aspects of his work, as a few examples will show. In order to illustrate the determination that ordinary persons are unacquainted with spiritual-intellectual pleasure, both Avicenna and Maimonides resort to the analogy of the blind person who cannot envisage visual beauty or the eunuch who cannot experience the pleasures of sex.[21] Both repeat the proof of the existence of spiritual pleasure as derived from the fact that people are willing to suffer in order to gain respect or praise from their peers,[22] and finally, both emphasize the pleasure derived by the separate

---

19 Ibid.
20 *Mishneh Torah, Laws* of Repentance 8:2. *Cf.* Gerald Blidstein, "The Concept of Joy in Maimonides," *Eshel Beer-Sheva* 2 (1980), 153, 162-163 [Heb]. Maimonides' doctrine of intellectual immortality as pleasure shaped the approach to immortality of the rationalist school in medieval Judaism. See, for example, in the early fourteenth century, David Kokhavi, *Sefer ha-Batim*, ed. Moshe Herschler, vol. 1 (Jerusalem: Regensburg Institute, 1983), 167 [Heb]. From the second half of the fourteenth century, see Samuel ibn Zarza, *Mikhlol Yofi*, MS Paris 729-730, vol. I, 189a. From the second half of the fifteenth century, see Abraham Shalom, *Neveh Shalom* (Venice, 1575), 123b.
21 *Kitāb al-Najāt*, 292; "Introduction," 38. Avicenna's analysis of the pleasure experienced by each and every faculty of the soul is lacking in Maimonides. Note that this discussion does appear briefly in the commentary of an early fifteenth century thinker, Ḥoter b. Shlomo, on Maimonides' thirteen principles that are enumerated in the "Introduction." See Ḥoter ben Shelōmō, *The Commentary of Ḥoter ben Shelōmō to the Thirteen Principles of Maimonides*, ed. David R. Blumenthal (Leiden: E. J. Brill, 1974), 305-306.
22 See *Kitāb al-Najāt*, 293; Abelson, "Introduction," 39.

intellects from their intellectual activity as an example of the very existence of spiritual pleasure.[23]

It is apparently unquestionable that the relevant passages from Avicenna's *Kitāb al-Najāt*, either in their original form or in paraphrase, were known to Maimonides, who formulated his doctrine of the intellect's or soul's experience in the afterlife in accordance with Avicenna's.[24] But we must not thereby conclude that Maimonides blindly followed Avicenna's lead. On the contrary, he parts ways with the Muslim thinker in certain essential details, as the next section will show.

The Substrate of Immortality

Avicenna's concept of immortality, as discussed, is not homogeneous. Its modes vary from absolute sorrow to absolute pleasure, depending on the personal achievements of the person in question. Some thought must now be given to one of the most difficult problems in Avicenna's philosophy. For Avicenna, immortality is personal and, in light of this determination, the eternal phenomena of pleasure and misery, are distinctly individual.[25] This stance entails a series of difficulties, such as the simultaneous existence of an infinite number of individual souls in the afterlife that remains after death given the doctrine of the eternity of the world. According to Aristotelian science, the simultaneous infinity of objects is impossible.[26] The particular difficulty that I will discuss here is the question of the substrate of immortality.

---

23 On Avicenna, see *Kitāb al-Najāt*, 292. On Maimonides, see Abelson, "Introduction," 38: "We are not sanctioned either by the Torah or by the divine philosophers to state that the angels, the stars, and the spheres enjoy no delights [*ladhdha*]. In truth they have exceeding great delight in respect of what they comprehend of the Creator (glorified be he!). This to them is an everlasting felicity without a break."

24 *Cf.* also Erwin I. J. Rosenthal, "Avicenna's Influence on Jewish Thought," in *Avicenna: Scientist and Philosopher—A Millenary Symposium*, ed. G. M. Wickens (London: Luzac, 1952), 70-71.

25 This assumption is compelled by the hierarchical structure of immortality according to the measure of pleasure and misery because affects, contrary to learning and speculative knowledge, are exclusively individual. Blumberg's position in "The Problem of Immortality" is therefore strange. On the one hand, he argues that Avicenna does not posit personal immortality (ibid., 170); on the other, he presents the hierarchy of immortality (ibid., 172-173). True, in Avicenna's many discussions of the theory of the soul, he also expounds on the impersonal theory of immortality but that is not the dominant trend in his writings. On the problems of Avicenna's theory of personal immortality, see Parviz Morewedge, *The Metaphysica of Avicenna* (London: Routledge and Kegan Paul, 1973), 254-255.

26 See Michael E. Marmura, "Avicenna and the Problem of the Infinite Number of Souls," *Medieval Studies* 20 (1960): 232-239; Oliver Leaman, *An Introduction to Medieval Islamic Philosophy* (Cambridge: Cambridge University Press, 1985), 94-96.

Both Avicenna and Maimonides claim that immortality involves pleasure. In other words, the intellectual soul experiences a certain affect of pleasure or enjoyment but the soul's intellectual faculty itself cannot provide the substrate for the pleasure. Some sort of animative and corporeal substrate is required for a pleasurable sensation, that is, for the external or internal senses to feel pleasure and for the imagination to envisage its effect.[27] In earthly life, the body and the external and internal senses provide the substrate for pleasure; but none of them survive after death. As shown below, this poses a particularly difficult question for Maimonides, whose epistemology teaches that knowledge contains nothing beyond the perceived forms, and the cognizing intellect is completely united with its material forms.[28] This approach presents problems for Avicenna as well since the intellect itself cannot serve as a substrate for a sensation of pleasure. The problem of the substrate of affects splits into two realms: the realm of eternal pleasure and the realm of eternal suffering. As for the latter, Maimonides' approach is essentially different from that of Avicenna, thereby rescuing Maimonides from the problems that Avicenna experiences. Maimonides does not recognize the possibility of eternal misery. For him, the knowledge that humans acquire endows their intellect with ontic reality, entailing it real existence after death and thus ensuring its survival in the afterlife. Every intellectually cognized object that is apprehended in earthly life, then, enhances the ontic status of the intellect's life after death and makes it more "stable." We can, therefore, infer its opposite as well: individuals who have not acquired knowledge or actualized their intelligence cannot survive after their death and are doomed to annihilation, to nothingness. They cannot attain durability (*la taḥṣīl bāqīyya*);[29] they are

---

27 See Leaman, *Introduction*, 95.
28 *Guide* I:68, 162.
29 "Introduction," 40. Cf. *Mishneh Torah*, Laws of Repentance 8:5. According to Davidson's analysis, Maimonides' may have adopted this view too on the basis of his interpretation of Avicenna. See Davidson, "Alfarabi and Avicenna," 174, and see the end of this section. Maimonides' solution too, whereby the punishment is identified with total nonexistence, was accepted by the rationalist school in medieval Judaism. See, for example, from the second half of the twelfth century Samuel Ibn Tibbon, *Ma'amar yiqqawu ha-mayim*, ed. M. L. Bisliches (Pressburg, 1837), 98; from the first half of the thirteenth century, Jacob Anatoli, *Malmad ha-talmidim* (Lueck, 1866), 52a; from the mid-thirteenth century, Isaac b. Jedaiah, "Commentary to Tractate Avot," in *Perushei Rishonim le-Massekhet Avot*, ed. Moshe Kasher and Yacakov Blecherowitz (Jerusalem: Machon Torah Shlemah, 1973), 62. Over the years, however, a trend developed among commentators who attempted to square Maimonides' views with those of Avicenna, claiming that Maimonides too assumed a dimension of suffering in immortality. See, for example, Joseph Caro, *Kesef Mishneh* on

nothing but perishable matter (*mādda*), lacking any ontic dimension that might assure their subsistence. Here too, Maimonides relies for his interpretation on biblical exegesis and argues that the total disappearance of persons who have failed to realize their intellectual potential is symbolized by that severest of punishments in the Torah—*karet,* "cutting off." *Karet* relates to the sinner's world to come, namely, to immortality, and means the sinner's absolute loss. Thus, Maimonides explains the verse, "that soul shall surely be cut off" (Numbers 15:31) as follows:

> This destruction [*karet*] it is to which the prophets metaphorically apply the terms … and all other expressions which denote cessation and destruction … because it is a ruin that is irreparable and a loss which is irrecoverable.[30]

In any event, the problem of the substrate of eternal pleasure in the afterlife affects Maimonides' thought too, since he claims that the soul acquires immortality through the intellect (*bi-baqā' ma'lūmihā*), and has no existence beyond that intellectual cognition.[31] Maimonides presented the following argument:

(1) The human intellect is identical to the intelligibles it has acquired.
(2) Only the intellect survives after death.

Laws of Repentance 3:6; Joseph Cohen, *Sefer ha-teshuvah* (Jerusalem, 1989), 256 (identifying the approaches of Maimonides and Nachmanides regarding immortality).

30 *Mishneh Torah: The Book of Knowledge*, ed. Moshe Hyamson (Jerusalem: Boys Town, 1962), Laws of Repentance 8:5, 90b. *Cf.* ibid., 8:l; 9:l. The Arabic term used in the introduction to *Perek Helek* for the parallel concept is *inqiṭāʿ* ("the cutting off of the soul") [Abelson, "Introduction," 40]. Maimonids also uses the Hebrew term *hefsek*, cessation, to translate *inqiṭāʿ*. See David H. Baneth, "On the Philosophic Terminology of Maimonides," *Tarbiz* 6 (1935), 18 [Heb].

31 In his words, "the merging of the two into one" (Abelson, "Introduction," 39—lit., "they become one thing," *shay' wāḥid*). There is no hint in Maimonides' discussion that he accepts Alfārābī's position, according to which the condition of the "acquired intellect" (*ʿaql al-mustafād*) converts the soul into a spiritual substance, making it immortal. See, for example, Alfārābī, *Arā' al-madīna al-fāḍila*, ed. Albīr Naṣrī Nādir (Beirut: al-Maktabah al-Kaṯhuliḳiyah 1959), 105. Abstract knowledge represents the soul according to Maimonides, and its intelligibles subsist without any material substrate. Incidentally, it is in this spirit that Maimonides interprets the famous mishnaic dictum, "All Israel have a share in the world to come," proposing the Thirteen Principles as a criterion for membership in the community of Israel. These principles include a series of philosophical/theological truths (God's attributes such as his unity, incorporeality, and eternity), religious truths (divine knowledge, providence and its consequences—messianism and resurrection), and finally, political truths (prophecy and Torah). All Jews, then, have some knowledge about intellectual truths of various sorts, which enable their survival after death. See Hyman, "Maimonides' 'Thirteen Principles,'"; Menachem Kellner, *Dogma in Medieval Jewish Thought: From Maimonides to Abravanel* (Oxford: Oxford University Press, 1986), 10-65.

(3) Aquiring intelligibles includes all the theoretical sciences and demands absolute devotion.
(4) The *karet* sinner is a rebel against his own society (this is a hidden premise, not clearly specified by Maimonides).
(5) The *karet* sinner cannot acquire intelligibles.
Therefore:
(6) The *karet* sinner does not acquire immortality.
(7) He who acquires intelligibles acquires immortality.

If all that survives of a person are only pure intelligibles, there is no room for any psychological substrate on which pleasure might leave its imprint. Unlike Avicenna, whose discussion of this problem is considered below, Maimonides entirely ignores it and does not address it, either directly or indirectly.

The difference between the two thinkers seems to widen given that Avicenna defines the soul as a spiritual substance while Maimonides never refers to or even hints at such a definition, though he does not propose any clear-cut definition of the human soul in his writings. Hence, it is easier for Avicenna to discuss the question of the substrate of pleasure since he is concerned with the survival of a substance, while Maimonides' brand of immortality relates exclusively to the knowledge that one has acquired during life. How, then, does Avicenna meet the challenge of providing a substrate for eternal pleasure and misery? He relies on the claim that a person's moral character and behavior create a habit (*malaka*).[32] This habit is an internal inclination of the soul, outwardly reflected in the person's moral behavior (for example, generosity or parsimony, and so forth). People must strive to behave in such a way that their actions will accustom them to the "middle way" or the mean (*malakat al-tawassut*).[33] A moderate, middle inclination implies that the soul's desire for concrete rewards (which is unnatural to it) and the concern with the material dimension will be neutralized. Individuals who have attained such a rank can devote themselves to the development of the goals and ideals of the soul's intellectual faculties because the body will no longer bother them with excessive demands. By contrast, individuals immersed in the incessant, insatiable demands of the body develop extreme forms of behavior that leaves their imprint on the soul. Avicenna applies these assumptions to his theory of immortality. In his view, the inclinations that

---

32 *Kitāb al-Najāt*, 296. Cf. A.M. Goichon, *Lexique de la langue philosophique d'Ibn Sina* (Paris: Desclée de Brouwer, 1938), 384-385.
33 See *Aḥwāl al-nafs*, 135.

individuals acquire during their lifetime will persist after death too, and they are the ones that determine the mode of the soul's immortality. On the basis of this principle, Avicenna proposes a hierarchy of varieties of immortality:

(I) Persons who do not acquire any knowledge at all in their lifetime. This category includes two classes of people:

(1) The soul of the wicked and ignorant maintains its lust for earthly pleasures after death as well except that, lacking a body to consummate these desires, it is doomed to eternal yearning, never to be satisfied.
(2) The soul of a morally honest person who is also ignorant merits a kind of ease or well-being (*rāḥa*) after death except that, lacking any intellectual achievement, it will not be able to experience pleasure.[34]

(II) Persons who realized the importance of knowledge as human perfection (*kamāl*). This category also includes two classes of people:

(1) The souls of individuals who have not realized their intellectual potential. In the afterlife, they will experience the torment of eternal yearning for the unattainable given that, despite their awareness of the importance of knowledge, they will still be unable to acquire it since there is no development after death.
(2) Individuals who have realized their intellectual potential will enjoy eternal and undisturbed pleasure.[35]

Avicenna, then, does not limit immortality to the intellectual faculty (*quwwat al-'aqlīyya*) alone. At least three elements do survive after death. One is the "habit" (*malaka*) that the soul has acquired owing to the person's moral behavior; the second is the yearning (*shawq*) of the soul, which may or may not reach fulfillment, and the third—eternal pleasure (*ladhdha*). These three elements clearly indicate that it is not only the intellectual faculty—the acquired intellect—that survives death. The yearning, for example, assumes some kind of will on the one hand, and imagination enabling the soul to construe the object of its yearning on the other. For Avicenna, then, the soul that subsists after death is clearly a substance possessing a distinct dimension of will and imagination, hence also of pleasure and pain.

---

34 *Kitāb al-Najāt*, 297.
35 *Ibid.*, 295. *Cf. Kitab al-shifā' (al-ilāhiyyāt)*, ed. G. C. Anawati & S. Zayed, vol. 2 (Cairo, 1960), 425-429; Davidson, "Alfarabi and Avicenna," 173-174.

Equating the surviving part of the soul with the "acquired intellect" alone is therefore not sufficient. The substance that is the soul after death includes animative aspects as well, such as the survival of the imagination and the will.

This approach is to some extent compatible with an argument found in other writings of Avicenna stating that, since the soul in the afterlife is a substance, it retains its imaginative faculty. This faculty causes the wicked to suffer an eternal, insatiable yearning of two varieties: souls that, when alive, recognized the value of acquiring knowledge continue to do so after death but are unable to attain it, whereas those that did not, yearn in vain to realize their earthly desires. Morally pious persons entirely lacking in knowledge merit quiet rest in that their imagination is untroubled by such everlasting desire.[36] Having postulated that the soul in the afterlife retains the imaginative faculty and perhaps also the faculty of volition, Avicenna does not entirely dismiss the possibility of happiness for souls that, although entirely ignorant of speculative knowledge (in the I.2 category above), are still familiar with the religious-popular idea of immortality in its materially oriented version, as in the resurrection of the dead idea.[37] While concerning those who have achieved perfection (the II.2 category), the intellectual element brings the soul and its imagination real happiness (sa'āda), believers in the mentioned theological notion may achieve pleasure—though indeed of an inferior kind—with the help of a celestial body—the eternal matter of the spheres (ajrām al-samāwīyya).[38] This matter serves as a kind of substratum for the imaginative faculty of the vulgar person's soul.

Avicenna's argument about the survival of the imaginative faculty thus offers a solution to the problem of the substrate, though not one free of difficulties. This solution, however, is incompatible with Maimonides'

---

36 For a comprehensive treatment of this question see Jean R. Michot, *La destinée de l'homme selon Avicenne: le retour à Dieu (ma'ād) et l'imagination* (Louvain: A. Peters, 1986). Incidentally, a similar interpretation of Avicenna was offered by Meir Aldubi, a Jewish thinker active in Spain in the second half of the fourteenth century: "And some have moreover stated that the imaginative faculty will survive after death as will the intellectual part, by the will of the Creator, blessed be He, through the active intellect, and they will conjoin with the intellectual faculty and become one so as to receive their just reward. But the other bodily faculties, such as those of nutrition, growth, reproduction and the like, have no part in immortality" (*Shvilei Emunah* [Warsaw, 1887], 73c).

37 Avicenna cites this idea in the name of the "theologians" ('ulamā'), *Kitāb al-Najāt*, 297. He was, nevertheless, accused of denying the doctrine of resurrection. See the next section and *cf*. Soheil M. Afnan, *Avicenna: His Life and Works* (London: Allen and Unwin, 1958), 182-183.

38 *Kitāb al-Najāt*, 298.

approach, which does not explain how the soul can experience pleasure after death. Contrary to Avicenna, then, who discussed the problem of the substrate at length, Maimonides chose not to tackle the problem at all.

Reactions

The preceding discussion could lead to the conclusion that Maimonides was influenced by Avicenna's description of immortality in terms of pleasure, as well as by the literary details of this discussion of pleasure. But Maimonides differs from Avicenna on two essential points:

(1) He does not acknowledge the survival of the soul after death as a substance but only the abstract survival of the intellect. If only a person's intellectual achievements enjoy immortality, this survival cannot be personal and the question of what substrate can possibly sustain pleasure in the afterlife emerges as unavoidable.
(2) Maimonides rejects the existence of eternal sorrow in the afterlife so that the problem of a substrate is irrelevant in that connection. By contrast, Avicenna holds that the soul survives *qua* substance, including the imaginative faculty, and therefore acknowledges eternal misery as well as eternal pleasure.[39]

Maimonides' account is more consistent than Avicenna's, as he grants the cognizing intellect a distinctly ontic status that enables its survival after death. Besides leaving the substrate problem unsolved, however, Maimonides falls into a theological difficulty regarding the righteous who have not acquired knowledge. For him, the fate of such individuals is no different from that of the wicked, condemned to absolute annihilation. Clearly, then, while Maimonides selectively borrowed and endorsed some of Avicenna's formal and philosophical motifs, he rejected several of Avicenna's central positions. This conclusion is in keeping with a passage in Maimonides' celebrated letter to Samuel Ibn Tibbon: "Though the books of 'Ali Ibn Sīnā show considerable accuracy and subtle study, they are not like the books of Abu Naṣr Alfārābī, but

---

[39] Pines interpreted this contrast as evidence that Maimonides, unlike Avicenna, "was not interested in apologetics at any price, or even in apologetics at all." See Shlomo Pines, "Translator's Introduction: The Philosophic Sources of *The Guide of the Perplexed*," *Guide*, xciii.

his books are useful, and he too is a person whose words should occupy you and whose works you should study."[40]

The reactions to the two thinkers' doctrines among extreme theologians of both religions doctrines were strikingly similar. Al-Ghazālī launched a fierce attack on Avicenna, whom he accused of denying the physical resurrection of the dead.[41] Maimonides was accused by two of his contemporaries—R. Meir Abula'fia in Spain and R. Samuel b. Eli in Baghdad—of precisely the same heresy. These sages spearheaded a movement of opposition to Maimonides and his teachings, generating a controversy that would later split Jewish communities into supporters and opponents of Maimonides. Abula'fia and Samuel b. Eli argued that the abstract notion of immortality need not negate its physical, corporeal dimension. Abula'fia's claim was that both bodily resurrection and the world to come can be upheld simultaneously, that is, that bodily resurrection can take place in the world to come:[42] "For I have explained that from the start I have spoken only of the resurrection of the dead that will take place in the world to come at the end of days."[43] But this claim refutes Maimonides' notion of the soul's "abstract" immortality. For Abula'fia, a speculative and entirely non-material immortality is clearly not enough. Nachmanides, by contrast, criticized the Maimonidean doctrine of the annihilation of the souls of the ignorant and the wicked after death:

> This is in keeping neither with the Torah nor with the views of our Sages, of blessed memory, but these are foreign views, expressed by those who think

---

40 "Letter to R. Shmuel ibn Tibbon on the translation of *Guide of the Perplexed*," in *Letters and Essays of Moses Maimonides*, ed. Yitzhak Shilat, vol. 2 (Ma'aleh Adumim: n. p., 1988), 653-654 [Heb]. On the impact of this letter on medieval Jewish philosophy, see Steven Harvey, "Did Maimonides' Letter to Samuel Ibn Tibbon Determine Which Philosophers Would Be Studied by Later Jewish Thinkers?" *Jewish Quarterly Review* 83 (1992): 51-70.

41 This is the subject of the last chapter in *Tahāfut al-falāsifa*. Cf. *Al-munqidh min al-ḍalāl*, ed. Jamāl Salībā & Kāmil 'Ayyād (Beirut: Dar al-Andalus, 1981), 106-107. Cf. Richard Joseph McCarthy, ed., *Freedom and Fulfillment: An Annotated Translation of Al-Ghazālī's al-Munqidh min al-Ḍalāl and Other Relevant Works of al-Ghazālī* (Boston: Twayne, 1980), 183, 203.

42 Meir Abula'fia, *Kitāb al Rasā'il*, ed. Yehiel Brill (Paris, 1871), 56-57. Cf. Daniel Jeremy Silver, *Maimonidean Criticism and the Maimonidean Controversy 1180-1240* (Leiden: Brill, 1965), 109-135; Bernard Septimus, *Hispano-Jewish Culture in Transition: The Career and Controversies of Ramah* (Cambridge, MA: Harvard University Press, 1982), 39-60.

43 Abula'fia, *Kitāb al-rasā'il*, 55. Abula'fia demands, as a matter of principle, that the resurrection be included in every messianic event. He holds that there will be resurrection not only in the world to come but also in the messianic age. Cf. ibid., 63.

themselves wise among the idolatrous nations, for it would follow that man is punished only with *karet,* but the Torah does not condemn every man to *karet,* and by this argument you would be exempting all other sinners from judgment and punishment.[44]

Thus, while Maimonides evaded the problematic nature of everlasting misery, he was attacked for the theological aspect of his doctrine. Both Avicenna and Maimonides were indeed accused of denying bodily resurrection. It is a plausible assumption that Avicenna's and Maimonides' attempts to present immortality as eternal pleasure and bliss were seen by their opponents as an attempt to offer an alternative to physical resurrection, which implies sensations and enjoyment. The zealots, however, objected to such a watered down alternative as Avicenna's pleasure *(ladhdha)* that, moreover, was dubious in respect of its underlying substrate. The resurrection of the dead in its simple, common sense meaning—as established in both Jewish and Muslim sources—implies the existence of a physical basis to sustain immortality. Finally, whether and to what extent were Maimonides' opponents influenced by al-Ghazālī's reaction in Muslim philosophy, is a matter for another occasion.

---

44 See, for example, "The Gate of Reward," in *Ramban (Nachmanides), Writings and Discourses,* vol. 2, trans. Charles B. Chavel (New York: Shilo, 1978), 474. On these grounds, Nachmanides explains the punishment of excision (*karet*) as "a form of afflictive punishment; it is not that the wicked man dies and his soul is destroyed and becomes like the eradicable soul of an animal" (ibid., 486; *cf.* ibid. 497-498. See also Dov Schwartz, *Messianism in Medieval Jewish Thought* (Boston: Academic Studies Press, 2017), 91-93.

Chapter 6

Maimonides: A Philosophical Theologian

In this concluding chapter, I will attempt to outline Maimonides' self-perception as a "philosophical theologian," a term describing a theologian who is not willing to renounce the Aristotelian paradigm with its Neoplatonic overtones but is willing to reconsider some of its basic assumptions. The cost of this reconsideration is the incorporation of basic assumptions from another paradigm, which relates to the world as having a starting point while acknowledging that the possibility of changing its order is limited.

What is a "Philosophical Theologian"?

Maimonides had so far split all thinkers into two groups: "Mutakallimūn" and philosophers. In the Jewish world, this split is reflected in "some Geonim" and Karaites on the one hand, and Andalusians on the other. Further on in the chapter from the *Guide* discussed below, however, Maimonides split the Mutakallimūn into two different groups: one is the early theologians (Christian, Greek, or Syrian) and the other, the later ones (the Muslim Kalām). My analysis addresses this Maimonidean division between earlier and later Mutakallimūn. This is how Maimonides presented these two groups:

> Know also that all the statements that the men of Islam—both the Mu'tazila and the Ash'arīyya —have made concerning these notions are all of them opinions founded upon premises that are taken over from the books of the Greeks and the Syrians who wished to disagree with the opinions of the philosophers and to reject their statements. The reason for this was that: inasmuch as the Christian community came to include those communities, the Christian preaching being what it is known to be, and inasmuch as the opinions of the philosophers were widely accepted in those communities in which philosophy had first risen,[1] and

---

1 Meaning that Christians conquered the pagan nations, where the philosophers' views had been widespread. All these views in general are philosophy and, therefore, the

inasmuch as kings rose who protected religion—the learned of those periods from among the Greeks and the Syrians saw that those preachings are greatly and clearly opposed to the philosophic opinions. Thus there arose among them this science of Kalām. They started to establish premises that would be useful to them with regard to their belief and to refute those opinions that ruined the foundations of their Law. When thereupon the community of Islam arrived and the books of the philosophers were transmitted to it, then were also transmitted to it those refutations composed against the books of the philosophers. Thus they found the Kalām of John Philoponus,[2] of Ibn 'Adi,[3] and of others with regard to these notions, held on to it, and were victorious in their own opinion in a great task that they sought to accomplish. They also selected from among the opinions of the earlier philosophers everything that the one who selected considered useful for him, even if the later philosophers had already demonstrated the falseness of these opinions—as for instance that affirming the existence of atoms and the vacuum. And they considered that these were conceptions common to all and premises that everyone who accepts a Law is obliged to admit. Afterwards they became wider in scope, and these people descended to other strange roads that had never been taken by the Mutakallimūn from among the Greeks and others, for these were near to the philosophers. Then there arose in Islam assertions of the Law that were particular to the members of that community and that they necessarily had need to defend. Furthermore, differences of opinion between them with regard to these questions made their appearance, so that every sect among them established premises useful to it in defence of its opinions.[4] There is no doubt that there are things that are common to all three of us, I mean the Jews, the Christians, and the Moslems: namely, [the statement about][5] the affirmation of the temporal creation of the world, the validity of which entails the validity of miracles and other things of that kind. As for the other matters that these two communities took the trouble to treat and were engrossed in—for instance, the study of the notion of trinity into which the Christians plunged and the study of the Kalām into which certain sects of the Moslems plunged[6]—so

---

statement "in which philosophy had first risen" should be read as the past that preceded the past—these views had been based on philosophy. See Harry A. Wolfson, *The Philosophy of the Kalam* (Cambridge, MA: Harvard University Press, 1976), 51-52.

2 See Herbert A. Davidson, "John Philoponus as a Source of Medieval Islamic and Jewish Proofs of Creation," *Journal of the American Oriental Society* 89 (1969): 357-391. See also *Guide*, "Translator's Introduction," lxxxv-lxxxvi.
3 Ibid., cxxvi, note 112.
4 *Rāy*. See below.
5 *qawl*.
6 Referring to the beliefs of the Orthodox Kalām, such as predestination and the eternity of the Quran.

that they found it requisite to establish premises and to establish, by means of these premises that they had chosen, the conceptions into the study of which they had plunged and the notions that are peculiar to each of the two communities, having been established in it: these are things that we do not require in any respect whatever.

To sum up: all the first Mutakallimūn from among the Greeks who have adopted Christianity and from among the Moslems did not conform in their premises to the appearance of that which exists, but considered how being ought to be in order that it should furnish a proof for the correctness of a particular opinion,[7] or at least should not refute it. And when such a fantasy held good, they assumed that what exists corresponds to that form and started to argue in order to establish the truth of the assertions from which are taken the premises that show the correctness of their doctrine or that at least do not refute it. This is the way of the men of intellect who first used this method, put it down in books, and claimed that speculation alone impelled them to do so and that they did not seek thereby to protect a doctrine[8] or a preconceived opinion.[9] Men of later periods who study these books know nothing about all this and consequently find in these ancient books a vigorous argumentation and a powerful endeavor to establish the truth of a certain thing or to refute a certain thing and think thereupon that its establishment or its refutation is in no way required for these foundations of the law that are required. They believe accordingly that their predecessors did what they did only in order to confuse the opinions of the philosophers and to make them doubt of what they regarded as demonstrations. Those who say this are not aware, and do not know, that matters are not as they thought, but that their predecessors toiled to establish the truth of what they desired to establish as true and to refute what they desired to refute because of the harm that would come if this were not done—even if it were after a hundred propositions—to an opinion whose recognition as correct was desired by them.[10]

---

7 *Rāy*. When previously describing the internal theological disputes in Islam, Maimonides referred to the views of each sect as *rāy* (Munk and Yoel 123, ln. 3). Later, by contrast, he used this term to refer to philosophical doctrines (ibid., 23). In other words, he left the decision as to whether this is a theological or philosophical view to the reader.
8 See TB Shabbat 13b; *Midrash on Psalms* (Buber edn.), 3a.
9 The reference is to an early argument. Crescas suggests that Maimonides hints here that the Mutakallimūn returned to pre-Socratic understandings, such as atomism and vacuum. Some commentators suggest that Maimonides had hinted here that the early Mutakallimūn did know they were not telling the truth and presented their claims only on apologetic grounds.
10 *Guide* I:71, 177–179.

In this passage, Maimonides creates three models of theologians:

(1) An ideal model of an early "Christian theologian"[11] (prior to the development of Muslim theology) or "the learned from among the Greeks and the Syrians," as Maimonides refers to them, free from the flaws of the Muslim Kalām of his time. This theologian belongs to the "Mutakallimūn from among the Greeks and others, for these were near to the philosophers."
(2) A model derived from the later theological interpretation that the "Moslem theologian" (the "Kalām," which includes the "Muʿtazila" and the "Ashʿarīyya") imposes on the model of the early theologian. This is a self-serving interpretation and, as such, also mistaken.
(3) The actual model of the later theologian. He selects alternative paradigms for existing science and adopts approaches such as vacuum and atomism.

I begin with the "authentic" description of the early (Greek or Syrian) Christian theologian according to Maimonides (note that Maimonides preferred the Christian to the Muslim theologian)[12] who is characterized as follows:

(1) He is well acquainted with philosophical traditions, and never doubts the scientific construct of the universe ("these were near to the philosophers").
(2) He is troubled by the confrontation between the scientific structure of the universe and special religious doctrines (creation, miracle, and beliefs specific to the great religions, such as the trinity and incarnation).
(3) He examines which of the various scientific models could solve this confrontation and endorses it.
(4) He does so even if the model is not suited to reality.
(5) Nevertheless, he does not allow the collapse of (1) and does not adopt theories such as atomism and vacuum.[13]
(6) He is driven by the search for truth.

---

11 In Wolfson's terminology, *The Philosophy of the Kalam,* 55. See Shlomo Pines, "Some Traits of Christian Theological Writing in Relation to Moslem Kalām and to Jewish Thought," in *Studies in the History of Arabic Philosophy by Shlomo Pines,* ed. Sarah Stroumsa (Jerusalem: Magnes Press, 1996), 79-99.
12 Maimonides sometimes preferred Christians, who preserve the holiness of the biblical text, to Muslims, who claim that the text was distorted. This issue has been extensively discussed.
13 Wolfson, *The Philosophy of the Kalam,* 55.

In this model, Maimonides appears to have created some tension. On the one hand, he claims that the early theologian was loyal to the received philosophical traditions, namely, to the Aristotelian Neoplatonic paradigms. On the other hand, he claims that the early theologian explains reality according to the demands of theology rather than according to the implications of reality, meaning that he adapts reality to his views. The solution, as noted, was to argue that the early theologian does indeed rely on the scientific paradigm but is ready to change parts of it in order to adapt it to the beliefs of religion.

The early theologian, according to the later (wrong) interpretation of the Muʻtazila and the Ashʻariyya, is characterized as follows:

(1) He adapts reality to his views.
(2) He endorses (1) on apologetic and "sophistic" grounds.
(3) He is well aware of (2). In other words, he does not delude himself for a moment that (1) is in any way an ontological statement.
(4) The reason for the previous steps is the will to challenge (Aristotelian) philosophy.

The key to the distinction between the Kalām interpretation of the Christian theologian and the "authentic" theologian is integrity. The Christian theologian aspires to reach truth while the Mutakallimūn interpreted him as a sophist and a dialectician. The Christian theologian does not cling to reality when it is shown to contradict religion but does not present an alternative paradigm either. Why did the Mutakallimūn distort the figure of the "Christian theologian"? They definitely resorted to tradition in order to show that theirs was a deeply rooted view and applied its features to the early theologian. According to Maimonides' historiosophical interpretation, the dialectic way of the Kalām and its typically confrontational style now targeted the early theologian.

I will argue that what the Kalām did to the "Christian theologian" is what Maimonides did as well—he applied his personal approach to the early theologian in his chapters on creation.[14] This matter needs

---

14 Note that the notion of creation that Maimonides presents in *Guide* II:13 is indeed a version of this theological approach. Maimonides emphasizes two aspects in this chapter: 1) Creation is the result of divine will. 2) Creation does not occur in time, because time itself is a characteristic of motion and, therefore, is not created. The latter determination shows that God did not precede creation since, before creation, temporal precedence was meaningless. Hence, the difference between the views of philosophy and

to be clarified because it is the key to Maimonides' self-perception. Maimonides did recognize the figure of the theologian who wishes to defend religion and preserve the standing of revelation. Such a theologian, who can be called "philosophical," accepts the Aristotelian structure of the world (in the version of Alfārābī and Avicenna, which includes Neoplatonic elements), but only after rigorously examining its assumptions. At times, he also finds that not all that philosophers present as proven is indeed so. On some matters, he is willing to adapt reality to his views as, for example, regarding the views on creation and on miracles.

According to Maimonides' description, the ideal theologian supports, in terms of content, a moderate type of "double faith theory,"[15] meaning a general correspondence between revelation and philosophy. Julius Guttmann refers to this as "metaphysics through revelation,"[16] and David Hartman as "a religious world view which does not negate the concept of nature in order to establish immediacy with God."[17] As for the arguments, this ideal theologian may present a specific alternative to the existing science, but without intending to undermine its foundations. The reexamination of the philosopher's views is evident in the *Guide* in the chapters on creation, as noted, and to some extent, in prophecy as well.

The early Mutakallimūn challenged the philosophical assumptions that seemed to contradict religion as part of their effort to grapple with the philosophical conception of reality. In the course of this effort, they developed approaches that do not fit Aristotelian science ("considered how being

---

the views of the Torah is only creation as an act of will. Since Maimonides noted in *Guide* II:12 that the divine act takes place through emanation, this is clearly a constant voluntary emanation. As it were, then, God chooses at a given point in time *a posteriori* (since time itself has already been created) to create the world. This is a version of a theological approach and the scholarship has dealt with it at length. Note that the connection between creation and prophecy is also a theological issue. See, for example, Lawrence Kaplan, "Maimonides on the Miraculous Element in Prophecy," *Harvard Theological Review* 70 (1977): 233-256; Herbert A. Davidson, "Maimonides' Secret Position on Creation," in *Studies in Medieval Jewish History and Literature*, vol. 1, ed. Isadore Twersky, (Cambridge, MA: Harvard University Press, 1979), 16-40; Warren Z. Harvey, "A Third Approach to Maimonides' Cosmogony-Prophetology Puzzle," *Harvard Theological Review* 74 (1981): 287-301.

15 See Harry Austryn Wolfson, "The Double Faith Theory in Clement, Saadia, Averroes, and St. Thomas and its Origin in Aristotle and the Stoics," *The Jewish Quarterly Review* 33 (1942-1943): 213-264.

16 Julius Guttmann, "Philosophy of Religion or Philosophy of Law," *Proceedings of the Israel Academy of Sciences and Humanities* 5 (1976), 191 [Heb].

17 David Hartman, *Maimonides: Torah and Philosophic Quest* (Philadelphia: Jewish Publications Society, 1976), 158.

ought to be in order that it should furnish a proof for the correctness of a particular opinion"). By contrast, the later Mutakallimūn hallowed controversy and, accordingly, they interpreted the early theologians as engaged in controversy for its own sake. From their perspective, the early theologians tried to refute the views of the philosophers in every possible way ("their predecessors did what they did only in order to confuse the opinions of the philosophers").[18] The distinction between early and later thinkers is not in their actual mistake but in the power of their intellectual and religious motivations: early thinkers strove to reach truth without renouncing the principles of their religion, whereas later ones merely strove to irritate the philosophers, that is, they hallowed polemical arguments per se.[19]

Maimonides sought to undermine the credibility of the (Muslim) Mutakallimūn by exposing their development. He thereby transposed Judah Halevi's distinction between truth-seeking philosophers and self-serving religious men to the realm of religious men themselves—some religious men (the early Mutakallimūn) see religious and scientific truth as their guiding principle while others (the late ones) are self-centered utilitarians. Through this split, Maimonides gained the model of the "positive Mutakallim." As Leo Strauss noted,[20] there are traces of a Kalām approach in the *Guide*, which was also meant to protect religion against challenges by philosophers (as, for example, on the matter of creation noted above). To the distinction between philosophers and Mutakallimūn, then, a new being can be added: a Mutakallim who seeks to reconcile his intellectual curiosity with the assumptions of religion and expose truth. In his own perception and possibly also in that of the reader, Maimonides is now represented by this new being. *Guide* I:71 henceforth presents three models:

(1) Some Geonim and Karaites, who are drawn to the "late Mutakallimūn" (revealed).
(2) Andalusians (revealed)
(3) Maimonides, who is drawn to the "early Mutakallimūn" (concealed).[21]

---

18 Resonating here is the notion of the decline of the generations. See Menachem Kellner, *Maimonides on the Decline of the Generations and the Nature of Rabbinic Authority* (Albany, NY: SUNY, 1996).
19 See Efodi's comments *ad locum*, *Sefer Moreh Nevukhim im Mefarshim* [Guide of the Perplexed with Commentators] (Jerusalem: offset, 1960), 108b.
20 See Leo Strauss, "How to Begin to Study *The Guide of the Perplexed*," in *Guide*, li-lii.
21 In his commentary on the *Guide ad locum*, Mordekhai Komtiyano saw the Andalusians as a variation of the Mutakallimūn.

As noted, Maimonides' closeness to the third model leads to its concealment between the lines. His innovation is the introduction of a type of theologian who does not merge with the "late Mutakallimūn."

Maimonides hints at this positive Mutakallim model elsewhere in the cited passage. He notes that his struggle with theologians is waged over beliefs common to the three religions. He does not intend to relate to the beliefs specific to each religion ("we do not require in any respect whatever") and focuses on "the affirmation of the temporal creation of the world … and other things of that kind," such as creation and the attributes. Although Maimonides explicitly noted he does not deal with beliefs such as the trinity, he did so in *Guide* I:50. This model of concealment is reiterated regarding Moses' prophecy—having said he would not consider it at all in the *Guide*, Maimonides devoted long discussions to it (for example, I:54 and II:35).[22] *Guide* I:71, then, hints to a model of "Mutakallim" capable of contending with special beliefs in philosophical ways, even though pure philosophy keeps away from interreligious controversy.

A Model Theologian

Maimonides, then, supported the approach of "early" theologians as opposed to the Muslim theology that he grapples with in the *Guide*. This is a new kind of confrontation between theology and philosophy: a distinction between "early" theology, which is more compatible with philosophy, and "late" theology, which contradicts it. Early theologians had sought, as it were, to change certain principles of philosophy without challenging its framework. From their perspective, the philosophical explanation of the universe's material structure is consistent and coherent, though we need not accept all its assumptions. Maimonides' self-perception, then, would appear to be that of an "early" theologian of this kind (or a "Christian theologian" who preceded the "Muslim theologian"). Maimonides sought to question the fundamental assumptions and implications of the Aristotelian paradigm, such as the eternity of the universe and the negation of the miracle of revelation, for example, but he did adopt this paradigm as a satisfactory explanation of the material order. Following is an examination of the ("early")

---

22 See, for example, Dov Schwartz, *Contradiction and Concealment in Medieval Jewish Thought* (Ramat-Gan: Bar-Ilan University, 2002), 59-80 [Heb].

Kalām theological moves adopted by Maimonides, so as to clarify his profile as a theologian.

Contending with the Proofs

In the chapters on creation, Maimonides set up a model of creation *ex nihilo* that does not fit the scientific structure of the universe but still preserves the frame of Aristotelian science with Neoplatonic overtones. More specifically, Maimonides claimed that creation is a move involving duality and even inner tension or contradiction. In his view, God created the world as ruled by scientific laws reflecting eternity. Observation of the universe as given, its structure and laws, points to eternity because the world was deliberately created in this fashion by God. For this purpose, Maimonides adopted the distinction between being and becoming, meaning coming into existence, presenting the parable of the difference between a fetus and a baby after birth and between the heart and the peripheral limbs in a fetus and in a baby.[23] A baby is full and complete because it was so created, but was preceded by a fetus that was entirely different. Maimonides, then, accepted the given scientific universe but incorporated the alternative assumption: it exists in this mode only since it was created. We thus face a kind of paradox: the world was created when, in itself, it is eternal, meaning that its order and its visible behavior are as those of an entity without a temporal beginning.

The rejection of Aristotle's proofs of the eternity of the world in *Guide* II:17 reveals an explication process for this "paradox" and exposes its meanings:[24]

(1) Aristotle's second proof: if we assume a matter that precedes the first matter, then the first matter came into existence. Whatever comes into existence, however, has form, and the first matter, by definition, has no form and is therefore eternal.

Maimonides' rejection:

For we do not maintain that the first matter is generated as man is generated from the seed or that it passes away as man passes away into dust. But we maintain that God has brought it into existence from nothing and that

---

23 *Guide*, II:17.
24 See Herbert Davidson, *Proofs for Eternity: Creation and the Existence of God in Medieval Islamic and Jewish Philosophy* (New York: Oxford University Press, 1987), 13-24, 28-30.

> after being brought into existence, it was as it is now—I mean everything is generated from it, and everything generated from it passes away into it; it does not exist devoid of form; generation and corruption terminate in it; it is not subject to generation as are the things generated from it, nor to passing-away as are the things that pass away into it, but is created from nothing. And its Creator may, if He wishes to do so, render it entirely and absolutely nonexistent.[25]

In other words, observation of the first matter leads to Aristotle's proof, but if we assume that the first matter was created so that its inherent order conveys eternity, the second proof is no longer valid.

> (2) Aristotle's first proof: if motion was created, we would have to assume a motion that preceded it that itself was preceded by another, thereby reaching an infinite simultaneous series, which is impossible. Motion is therefore eternal. Maimonides' rejection:

> For we maintain that after motion has come into existence with the nature characteristic of it when it has become stable, one cannot imagine that it should come into being as a whole and perish as a whole, as partial motions come into being and perish. This analogy holds good with regard to everything that is attached to the nature of motion. Similarly the assertion that circular motion has no beginning is correct. For after the spherical body endowed with circular motion has been brought into being, one cannot conceive that its motion should have a beginning.[26]

Maimonides reiterated the previous rejection: the observation of motion per se leads to this conclusion. At the same time, however, we may assume that motion was created with its eternal laws. Here, however, Maimonides already added the stylistic use of "nature" (*tabī'ah*), that is, he noted more clearly the dual nature of the object (created as eternal) and of its physical laws.

> (3) Aristotle's fourth proof: chronologically, possibility precedes the appearance and motion of the object, since generation and straight movement are both included in "motion." By contrast, the circular movement of the spherical body was not preceded by possibility and, therefore, has no beginning. The "late" theologians added the modal

---
25 *Guide*, II:17, 297.
26 Ibid.

categories to it and claimed that the category of possibility compels a substratum, which would then be eternal. Maimonides' rejection:

> We shall make a similar assertion with regard to the possibility that must of necessity precede everything that is generated. For this is only necessary in regard to this being that is stabilized—in this being everything that is generated, is generated from some being. But in the case of a thing created from nothing, neither the senses nor the intellect point to something that must be preceded by its possibility.[27]

At this stage, Maimonides added a clarification about the previous rejections: contrary to the existing universe, which is subject to scientific understanding, creation cannot possibly be. Being is subject to scientific analysis, but becoming is not, since there is no sensory or intellectual analogy to the act of creation. According to Aristotle, knowledge relies on sensory apprehension.[28] Creation, then, cannot be subject to scientific apprehension.

(4) Aristotle's third proof: there are no contraries in the heavenly matter and, therefore, it is eternal.

Maimonides' rejection:

> We make a similar assertion with regard to the thesis that there are no contraries in heaven. That thesis is correct. However, we have not claimed that the heavens have been generated as the horse and palm tree are. Nor have we claimed that their being composite renders necessary their passing-away as is the case with plants and animals because of the contraries that subsist in them.[29]

Maimonides refined his clarification and argued that the act of creation also involves a hierarchy, meaning it has an inner tension: its order (if any) cannot be understood because it has no cognitive parallel, but a distinction can be drawn between higher and lower creatures, all created in different ways.

Maimonides, then, exposed his Kalām argument in a step by step process, in the model of the early Kalām. He clarified that he accepts

---

27 Ibid.
28 See, for example, *De Anima* 432a7. See Jonathan Barnes, "Aristotle's Concept of Mind," in *Articles on Aristotle*, ed. Jonathan Barnes, Malcolm Schofiled and Richard Sorabji (London: Duckworth, 1979), 39-40.
29 *Guide*, II:17, 297.

the scientific universe as is and does not doubt its order and the arguments deriving from it. Yet, he replaced the scientific paradigm about the source of the universe with a Kalām model in the sense that it has other, paradoxical, laws that are not sensorially or rationally perceived. These laws, however, do have an inner structure and order, which distinguishes the creation of heaven from the creation of "the horse and palm tree." Maimonides, therefore, chose a chiastic structure and changed the order of Aristotle's arguments, or at least the arguments enumerated in *Guide* II:14. Proofs are now presented on the way that arguments about matter begin and end (1, 4), with arguments about motion and change (2, 3) in between. Maimonides indicated to the reader that he is about to present a special conception of creation.

"Early" and "Late"

Maimonides' introduction to Aristotle's arguments about the eternity of the world (mentioning both philosophers and theologians) merits reconsideration. Usually, when Maimonides compares divergent issues, some ulterior meaning is involved. He writes:

> I shall not write at length, but only draw your attention to the methods that they [the philosophers] aim at, as I did for you regarding the opinions of the Mutakallimūn. I shall pay no attention to anyone who besides Aristotle has engaged in speculative discourse, for it is his opinions that ought to be considered. And if there are good grounds for refuting him or raising doubt with regard to these opinions as to some point on which we make a reflection or raise doubts, these grounds will be even firmer and stronger with respect to all the others who disagreed with the fundamental principles of the Law.[30]

Discerning readers will note the tensions in this passage. Ostensibly, a latent tension prevails between theologians and philosophers: the views of theologians (Mutakallimūn) are cited without differentiating between the founders (such as Wāṣil ibn 'Atā') and the Ash'arīyya, whose views are detailed at the end of Part I of the *Guide*. Maimonides would appear to view theologians as unworthy of the fine distinctions he applies to philosophers ("Aristotle … and all the others").[31] But we do know that is not the case

---

30 *Guide* II:14, 285-286.
31 Note the order of the discussion. *Guide* II:14 opens with Aristotle's proofs of eternity, as detailed above, followed by four additional proofs suggested by his followers. The fourth Aristotelian proof rests on the concept of possibility. In this proof, Maimonides had

and, in *Guide* I:71, Maimonides does separate the early theologians, who challenged philosophers, from his own contemporaries.

Furthermore, Maimonides created a kind of symmetry regarding claims about the eternity of the world between the Kalām and philosophers. In *Guide* II:14, he cited four Aristotelian proofs of eternity, as discussed above. These proofs are based on the actual universe and its laws, according to the Aristotelian approach. Maimonides then cited a series of proofs adduced by Aristotle's followers, all of which affirm eternity relying on the concept of divine perfection. In Chapter 16, Maimonides claimed that Aristotle had never held he had proved eternity. In other words, Aristotle was a man of integrity and admitted he had no absolute solution to this question. Again, then, we find a distinction between the honest historical source and the followers who distort it for self-serving reasons. A symmetry thus emerges between the early (honest) Kalām and the Mutakallimūn who followed and Aristotle and his commentators, the Peripatetics. Moreover, Aristotle's interpreters were apparently religious, since Aristotle had not dwelt at length on the concept of God addressed by his Christian and Muslim commentators. Maimonides, then, tried to hint that it is possible to develop a theology that takes into account philosophical assumptions, so long as scientific integrity is suitably preserved.

As for the tension in the passage cited, note that it begins with a comparison between philosophers and theologians ("as I did for you regarding the opinions of the Mutakallimūn") and then draws a distinction between them—concerning the theologians, any genuine hierarchy between founders and followers was "dismissed" by the Kalām of the Muʿtazila and the Ashʿarīyya, whereas concerning the philosophers, the hierarchy is preserved (Aristotle prevails over his followers). Maimonides, then, tried to create the impression that they are different, whereas he himself intended to follow the early theologians regarding creation while changing some details of the scientific and philosophical paradigm. This examination of the attitudes of theology and philosophy appears to be subtly present in other questions in the *Guide* too, as shown below.

---

already included the views of Aristotle's followers and introduced the modal distinction (possible, necessary, and impossible). He also noted that this proof is "very powerful." The followers, then, strengthen Aristotle's position and perfect additional aspects. Maimonides wanted to create a narrative of historical development through Aristotle's arguments to his followers, parallel to the historical processes of the Kalām. Aristotelian tradition, however, shows development, whereas theological tradition shows retreat.

The Purpose of the *Guide*

Strauss considered the genre of the *Guide*, posing the question of whether the *Guide* is a book of philosophy or of theology and answering it at various stages of his thought.[32] He outlined the method for discussing the genre and purpose of the *Guide* in the research of Maimonides. Many followed him, but others strongly opposed him. Strauss is largely recognized as the scholar who tied the discussion about the purpose of the *Guide* to the connection between philosophy and theology.

The introductions to the *Guide* present several versions of its purpose, including hidden messages concerning the tension between theology and philosophy. In this chapter, I attempt to trace the attitude toward theology according to the "Epistle Dedicatory" and according to the Introduction.

Maimonides expressed views on the purpose of the *Guide* in several places. Furthermore, if we consider the name of the treatise, we find that Maimonides relates to certain issues as "perplexities" (particularly in the context of creation) while ascribing others to "the perplexed."[33]

Maimonides explicitly discusses the purpose of writing the *Guide* in three different places, all logically located at the beginning of the work: one is found in the "Epistle Dedicatory," and two in the Introduction. In all three, Maimonides presents a model of a primary and a secondary purpose and challenges the reader with their implications. Considering the concealment techniques used in the *Guide*, it is a plausible assumption that the secondary purpose is actually the important one for understanding the author's view. I detail the literary model below and consider its implications for the relationship between philosophy and theology.

Between Rabbi and Disciple

The Epistle that Maimonides sent to his disciple, Joseph b. Judah, is a well-known philosophical document. The Epistle attached to the *Guide* became a paradigm of philosophical communication between teacher and student. This Epistle has not been intensively researched, which is puzzling since the style and aims of the *Guide* have been addressed in numerous studies and the Epistle offers the author's direct testimony on these issues. Worth noting are the interpretation of Daniel Frank, who focused on Joseph's passion for metaphysics and on the fact that he was not sufficiently worthy

---

32 See, for example, Leo Strauss, *Persecution and the Art of Writing* (Glencoe, IL: Free Press, 1952), 42-46.
33 See *Guide* II:24, 25; III:13, 22, 23, 28.

of studying it,[34] and Sarah Stroumsa's discussion on Maimonides' connection with the Mutakallimūn according to the Epistle.[35] In another work, Stroumsa cites evidence of the attraction that the Kalām held for Joseph.[36] Steven Harvey emphasized the change in Maimonides' evaluation of his disciple and analyzed the causes of his disappointment.[37]

The Epistle points to the distinction between Joseph's expectation from the *Guide* and Maimonides' intention. The disciple sought knowledge about the foundations of both metaphysics and theology. Maimonides attests to this request from Joseph:

> Thereupon I began to let you see certain flashes and to give you certain indications. Then I saw that you demanded of me additional knowledge and asked me to make clear to you certain things pertaining to divine matters, to inform you of the intentions of the Mutakallimūn in this respect, and to let you know whether their methods were demonstrative and, if not, to what art (*ṣinā'ah*) they belonged.[38]

The disciple, then, assumed *ab initio* that philosophy and theology are mutually complementary, seeing no contradiction between "divine matters" (as metaphysics was called),[39] and theological doctrines. But he thereby incurred a grave error, which led to his perplexity. Maimonides had subtly clarified to Joseph in their meetings that the (Islamic) Kalām rests on non-philosophical foundations. He then probably added and explained that Kalām sages are concerned with their own interests, as evident from the tone of his formulations in *Guide* I:71. The theologians' logic is dialectical, and their arguments are therefore unreliable.

---

34 See Daniel H. Frank, "The Elimination of Perplexity: Socrates and Maimonides as Guide of the Perplexed," in *Autonomy and Judaism: The Individual and the Community in Jewish Philosophical Thought*, ed. Daniel H. Frank (Albany, NY: SUNY Press, 1992), 130-135.

35 See Sarah Stroumsa, *Maimonides in His World: Portrait of a Mediterranean Thinker* (Princeton, NJ: Princeton University Press, 2009), 36-38.

36 See Sarah Stroumsa, *The Beginnings of the Maimonidean Controversy in the East: Yosef Ibn Shimcon's Silencing Epistle Concerning the Resurrection of the Dead* (Jerusalem: Yad Izhak Ben-Zvi, 1999), 14-15 [Heb].

37 Steven Harvey, "Maimonides and the Art of Writing Introductions," *Maimonidean Studies* 5 (2008), 96-100.

38 *Guide*, "Epistle Dedicatory," 3-4.

39 According to Maimonides, metaphysics deals with non-material existents. See, for example, Armand A. Maurer, "Maimonides and Aquinas on the Study of Metaphysics," in *A Straight Path: Studies in Medieval Philosophy and Culture—Essays in Honor of Arthur Hyman*, ed. Ruth Link-Salinger (Washington, DC: Catholic University of America Press, 1988), 206-215.

According to the disciple's intention, then, the aim of the *Guide* was to solve the perplexity of the Kalām, meaning that Joseph hesitated between theology and philosophical truth. Maimonides, therefore, writes, "the truth should be established in your mind according to the proper methods and that certainty should not come to you by accident."[40] In other words, even if the views of the Kalām are true, such as creation *ex nihilo*, their method is wrong because it is dialectical, meaning it is based on premises that are factually and scientifically dubious. Demonstrations of creation are therefore pointless unless they are well-grounded and deliberate ("by accident"). Maimonides' disciple held that his illustrious teacher would reconcile theology and philosophy.

That was not Maimonides' intention. He explicitly noted his own expectations in the Epistle, as follows:

> When thereupon you read under my guidance texts dealing with the science of astronomy and prior to that texts dealing with mathematics, which is necessary as an introduction to astronomy, my joy in you increased because of the excellence of your mind and the quickness of your grasp. I saw that your longing for mathematics was great, and hence I let you train yourself in that science, knowing where you would end. When thereupon you read under my guidance texts dealing with the art of logic, my hopes fastened upon you, and I saw that you are one worthy to have the secrets of the prophetic books revealed to you so that you would consider in them that which perfect men ought to consider.[41]

Maimonides chose to present Joseph's acquisition of the sciences in reverse order:

(1) Astronomy (*hay'a*).
(2) Mathematics (*riyāḍah*).
(3) Logic ("the art of logic"—*ṣinā'ah almanṭiq*)

The purpose is to show, on the one hand, that the disciple does not give up any rung in the ladder of the sciences and, on the other, that his ladder of knowledge is unbalanced and is the key to his mistakes. In any event, since the student is diligent and has acquired the preparatory sciences (logic and mathematics), Maimonides held that he is worthy of studying physics and

---

40 *Guide*, "Epistle Dedicatory," 4.
41 Ibid., 3.

metaphysics. According to Maimonides, then, the purpose of the *Guide* is to impart "the secrets of the prophetic books."

Were we to sum up the aim of the *Guide* according to the Epistle, we would find that the main and primary purpose is the acquisition of metaphysics, meaning a pure philosophical pedagogical intention. Noting the order of the sciences that the student had acquired attests that "the secrets of the prophetic books" mean physics and mathematics. The secondary purpose of the *Guide* is to clarify the distinction between philosophy and theology. The first purpose is the teacher's intention, and the second is set against the teacher's wishes in the wake of the student's demand and of the circumstances that had attracted many young people or intellectuals to follow the Kalām. This model is largely reminiscent of Part Five in *The Kuzari*, where the Rabbi sought to teach philosophy whereas the king insisted on studying theology. Part Five opens with the king's request: "I must trouble thee to give me a clear and concise discourse on religious principles and axioms according to the method of the Mutakallims" (V, 1). The difference is that, for Halevi, the entire discussion (including the philosophical dimension) is *ex post factum*, but for Maimonides, it is a fundamental and significant concern both for life in this world and for the immortality of the intellect.

The Terms and Metaphysics

I turn now from the Epistle to Maimonides' declaration about the aim of the treatise in the Introduction to the *Guide*.[42] The model of a primary and a secondary purpose recurs at the very beginning of the introduction, which opens with the following sentence: "The first purpose [*gharaḍ*] of this Treatise is to explain the meanings of certain terms occurring in books of prophecy."[43] Maimonides relates specifically to equivocal, derivative, or amphibolous terms while ostensibly referring to the lexicographical chapters in Part I of the *Guide*, that is, to the negation of corporeality. He then presents the "second purpose (*gharaḍ*)": "the explanation of very obscure parables occurring in the books of the prophets, but not explicitly identified

---

42 See the discussions in Herbert A. Davidson, *Moses Maimonides: The Man and His Work* (Oxford: Oxford University Press, 2005), 327-329; Harvey, "Writing Introductions," 100-104.
43 *Guide*, "Introduction to the First Part," 5.

there as such. Hence an ignorant or heedless individual might think that they possess only an external sense, but no internal one."[44]

The first purpose conveys a clear message: the literal meaning of the biblical terms contradicts philosophical thought and, therefore, constitutes a "perplexity." The handling of this perplexity is also clear: Maimonides will interpret these terms according to the theory of names in the logical texts. The second purpose, by contrast, reflects a completely different message—entire biblical issues, which appear as real historical events, are actually parables; they have a deep interpretive layer (*bāṭin*, which is added to or replaces the literal meaning. The political element is particularly evident in the second purpose of the treatise. Here, the subject is no longer some divine attribute that is not to be interpreted in anthropomorphic terms but a biblical historical event, which is merely "a cover" (symbol, metaphor) of the scientific and philosophical meaning. Maimonides was indeed targeted for strong criticism in the thirteenth century for this determination and its applications, such as the claim that the three people or angels who appeared to Abraham were a prophetic vision.[45]

Further in the introduction, Maimonides again presents a primary and secondary purpose for the book, although this time less openly. Addressing M. Hagigah 2:1, Maimonides presents the purpose of the *Guide* as a discussion of metaphysics (primary purpose) and of physics (secondary purpose):

> … and have explained the rabbinic saying: "The Account of the Chariot ought not to be taught even to one man, except if he be wise and able to understand by himself, in which case only the chapter headings may be transmitted to him."[46] Hence you should not ask of me here anything beyond the chapter headings.[47] And even those are not set down in order or arranged in coherent fashion in this Treatise, but rather are scattered and entangled with other

---

44 Ibid., 6. See Abraham Nuriel, "Maimonides on Parables Not Explicitly Identified As Such," *Daat* 25 (1990): 85-91 [Heb]; Yair Lorberbaum, "On Allegory, Metaphor, and Symbol in *The Guide of the Perplexed*," in *Jewish Culture in the Eye of the Storm: A Jubilee Book in Honor of Yosef Ahituv*, ed. Avi Sagi and Nahem Ilan (Tel Aviv: Hakibbutz Hameuchad, 2002), 396-422 [Heb]; idem, "On Maimonides Conception of Parables," *Tarbiz* 71, 1-2 (2001): 87-132 [Heb].

45 *Guide*, II:42, 388.

46 BT Hagigah 13a.

47 In *Guide* II:2, 253, Maimonides writes that the aim of the book is "to elucidate the difficult points of the Law and to make manifest the true realities of its hidden meanings, which the multitude cannot be made to understand because of these matters being too high for it." He therefore argued that he relies on physical and metaphysical determinations that can be demonstrated. In other words, Maimonides avoided dealing with equivocal questions and focused on the proven truths.

> subjects that are to be clarified. For my purpose is that the truths be glimpsed and then again be concealed, so as not to oppose that divine purpose which one cannot possibly oppose and which has concealed from the vulgar among the people those truths especially requisite for His apprehension. As He has said [Psalms 25:14]: "The secret of the Lord is with them that fear Him." Know that with regard to natural matters[48] as well, it is impossible to give a clear exposition when teaching some of their principles as they are. For you know the saying of [the Sages], may their memory be blessed: "The Account of the Beginning ought not to be taught in the presence of two men." Now if someone explained all those matters in a book, he in effect would be teaching them to thousands of men. Hence those matters too occur in parables in the books of prophecy. The Sages, may their memory be blessed, following the trail of these books, likewise have spoken of them in riddles and parables, for there is a close connection between these matters and the divine science, and they too are secrets of that divine science.[49]

Maimonides then cites the parable of lightning to clarify that he is returning to the first topic, meaning metaphysics, where only "chapter headings" are transmitted. Metaphysics is characterized by two features of disorder following from different needs, which create contradictory actions:

(1) A methodological need: metaphysics is learned from an eclectic mixture of *Guide* chapters entailing the gathering and concentration of details.
(2) A political need: the gathering of metaphysical truths is followed by their renewed dispersal so as to prevent the multitude from confronting these truths and causing harm or being harmed.

The implied purpose of the *Guide*, then, is to deal above all with metaphysics, hence the style rich in hints and allusions that Maimonides would endorse. After noting the primary purpose, Maimonides added a secondary one, which is physics and, more precisely "some of their principles" (*mabādī*), referring to natural matters. The matters he would be dealing with, then, are not the laws of physics as such but their foundations or principles.

Furthermore: Maimonides clarified that the truths of physics and metaphysics should not be inferred from the *Mishneh Torah* and applied to the *Guide*, or vice-versa. He claimed that a distinction must be drawn

---

48 *Al-amūr al-ṭabīʿiya*.
49 *Guide*, "Introduction to the First Part," 6-7.

between a treatise dealing with norms and one dealing with scientific truths, thus indirectly creating a distinction between a theological and a philosophical work. Maimonides noted that, in his youth, he had planned to write two treatises—a "Book of Prophecy," dealing with prophecy matters, and a "Book of Correspondence," devoted to the explanation of rabbinic midrashim, but decided against it:

> We also saw that if an ignoramus among the multitude of Rabbanites should engage in speculation on these Midrashim, he would find nothing difficult in them, inasmuch as a rash fool, devoid of any knowledge of the nature of being, does not find impossibilities hard to accept.[50] If, however, a perfect man of virtue[51] should engage in speculation on them, he cannot escape one of two courses: either he can take the speeches in question in their external sense and, in so doing, think ill of their author[52] and regard him as an ignoramus—in this there is nothing that would upset the foundations of belief (*qawa-'id al-i'tiqa-d*); or he can attribute to them an inner meaning, thereby extricating himself from his predicament and being able to think well of the author whether or not the inner meaning of the saying is clear to him. With regard to the meaning of prophecy, the exposition of its various degrees, and the elucidation of the parables occurring in the prophetic books, another manner of explanation is used in this Treatise. In view of these considerations, we have given up composing these two books in the way in which they were begun. We have confined ourselves to mentioning briefly the foundations of belief (*qawa-'id al-i'tiqa-d*) and general truths, while dropping hints that approach a clear exposition, just as we have set them forth in the great legal compilation, *Mishneh Torah*.[53]

---

50 An impossibility is the assumption of an object whose existence leads to a contradiction. Impossibilities can be physical or logical. Maimonides' example of a physical impossibility is an iron ship flying in the air, mentioned in the introduction to Tractate Avot. Assuming such a ship leads to a contradiction since, according to Aristotelian physics, the natural place of heavy objects is below. The example of a logical impossibility is a square whose diagonal is smaller than its side. The theologian sustained the existence of impossibilities, on the grounds that denying them detracts from God's omnipotence. Impossibilities surface as entities that God cannot create, and the theologian therefore affirms them. Midrashim, where formulations are often hyperbolical, sustain impossibilities, and "an ignoramus among the Rabbanites" follows the theologians, but Maimonides, as a philosopher, rejects their existence.
51 Meaning an intellectual.
52 Whoever articulated the Midrash. Maimonides clarified that the problem with Midrashim is the affirmation of impossibilities.
53 *Guide*, "Introduction to the First Part," 10.

Many midrashim are products of the creative imagination and contain hyperboles. Maimonides described two approaches of the intellectual to midrashim:[54] one ascribes to the rabbis faith in the existence of impossibilities and therefore claims that midrashim should be interpreted literally. According to his view, the rabbis were primitive people who held that divine omnipotence enables impossibilities. The other approach ascribes deep, allegorical significance to aggadic statements ("inner meaning"). The former approach views the rabbis as theologians (preachers who are not philosophers), and the latter—as philosophers.

Maimonides declared that admitting impossibilities (or, more precisely, ascribing them to the rabbis) does not contradict the foundations of faith. Presenting the rabbis as theologians who lack elementary scientific knowledge, then, is compatible with "the foundations of faith." Moreover, Maimonides ascribed to the *Mishneh Torah* the status of "foundations of faith." *Mishneh Torah* is thus meant for theologians or, at least, is compatible with their views whereas, about the *Guide*, he said that it is meant for "one who has philosophized."[55] Maimonides, then, tried to separate the philosophical chapters and issues in the *Mishneh Torah* (such as the first chapters of the Laws of the Foundations of Faith) from the *Guide*. He thereby

---

54 These approaches also appear in Maimonides' introduction to *Perek Helek* (Chapter 10 in Tractate Sanhedrin) in *Commentary to the Mishnah*, though his formulation there is much sharper than the one he endorsed in the relatively restrained tones of the cited passage from the Guide. On the first approach, he writes in the introduction to *Perek Helek* that, "as far as I have seen, [it is] the largest in point of their numbers and of the numbers of their compositions; and it is of them that I have heard most" (Abelson, "Introduction," 34). Maimonides also detailed at length the harm caused by this class. About the second class, whose action he describes as "nothing that would upset the foundations of belief," Maimonides writes that it characterizes the "perfect man of virtue." By contrast, in the Introduction to *Perek Helek*, he strongly condemns them as "men who in their own estimation are sages and philosophers. But how far removed are they from humanity when placed side by side with the true philosophers!" (ibid., 36). In the introduction to *Perek Helek*, then, members of the second class are not included in the "perfect" category. Maimonides' easy tone in the introduction to the *Guide* could be due to one of two (contrary) reasons: first, he himself noted that the "Book of Correspondence" entails objective difficulties and that explaining Midrashim is an extremely problematic task. No matter how hard he tried, he came to realize that explanations of midrashim are no less vague than the midrashim themselves. Second, when writing the *Commentary to the Mishnah* in his youth, Maimonides had still believed that the multitude could be educated to change its view if exposed to the truth. By contrast, when he came to write the *Guide*, he no longer held this was possible and felt less perturbed by it. See Yair Lorberbaum, "Changes in Maimonides' Approach to Aggadah," *Tarbiz* 78, 1 (2008): 81-122 [Heb]; idem, "Criticism of Aggadah in *The Guide of the Perplexed*," *Tarbiz* 78, 2 (2009): 203-230.

55 *Guide*, "Introduction to the First Part," 10.

warned as it were, against the temptation to read his writings as one whole, inferring from one to another. We also learn that theology should not be mixed with philosophy and each deserved separate discussion. Taking into account the ideal figure of the theologian, then, we can determine that, according to Maimonides, a theology that does not rely on philosophical foundations (such as that of the "Rabbanites" or of the Kalām) and is compatible with the *Mishneh Torah*, should not be mixed with a theology that does rely on such foundations, which are detailed only in the *Guide*.

The end of the cited passage suggests that the principles of the Book of Prophecy and of the Book of Correspondence were incorporated into the *Mishneh Torah* so that the essence of the "inner meaning" can be assumed to appear in the *Mishneh Torah* as well. Since the *Mishneh Torah* is fundamentally a halakhic treatise, its "inner meaning" probably refers to ethics, whereas that of the *Guide* refers to science. Be that as it may, the purpose of the *Guide* is metaphysics (primary) and physics (secondary), in the sense of secrets and mysteries of the Torah.

The Aim of the Guide

To sum up: Maimonides presented three versions of its purpose at the opening of his book, each including a primary and a secondary aim:

(1) In the Epistle: the primary purpose is the revelation of prophetic secrets, and the secondary is the distinction between the Kalām and philosophical truth.
(2) At the opening of the Introduction to the *Guide*: the primary purpose is the clarification of terms in prophetic books, and the secondary is "the explanation of very obscure parables occurring in the books of the prophets, but not explicitly identified there as such."
(3) Further in the Introduction: the primary purpose is the explanation of metaphysics, and the secondary is the "open" secrets of physics.

Given the instructions to the interactive reader ("wise and able to understand by himself") at the opening of the *Guide*, we could interpret that the secondary purpose is actually the important one. The Epistle already hints that the study of metaphysics ("divine matters") is problematic. I will not enter the discussion about the possibility of metaphysical knowledge according to the *Guide*.⁵⁶ The text of *Guide* II:24 will suffice to conclude that its knowledge is problematic because astronomy, on which it is founded, is itself dubious and a kind of "perplexity." In the third version, Maimonides appears committed to play down his view that apprehending metaphysics is problematic. He hints that, since the order of the sublunar world can be learned and its description is in no way questionable, it is preferable to focus on it rather than on metaphysics. Hence, the statements in the *Guide* relating to physics are actually the purpose of the book.

I return now to the first version, which appears in the Epistle. According to this line of argument, the *Guide* was meant to distinguish theology from philosophy. Specifically, Maimonides sought to differentiate "bad" theology (such as that of the "late," Islamic theologian), which does not take philosophy into account, from the "improved" version (of the "early" Christian theologian), which is the one he suggests. And indeed, as noted, Strauss persuasively argued that the *Guide* is fundamentally a theological (Kalām) work.⁵⁷ The dispute between Strauss and Guttmann reveals even more explicitly Guttmann's view that Maimonides integrated religious motifs into philosophy,⁵⁸ bringing Maimonides' approach closer to theology.

Consider now Maimonides' stance in the second version. According to the secondary purpose, the biblical stories are parables or, in Strauss' terms, "noble myths." More than the other two, this version clarifies how far Maimonides had drawn away from Muslim theology. In establishing the biblical stories on the "inner" interpretation, he presented the contents of revelation as scientific according to one alternative, and as a political foundation for the creation of a lofty state based on a personal God who protects and punishes according to the other. Whereas the former alterna-

---

56 See, for example, Pines, "The Limitations of Human Knowledge," 82-102; Herbert A. Davidson, "Maimonides on Metaphysical Knowledge," *Maimonidean Studies* 3 (1992/1993), 49-103.

57 For a discussion of Strauss' view, see Warren Z. Harvey, "Why Maimonides Was Not a Mutakallim?," in *Perspectives on Maimonides*, ed. Joel L. Kramer (Oxford: Oxford University Press, 1991), 105-114; Aviram Ravitzky, "Saadia's Theology and Maimonides' Philosophy: The Characteristics of Medieval Jewish Thought," in *Religion and Politics in Jewish Thought: Essays in Honor of Aviezer Ravitzky*, vol. 1, ed. Benjamin Brown et. al. (Jerusalem: Israel Democracy Institute, 2012), 298-303. The typical characteristic of Strauss' approach throughout his writings is a perception of the political law as the key to the understanding of philosophical approaches.

58 See Guttmann, "Philosophy of Religion or Philosophy of Law"; idem, "Die religiösen Motive in der Philosophie des Maimonides," in *Entwicklungsstufen der Jüdischen Religion* (Giessen: A. Töpelmann, 1927), 61-90.

tive suits the rationalist medieval interpretation of this matter, the latter fits the studies of Strauss and Pines on Maimonides' esoteric style.[59] If, according to the first two versions, Maimonides drew away from his theologian contemporaries in scientific terms, this time he did so in terms of the revelation concept as well. Henceforth, what is revealed is not only the law but also scientific secrets, and possibly also noble myths. Maimonides' attitude toward theology is thus complex:

(1) Maimonides rejected the prevalent (Muslim) theology.
(2) Maimonides believed in the existence of an (ideal) theology compatible with philosophy.
(3) In order to build such a theology, the status of philosophy or of science and its connection to the interpretation of texts should be clarified according to its "inner meanings."
(4) This was the task that occupied Maimonides in the *Guide* and, possibly, he held that he had completed it.

The *Guide*, then, was intended as a critique of theology. The purpose of this critique, however, was not to replace it with philosophy but to suggest a new theology based on philosophical considerations. In this sense, the *Guide* is a "theological" treatise. The new theology is founded on knowledge about the laws of the material world (physics), based on the Aristotelian paradigm with Neoplatonic overtones, and unhesitatingly endorses "*ta'wīl*," meaning an interpretation added to the literal one.

Self-Perception

My focus so far has been on Maimonides' declarations about the purpose of the *Guide* as conveyed, *inter alia*, in the "Epistle Dedicatory" to R. Joseph b. Judah and in the Introduction to the book. At the end of the Introduction, however, we find that Maimonides added significant data about the standing of the theologian vis-à-vis the philosopher, which may add details about his self-perception.

---

59 On this issue, see Aviezer Ravitzky, "The Secrets of *The Guide of the Perplexed*: Between the Thirteenth and the Twentieth Centuries," in *Studies in Maimonides*, ed. Isadore Twersky (Cambridge, MA: Harvard University Press 1990), 159-207.

Contradictions

Maimonides placed an "Introduction" at the end of the "Introduction to the First Part," where he enumerates the seven types of contradictions or contrary statements found in books, an issue whose content and language has occupied many scholars.[60] In the course of the discussion, Maimonides drew a distinction between the philosophers and himself, that is, between the philosophy and the unique theology typical of his approach. Toward the end of this Introduction, he writes:

> As for the divergences ['*ikhtilāf*][61] occurring in the books of the philosophers, or rather of those who know the truth, they are due to the fifth cause.... Divergences that are to be found in this Treatise are due to the fifth case and the seventh. Know this, grasp its true meaning, and remember it very well so as not to become perplexed by some of its chapters.[62]

The fifth cause is pedagogical. Its meaning is that an obscure issue is a presumption for an easier one but, insofar as understanding ability is concerned, one should begin with what is easier. Hence, the author opens with the obscure issue but presents it "in accord with the listener's imagination."[63] This contrast is found both in the books of the philosophers and in the *Guide*.

The *Guide*, however, presents the divergence not only according to the fifth cause but also according to the seventh, which implies that "in speaking about very obscure matters it is necessary to conceal some parts and to disclose others."[64] This cause relates to issues founded on contradictions. The author, therefore, uses a "device" involving the use of partial knowledge, which is helpful in abstract apprehension.[65] Devices are generally used to apprehend metaphysics. The seventh cause has a political aspect, as conveyed in Maimonides' instruction: "the vulgar must in no way be aware of the contradiction; the author accordingly uses some device to conceal it by all means." But this contradiction entails a pedagogical aspect as well, as denoted by the term "device."

---

60 Yair Lorberbaum, "The 'Seventh Cause': On Contradictions in Maimonides' 'Guide of the Perplexed,'" *Tarbiz* 69, 2 (2010): 211-237 [Heb].
61 See Marvin Fox, *Interpreting Maimonides: Studies in Methodology, Metaphysics, and Moral Philosophy* (Chicago: University of Chicago Press, 1990), 74-75.
62 *Guide*, "Introduction to the First Part," 19-20.
63 Ibid., 18.
64 Ibid.
65 Ibid. See Amira Eran, "'Artifice' as a Device for the Study of the Divinity in the Writings of Maimonides and Averroes," *Pe'amim* 61 (1994): 109-131[Heb].

Maimonides, therefore, held that philosophers do not use the seventh cause, contrary to a "philosophical theologian" like himself, who does. In some senses, then, the *Guide* is preferable to the books of the philosophers, and its author is not exactly a philosopher.[66] The implication for Maimonides' self-perception is clear and, incidentally, Maimonides ranked prophetic books and rabbinic midrashim in the other causes, unrelated to the fifth and seventh ones.

Dual Purposes

Concerning contradictions, Maimonides adopted the model of primary and secondary purposes that appears in the "Epistle Dedicatory" and in the "Introduction to the First Part" of the *Guide*. The primary purpose of the list of contradictions and contrary statements was to present their appearance in the books of prophecy. The focus of the list as a whole, therefore, is on the third and fourth causes, as he explicitly notes: "That some passages in every prophetic book, when taken in their external sense, appear to contradict or to be contrary to one another is due to the third cause and to the fourth. And it was with this in view that this entire introduction was written."[67]

The primary purpose, then, was to explain the contradictions and contrary statements in the books of prophecy, whereas the secondary purpose was to present the contradictions and contrary statements in the *Guide*, contrasting them with the books of the philosophers and focusing on the fifth and seventh causes. The model here is again that of the Epistle. Prophecy and its secrets are only the primary purpose, and the confrontation with theology—the secondary purpose. According to the philosophical model that Maimonides sought to create, the central purpose is indeed to create "an early theologian," who relies on philosophy.

Maimonides' attitude toward the rabbis and toward biblical and tannaitic esotericism is complicated and has been extensively discussed, including

---

66 In the chapters on providence in the *Guide*, Maimonides adopted a similar model. On the one hand, as noted, he determined that the Torah's view regarding providence is that it watches over humans as well as animals (III:17); on the other, he presented his own view—"as for my own belief" (ibid., 471)— that providence watches only over humans. Despite the objections voiced in this regard—how could he claim to hold a view different from that of the Torah?—this was definitely his thought. In any event, here too, Maimonides included himself in the fifth cause among the philosophers, and then separated himself from them in being the only one using the seventh cause. I have no doubt that he saw himself as a special model of a philosopher and, in fact, as a theologian philosopher.

67 *Guide*, "Introduction to the First Part," 19.

in Chapters 1 and 2 above.[68] Maimonides clearly ranked the philosophical theologian (who relies on the Aristotelian vision of the universe) above the philosophers regarding the depth of the writing and of the issues involved. The philosophical theologian, as noted, challenges philosophy with assumptions that are not philosophical, such as revelation and creation, but without collapsing the scientific Aristotelian framework. The philosophical theologian creates an "improved" philosophy, which takes these assumptions into account and thus ultimately represents an intellectual of the highest quality. This inference follows the instructions in the *Guide*: accept the conclusions in I:71 and, in their light, read the Introduction to the treatise. The relationship between theology and philosophy then emerges as crucial for the understanding of the *Guide*'s teachings.

Maimonides and Judah Halevi

Prima facie, no greater opposition could be construed than that between *The Kuzari* and *The Guide of the Perplexed*, another widely researched topic. Formally, one is an aesthetic treatise while the other lacks any aesthetic dimension. Substantively, one supports evidence as the only criterion of truth and the other rationality and a subtle approach to the canonical texts. Concerning the sources, one relies mainly on philosophy's critics and rejects any scientific paradigm except for the purposes of the discourse, while the other relies mainly on its supporters. Nevertheless, the discussion on the relationship between philosophy and theology points to the lines connecting the two different treatises that emerged in Andalusian culture. This relationship created a pattern of reactions that brings together even the most prominent opponents.

Regarding the discourse, Halevi's approach is characterized by conceptual and philosophical openness because, paradoxically, basing truth on historical evidence a priori precludes any fixed thought constructs. Absolute rejection of the authority of reason regarding truth enables the thinker to choose freely between philosophical styles in order to create the polemic. Halevi's extreme theological conception enabled him conceptual openness

---

68 See also, for example, Sarah Stroumsa, "Elisha ben Abuyah and Muslim Heretics in Maimonides' Writings," *Maimonidean Studies* 3 (1992-1993): 175-183; Sara Klein-Braslavy, *King Solomon and Philosophical Esotericism in the Thought of Maimonides* (Jerusalem: Magnes, 1996), Part One [Heb]; James A. Diamond, "The Failed Theodicy of a Rabbinic-Pariah: A Maimonidean Recasting of Elisha ben Abuyah," *Jewish Studies Quarterly* 9 (2003): 353-380; Menachem Kellner, *Maimonides' Confrontation with Mysticism* (Oxford: Littman Library, 2006).

and freedom, and he indeed chose how to conduct his discourse. Not so Maimonides. Maimonides, who upheld reason as the truth criterion, could not be tolerant of other approaches but regained to some extent his freedom of thought by viewing himself as not entirely bound by the absolute Aristotelian paradigm. In his view, science is a framework that enables the inclusion of basic assumptions that are not part of it. Only in this fashion can we understand a "dual" and paradoxical conception—the creation of a universe whose order is eternal and not created. Other conceptions, which were not discussed here, also endorse this view. One example is the concept of accidental existence, meaning that of existence as an attribute that is unsuited to the Aristotelian paradigm. According to this view, essence and existence are equal only in the deity. Maimonides drew on Avicenna for this view, and possibly also on Alfārābī.[69] The model of changing some of the scientific paradigm's basic assumptions brought Maimonides to adopt an approach that, at least a first glance, entails contradictions. He unhesitatingly determined an alternative order to the act of creation itself, qualitatively ranking various objects. Maimonides' philosophy too, then, enabled freedom of thought, allowing for the comparison with Halevi.

More on the Maimonides-Halevi Connection

The Epistle in the *Guide* also resembles, in structural terms, the dialogue on the attitude toward theology. Maimonides' writings show him struggling against the discourse of the Kalām. The disciple's demand and Maimonides' disappointment in return turn the Epistle from a functional introductory document into an actual confrontation. Even throughout the *Guide*, Maimonides did not devote long discussions to a direct rejection of the Kalām. Like Halevi in *The Kuzari* (V:18), Maimonides too detailed the principles of the theology. More extensively than Halevi, however, and particularly in the explanation of atomism and admissibility, he allowed readers to choose for themselves and, more precisely, to understand by themselves why theology's scientific pretensions are doomed to fail. Obviously, Maimonides' strongly critical nuances concerning all Kalām doctrines is missing from Halevi's texts. Whereas Halevi guided readers to understand the complexity entailed by the Aristotelian philosophical discourse—made redundant by revelation but, nevertheless, still preferable

---

69 See, for example, Alexander Altmann, *Studies in Religious Philosophy and Mysticism* (London: Routledge & Kegan Paul, 1969), 108-127.

to the theological discourse—Maimonides' readers have no hesitations concerning their choice. In this regard, Maimonides actually left no room for the interactive reader. He unequivocally supported the philosophical side and presented theology as a self-serving field that is not at all in competition with philosophy. Readers of the *Guide* never doubt whether to choose a world of accident or one composed of essences. But Maimonides left his precise attitude toward theology (contrary, for example, to Saadia Gaon) shrouded in secrecy as, for example, regarding the primary and secondary aims of the book, when the secondary aim is probably the more significant one. The purpose of the *Guide* was to dispel doubts, and the absurdity is that a tangle of contradictions and contrary statements was construed as a solution to a tangle of doubts.

Both Halevi and Maimonides acknowledged Kalām theology as a realm of reference and as a (problematic) alternative that thinking individuals (Al Khazari, Joseph b. Judah) support. Furthermore, both wrote treatises with strong theological emphases, if we take into account the theological feature of defending religion and the use of non-scientific assumptions according to the scientific Aristotelian paradigm with Neoplatonic overtones. The title of *The Kuzari* conveys it as a defense of the "despised faith," and is entirely apologetic. The *Guide* was meant to show that the Aristotelian paradigm does not contradict Jewish religion so that this work too is largely a defense brief. One instance of its critical view of this paradigm is, obviously, the challenge it poses to the notion of the world as eternal. Yet both these thinkers, indeed in different measures, still prefer the philosophical discourse to the prevailing theological one. Halevi explained this as the advantage of the honest individual (the philosopher, who has no tradition but is a sincere and ethical person), while Maimonides presented an ideal model of defending religion without renouncing the philosophical context.

These two twelfth-century thinkers created the ideal figure of an "improved" theologian who is not lured by the accidental quality of objects (Halevi) or by the alternative science as a whole (Maimonides). Largely, both continued in the line of Saadia, who had sought a new model of thought out of the Kalām style that he adopted. Saadia too strove to create an "improved" theologian, who acknowledges the stable structure of the universe and its interrelationships. The distinction still remains: Halevi preferred the evidence of revelation even over the "improved" theologian (who knows how to protect religion relying on balanced philosophical assumptions), whereas Saadia and Maimonides viewed such a defense as the ideal course.

Saadia, Halevi, and Maimonides all favored the universe of essences typical of the Aristotelian paradigm over the theological conception that presented only God as an essence. Nevertheless, both Halevi and Maimonides, in one way or another, adopted the distinction between essence and existence to distinguish the "essentiality" of God from that of all other existents.[70] According to this view, the being of an essence (let us say, within divine knowledge) does not compel its actual existence. Existence becomes only possible and is perceived as an attribute that is added to the essence. Only regarding one existent, essence is not added to but is identical to existence, and that is obviously God. Philosophers attacked theologians for this distinction and claimed that it is "theological" because, in their view, it was actually meant to legitimize the conception of creation. Grappling with the approach that denies essences is nevertheless typical of both Halevi and Maimonides.

Transition

We can now glance at the historical process of twelfth-century Jewish thought, that is, at the transition from the Kalām to Aristotelianism (the Neoplatonic treatise translated by Ibn Hisdai and the treatise of Ibn Gabirol were transient episodes, but the Kalām was constantly in the background). Halevi confronted Muslim theological tradition. He recoiled from the Kalām paradigm and opposed its explanations on the behavior of the universe. Hence, he tried to replace it with the Aristotelian philosophical paradigm (with Neoplatonic overtones) that he admired and, as Strauss and Yohanan Silman claimed, he probably adhered to philosophy during a limited period of this life. Halevi introduced the Aristotelian paradigm into his dialogue about the religion of truth. His hesitations are evident both in his indirect reliance on Ibn Gabirol and in his dialectic relationship with the Kalām conveyed in the exchange between Al Khazar (the theologian) and the Rabbi (the philosopher).

Neither did Maimonides dare to advocate the absolute rejection of the theological course. Although he did continue Halevi's endeavor and was disgusted by the nature and the psychology of Muslim theology, he did not reach the stage of endorsing a pure philosophy. He still wrote a defense

---

70 Yohanan Silman, *Philosopher and Prophet: Judah Halevi, The Kuzari, and the Evolution of His Thought*, trans. Lenn J. Schramm (Albany, NY: SUNY Press, 1995), 34-35. See also Altmann, *Studies*, 108-127.

brief, drawing close to a pure philosophical stance but presenting a "philosophical theologian" or a "Christian Mutakallim" (Philoponus) instead of the Aristotelian and Neoplatonic philosopher and scientist. In the discussion about the contradictions in the Introduction to the *Guide*, as noted, Maimonides ascribed greater importance to philosophical theology than to philosophy per se, which does not necessarily deal with "deep" issues. Gersonides would come closer to a pure philosophical stance, but a Jewish religious philosopher apparently cannot identify, absolutely and unequivocally, with a philosophical position.

Guttmann argued that, contrary to Muslim philosophers from the tenth to the twelfth centuries, the concern of most Jewish philosophers "was definitely a philosophy of religion"—whereas Muslim philosophers dealt with the structure and function of the universe as such, Jewish philosophers dealt mainly with religious philosophical questions.[71] Although this determination was formulated before most historians of science in the medieval Jewish world exposed the curiosity common to Jewish philosophers and their surroundings, it still shows that theology is an important factor in Jewish thought. Many writings can be defined as theology and as a theology based on philosophy. The approaches of Halevi and Maimonides point to the different results of the confrontation between theology and philosophy: according to Halevi, philosophy prevails over Halakhah in theory but not in practice, whereas according to Maimonides, philosophy prevails but its victory is not absolute, since only philosophical theology ensures the development of a stance free from most of the difficulties.

---

71 Julius Guttmann, *Philosophies of Judaism: The History of Jewish Philosophy from Biblical Times to Franz Rosenzweig*, trans. David W. Silverman (New York: Holt, Rinehart, and Winston, 1964), 55.

Epilogue

For generations, traditional commentators, scholars, and thinkers have offered numerous interpretations of Maimonides' thought. At times, this multiplicity leads the student to despair: Maimonides' "authentic" view recedes further and further away when so much is invested in the eager pursuit of its foundations. This multiplicity of interpretations is indeed a distinctive sign or perhaps we should say an anticipation of postmodernism, but we may assume Maimonides' interpreters and scholars to be genuinely interested in delving into the depths of his thought.

One dimension evoking hope among scholars is the study of the sources. Thinkers develop in the context of scholarly, scientific, and intellectual traditions, and their views are therefore judged against a specific background. Concerning Maimonides, a dual body of sources is involved: on the one hand, the biblical sources in their rabbinic interpretation, and on the other, the Muslim philosophy whose representatives Maimonides himself details in the letter he sent to his translator, Samuel Ibn Tibbon. Maimonides was certainly acquainted with Jewish works, and even related to them implicitly in his writings. The more significant influence on the shaping of his views, however, is that of scientific and philosophical approaches that emerged in the Muslim world.

In this work, therefore, I have tried to highlight Maimonides' views according to his sources. On the study of metaphysics and regarding astral magic, I emphasized the role of the rabbis beside the Muslim influence. On the view of idolatry as mediation and on the immortality of the soul, I focused mainly on Muslim sources. On the matter of the separate intellects, I examined Maimonides' attitude toward his rabbinic sources. In Shlomo Pines' classic article on the sources of the *Guide*, which appeared as a preface to his translation of the book, he reviewed Maimonides' direct sources. Although his indirect sources and his approach to them is extensively considered, these issues still require further discussion.

The contribution of the current work to the study of Maimonides' sources ultimately prepared the ground for defining the type of thinker he created. I argued in chapter 6 that Maimonides was a theological philosopher or a philosophical theologian. Contrary to radical views claiming that

Maimonides was a "pure" philosopher who interpreted religion solely in political terms, this work shows that the religious stance was an integral aspect of his personality and also carried metaphysical significance. My discussions, though focused on a limited number of issues, suffice to trace the contours of Maimonides' philosophical concern, and if this book helps to open up research horizons, it can be said to have succeeded in its task.

Bibliography

Primary Sources

'Abd al-Jabbār al-'Asādabādī, *Kitāb al-Mughni fi 'abwāb al-Tawḥīd wal-'Adl*, Part 5, "The Non-Muslim Sects" ed. by Tāhā Ḥusayn and Ibrāhīm Madkūr. Cairo: Wizārat al-Thaqāfa wa-'l-Irshād al-Qawmī, al-Idāra al-'Āmma li-'l-Thaqāfa, 1961.

Abelson, J. "Maimonides on the Jewish Creed." *Jewish Quarterly Review* 19 (1906): 24-58.

Abraham ibn Daud. *Das Buch Emunah Ramah, oder Der Erhabene Glaube*. Translated by Simson Weil. Frankfurt am Main: Druck, 1852.

Abraham Ibn Ezra. *Be'ur Ibn Ezra le-Sefer Shemot (ha-Perush ha-Katsar)*, edited by Judah Leib Fleischer. Vienna, 1926 [Heb].

Abraham Ibn Ezra. *Perushei ha-Torah le-Rabbenu Abraham ibn Ezra*, vol. 2, edited by Asher Weiser. Jerusalem: Mosad Harav Kook, 1977 [Heb].

Abraham Shalom. *Neveh Shalom.* Venice 1575.

Abū Ma'šar. *The Abbreviation of the Introduction to Astrology*, edited and translated by Charles Burnett, Keiji Yamamoto, and Michio Yano. Leiden and New York: Brill, 1994.

Alfārābī, *Arā' al-madīna al-fāḍila*, edited by Albīr Naṣrī Nādir. Beirut: al-Maktabah al-Kāthūlīkīyah 1959.

Al-Ghazālī. *Mizān al-'amal*, edited by Suleimān Dunyā. Cairo: Dār al-Ma'ārif, 1964.

Al-Ghazālī. *Al-munqidh min al-ḍalāl*, edited by Jamāl Salībā & Kāmil 'Ayyād. Beirut: Dar al-Andalus, 1981.

al-Shahrastānī, *Kitāb Al-Milal wa al-Nihal*, edited by Ṣidqī Jamīl al-'Aṭṭār. Beirut, 1997. Based on 'Abd al-'Azīz Muḥammad al-Wakīl's edition. Cairo, 1967

'Ali ibn 'Ali Ibn Abī al-'Izz. *Sharhal-'aqīda al-tahāwiyya*, edited by 'Abdallāh ibn 'Abd al-Muḥsin al-Turki and Shu'ayb al-Arna'ūṭ. Beirut, 1991.

Aristotle, *The Metaphysics*. Translated by Hugh Tredennick. Cambridge, MA: Harvard University Press, 1947.

Averroes. *Kitzur Sefer ha-Hush ve-ha-Muhash le-Ibn Rushd (Averrois Cordubensis: Compendia Librorum Aristotelis qui Parva Naturalia vocantur)*, edited by Henricus (Zevi) Blumberg. Cambridge, MA: Mediaeval Academy of America, 1954 [Heb].

Avicenna. *Kitāb al-Najāt*, edited by Muḥyiddīn al-Din Ṣabrī al-Kurdī. Cairo: Sa'adat Press, 1938.

Avicenna. *Aḥwāl al-nafs*, edited by Ahmad Fuād al-Ahwānī. Cairo: Īsā al-Bābī al-Ḥalabī, 1952.

Avicenna. *Al-ishārāt wal-Tanbihāt*, vol. 3, edited by Suleimān Dunyā. Cairo: Dār al-Ma'ārif, 1960.

Avicenna. *Kitāb al-shifā' (al-ilāhiyyāt)*, edited by G. C. Anawati & S. Zayed, vol. 2. Cairo, 1960.

David Kokhavi. *Sefer ha-Batim*, edited by Moshe Herschler, vol. 1. Jerusalem: Regensburg Institute, 1983 [Heb].

Hiddushei Talmidei Rabbenu Yona al Masekhet Avodah Zarah, edited by Zvi Hacohen Zashrakovsky. New York: 1956 [Heb].

Hoter ben Shelōmō, *The Commentary of Hoter ben Shelōmō to the Thirteen Principles of Maimonides*, edited by David R. Blumenthal. Leiden: E. J. Brill 1974.

Isaac b. Jedaiah. "Commentary to Tractate Avot." In *Perushei Rishonim le-Massekhet Avot*, edited by Moshe Kasher and Yaakov Blecherowitz. Jerusalem: Machon Torah Shlemah, 1973.

Isaac b. Shem Tov. *Lehem ha-Panim*, MS. London 912.

Jacob Anatoli, *Malmad ha-Talmidim*. Lueck: Mekizei Nirdamim, 1866.

Joseph Kaspi, *Ammudei kesef u-Maskiyyot Kesef*, edited by S. Werbluner. Frankfurt am Main, 1848.

Judah Halevi. *The Kuzari*. Translated by Hartwig Hirschfeld. New York: Schocken, 1964.

Judah Halevi. *Al-Kitāb Al-Khazarī*, edited by D. Z. Baneth and H. Ben-Shammai. Jerusalem: Magnes Press, 1977.

Lerner, Ralph and Muhsin Mahdi, eds. "Maimonides' Letter on Astrology." In *Medieval Political Philosophy: A Sourcebook*, 227-236. Ithaca, NY: Cornell University Press, 1963.

Lewin, B. M. *Otzar ha-Geonim: Thesaurus of the Gaonic Responsa and Commentaries*, vol. 4, *Chagiga*. Jerusalem: Hebrew University Press Association, 1984 [Heb].

Maimonides, Moses. *Dalālat al-Ha'irīn*, edited by Salomon Munk and Issachar Yoel. Jerusalem: Yunovits, 1931.

Maimonides, Moses. *Moreh Nebukim: Guide for the Perplexed*, edited with vocalized and emended text with a new and full commentary based upon the results of literary and philosophic research by Dr. Yehudah Even Shmuel, Part One (1). Tel Aviv: Shvil (Mosad Harav Kook), 1935 [Heb].

Maimonides, Moses. *Mishnah Im Perush Rabbenu Moshe ben Maimon* [Mishnah with the Commentary of Our Master Moses ben Maimon], edited by Yosef Qafih. Jerusalem: Mossad Harav Kook, 1963 [Heb].

Maimonides, Moses. *The Guide of the Perplexed*. Translated by Shlomo Pines. Chicago: University of Chicago Press, 1963.

Maimonides, *Commentary to the Mishnah*, edited by Yosef Qafih. Jerusalem: Mosad Harav Kook, 1967 [Heb].

Maimonides, *Sefer Mishneh Torah*, first edition according to Yemen MSS with a comprehensive commentary by Yosef b. David Qafih (Kiriyat Ono: Machon Mishnat ha-Rambam, 1984) [Heb].

Maimonides, Moses. *Epistles*, edited by David Hartwig Baneth. Jerusalem: Magnes, 1985 [Heb].

Maimonides. "The Epistle to Yemen." In *Crisis and Leadership: Epistles of Maimonides*. Translated by Abraham Halkin, with discussions by David Hartman. Philadelphia/Jerusalem: Jewish Publication Society of America, 1985.

Maimonides. *The Guide of the Perplexed*. Translated by Michael Schwarz. Tel Aviv: Tel Aviv University Press, 2002 [Heb].

McCarthy, Richard Joseph, ed. *Freedom and Fulfillment: An Annotated Translation of Al-Ghazali's al-Munqidh min al-dalal and Other Relevant Works of al-Ghazali*. Boston: Twayne, 1980.

Meir Abula'fia. *Kitāb al Rasā'il*, edited by Yehiel Brill. Paris, 1871.

Meir Aldubi. *Shvilei Emunah*. Warsaw, 1887.

Menachem Meiri. *Beith ha-Behirah al Masekhet Avodah Zara*, edited by Abraham Sofer. Jerusalem, 1964 [Heb].

Moses of Narbonne. *Ma'amar bi-Shlemut ha-Nefesh* [Treatise on the Perfection of the Soul], edited by Alfred L. Ivry. Jerusalem: Israel Academy of Sciences and Humanities, 1977 [Heb].

Nachmanides, Moses. *Ramban (Nachmanides): Writings and Discourses,* vol. 2. Translated by Charles B. Chavel. New York: Shilo, 1978.

Saadia Gaon. *Sefer ha-Nivhar be-Emunot u-be-Deot*, edited by Yosef Qafih. Jerusalem: Sura Institute, 1970 [Arabic and Hebrew].

Saadia Gaon. *The Book of Beliefs and Opinions*. Translated by Samuel Rosenblatt. New Haven CT: Yale University Press, 1948.

Samuel Ibn Tibbon. *Ma'amar yiqqawu ha-mayim,* edited by M. L. Bisliches. Pressburg, 1837.

Samuel ibn Zarza, *Mikhlol Yofi,* MS Paris, vol. I.

Schwartz, Dov and Esti Eisenmann, *Commentary on Guide of the Perplexed: The Commentary of R. Mordekhai ben Eliezer Komtiyano on Maimonides' Guide of the Perplexed*. Ramat-Gan: Bar-Ilan University Press, 2016.

Sefer Moreh Nevukhim with Four Commentaries: Ephodi, Shem Tov, Crescas, Abravanel, vol. 2. Jerusalem, 1960 [Heb].

Shem Tov ibn Falaquera. *Moreh ha-Moreh*, edited by Yair Shiffman. Jerusalem: World Union of Jewish Studies, 2001 [Heb].

Shilat, Itzhak, ed. *The Letters and Essays of Moses Maimonides*. Jerusalem: n. p., 1995.

Secondary Sources

Abrahamov, Binyamin. "Ibn Sina's Influence on Al-Ghazali's Non-Philosophical Works." *Abr-Nahrain* 29 (1991): 1-17.

Abrahamov, Binyamin. "'Abd al-Gabbar's Theory of Divine Assistance (*Lutf*)." *Jerusalem Studies in Arabic and Islam* 16 (1993): 41-58.

Abrahamov, Binyamin. "The Appointed Time of Death (*Ağal*) According to 'Abd al-Ğabbār." *Israel Oriental Studies* 13 (1993): 7-38.

Abrahamov, Binyamin. *Divine Love in Islamic Mysticism: The Teachings of al-Ghazālī and al-Dabbāgh*. London: Routledge Curzon, 2003.

Abrams, Daniel. *The Female Body of God in Kabbalistic Literature*. Jerusalem: Magnes, 2005 [Heb].

Adamson, Peter. "Correcting Plotinus: Soul's Relationship to Body in Avicenna's Commentary on the Theology of Aristotle." *Bulletin of the Institute of Classical Studies* 47 (2004): 59-75.

Afnan, Soheil M. *Avicenna: His Life and Works*. London: Allen and Unwin, 1958.

Altmann, Alexander. *Studies in Religious Philosophy and Mysticism*. London: Routledge and Kegan Paul, 1969.

Altmann, Alexander. "Maimonides on the Intellect and the Scope of Metaphysics." In *Von der mittelalterlichen zur modernen Aufklaerung: Studien zur juedischen Geistesgeschichte*, edited by Alexander Altmann, 61-129. Tübingen: JCB Mohr, 1987.

Alves Carrara, Angelo. "Geoponica and Nabatean Agriculture: A New Approach into Their Sources and Authorship." *Arabic Sciences and Philosophy* 16 (2006): 103-132.

Arberry, Arthur J. *The Koran Interpreted*. London: Oxford University Press, 1964.

Attias, Jean-Christophe. *Le commentaire biblique: Mordekhai Komtino ou l'herméneutique du dialogue*. Paris: Cerf, 1991.

Baneth, David H. "On the Philosophic Terminology of Maimonides." *Tarbiz* 6 (1935): 254-284 [Heb].

Bar-Ilan, Meir. "Astrology and Magic in the Middle Ages." Review of *Astral Magic in Medieval Jewish Thought*, by Dov Schwartz, *Kabbalah* 7 (2002): 361-384 [Heb].

Barnes, Jonathan. "Aristotle's Concept of Mind." In *Articles on Aristotle*, edited by Jonathan Barnes, Malcolm Schofiled, and Richard Sorabji. London: Duckworth, 1979.

Ben-Menahem, Naphtali. *Ibn Ezra Topics*. Jerusalem: Mosad Harav Kook, 1978 [Heb].

Berman, Lawrence V. *Ibn Bājjah and Maimonides*. Ph.D. dissertation: Hebrew University of Jerusalem, 1959) [Heb].

Berman, Lawrence V. "Maimonides, the Disciple of Alfārābī." *Israel Oriental Society* 4 (1974): 154-178.

Bland, Kalman P., ed., *The Epistle on the Possibility of Conjunction with the Active Intellect by Ibn Rushd with the Commentary of Moses Narboni*. New York: Jewish Theological Seminary of America, 1982.

Bland, Kalman P. *The Artless Jew: Medieval and Modern Affirmations and Denials of the Visual*. Princeton, NJ: Princeton University Press, 2001.

Blidstein, Gerald. "The Concept of Joy in Maimonides." *Eshel Beer-Sheva* 2 (1980): 145-163 [Heb].

Blumberg, Harry. "The Problem of Immortality in Avicenna, Maimonides and St. Thomas Aquinas." In *Harry Austryn Wolfson Jubilee Volume on the Occasion of His Seventy-Fifth Birthday*, edited by Saul Lieberman, 165-185. Jerusalem: American Academy of Jewish Research, 1965.

Blumberg, Harry. "The Separate Intelligences in Maimonides's Philosophy." *Tarbiz* 40 (1971): 216-225 [Heb].

Blumenthal, David R. *Philosophic Mysticism: Studies in Rational Religion*. Ramat Gan: Bar-Ilan University Press, 2006.

Blumenthal, H. J. "Neoplatonic Elements in the *de Anima* Commentaries." In *Aristotle Transformed: The Ancient Commentators and Their Influence*, edited by Richard Sorabji, 327-348. Ithaca, NY: Cornell University Press, 1990.

Burrell, David B. "Creation or Emanation: Two Paradigms of Reason." In *God and Creation: An Ecumenical Symposium*, edited by David B. Burrell and Bernard McGinn, 27-37. Notre Dame, ID: University of Notre Dame Press, 1990.

Corbin, Henry. *Avicenna and the Visionary Recital*. Translated by Willard R. Trask. Princeton: Princeton University Press, 1960.

Dales, Richard C. *Medieval Discussions of the Eternity of the World*. Leiden: Brill, 1990.

Davidson, Herbert A. *The Philosophy of Abraham Shalom: A Fifteenth-Century Exposition and Defence of Maimonides*. Berkeley, CA: Universtiy of California Press, 1964.

Davidson, Herbert. *Proofs for Eternity: Creation and the Existence of God in Medieval Islamic and Jewish Philosophy*. New York: Oxford University Press, 1987.

Davidson, Herbert A. *Alfarabi, Avicenna and Averroes on Intellect: Their Cosmologies, Theories of the Active Intellect, and Theories of Human Intellect*. New York: Oxford University Press, 1992.

Davidson, Herbert A. *Moses Maimonides: The Man and His Work*. Oxford: Oxford University Press, 2005.

Davidson, Herbert A. "John Philoponus as a Source of Medieval Islamic and Jewish Proofs of Creation." *Journal of the American Oriental Society* 89 (1969): 357-391.

Davidson, Herbert A. "Alfarabi and Avicenna on the Active Intellect." *Viator* 3 (1972): 171-175.

Davidson, Herbert A. "Maimonides' Secret Position on Creation." In *Studies in Medieval Jewish History and Literature*, vol. 1, edited by Isadore Twersky, 16-40. Cambridge, MA: Harvard University Press, 1979.

Davidson, Herbert A. "Averroes and the Material Intellect," *AJS Review* 9 (1984): 174-184.

Davidson, Herbert A. "Maimonides on Metaphysical Knowledge." *Maimonidean Studies* 3 (1992/1993): 49-103

Davis, Eli, and David A. Frenkel, *The Hebrew Amulet: Biblical-Medical-General*. Jerusalem: Institute for Jewish Studies, 1995 [Heb].

Diamond, James A. "The Failed Theodicy of a Rabbinic Pariah: A Maimonidean Recasting of Elisha ben Abuyah." *Jewish Studies Quarterly* 9 (2003): 353-380.

Dillon, John. "Image, Symbol and Analogy: Three Basic Concepts of Neoplatonic Allegorical Exegesis." In *The Significance of Neoplatonism*, edited by R. Baine Harris, 247-262. Norfolk, VA: Old Dominion University, 1976.

Dunphy, William. "Maimonides' Not-So-Secret Position on Creation." In *Moses Maimonides and His Time*, edited by Eric L. Ormsby, 151-172. Washington, DC: Catholic University of America Press, 1989.

Eran, Amira. "'Artifice' as a Device for the Study of the Divinity in the Writings of Maimonides and Averroes." *Pe'amim* 61 (1995): 109-131 [Heb].

Eran, Amira. "Al-Ghazālī and Maimonides on the World to Come and Spiritual Pleasures." *Jewish Studies Quarterly* 8, 2 (2001): 137-166.

Eran, Amira. "The Ladder of Delight in Al-Ghazālī's and Maimonides's Metaphors." In *Alei Asor: Proceedings of the Tenth Conference of the Society for Judaeo-Arabic Studies*, edited by Daniel J. Lasker and Haggai Ben-Shammai, 183-191. Beer-Sheva: Ben-Gurion University of the Negev Press, 2008 [Heb].

Even-Chen, Alexander. "Maimonides's Theory of Positive Attributes." *Daat* 63 (2008): 19-45 [Heb].

Faur, José. *Studies on Maimonides's Code (The Book of Knowledge)*. Jerusalem: Mosad Harav Kook, 1978 [Heb].

Fox, Marvin. *Interpreting Maimonides: Studies in Methodology, Metaphysics, and Moral Philosophy*. Chicago: University of Chicago Press, 1990.

Frank, Daniel H. "The Elimination of Perplexity: Socrates and Maimonides as Guide of the Perplexed." In *Autonomy and Judaism: The Individual and the Community in Jewish Philosophical Thought*, edited by Daniel H. Frank. Albany, NY: SUNY Press, 1992.

Frede, Michael. *Essays in Ancient Philosophy*. Oxford: Clarendon Press, 1987.

Freudenthal, Gad. "Maimonides' Stance on Astrology in Context: Cosmology, Physics, Medicine and Providence." In *Moses Maimonides: Physician, Scientist, and Philosopher*, edited by Fred Rosner and Samuel S. Kottek. Northvale, NJ: Ktav, 1993.

Freudenthal, Gad. "Maimonides on the Scope of Metaphysics *alias Maʻaseh Merkavah*: The Evolution of His Views." In *Maimonides y su época*, edited by Carlos del Valle, Santiago Garcia-Jalon, and Juan Pedro Monferrer, 221-230. Madrid: Sociedad Estatal de Conmemoraciones Culturales, 2007.

Freudenthal, Gad. "Four Observations on Maimonides's Four Celestial Globes (*Guide* II:9-10)." In *Maimonides: Conservatism, Originality, Revolution*, edited by Aviezer Ravitzky. 499-527. Jerusalem: Zalman Shazar Center, 2008 [Heb].

Gevaryahu, Hayyim."Maimonides' Concept of Paganism." In *Sefer Karl*, edited by Asher Weiser and Ben Zion Luria, 351-363. Jerusalem: Kiriyat Sefer, 1960.

Goichon, A.M. *Lexique de la langue philosophique d'Ibn Sina*. Paris: Desclée de Brouwer, 1938.

Goodman, Lenn E. *Avicenna*. London and New York: Routledge, 1992.

Gurfinkel, Eli. "Maimonides: Between Dogmatism and Liberalism." *Daat* 60 (2007): 5-28 [Heb].

Gutas, Dimitri. "Avicenna: The Metaphysics of the Rational Soul." *The Muslim World* 102 (2012): 417-425.

Guthrie, W. K. C. *A History of Greek Philosophy*, vol. 6, *Aristotle: An Encounter*. Cambridge: Cambridge University Press, 1981.

Guttmann, Julius. "Die religiösen Motive in der Philosophie des Maimonides." In *Entwicklungsstufen der Jüdischen Religion* (Giessen: A. Töpelmann, 1927), 61-90.

Guttmann, Julius. *Philosophies of Judaism: The History of Jewish Philosophy from Biblical Times to Franz Rosenzweig*. Translated by David W. Silverman. New York: Holt, Rinehart, and Winston, 1964.

Guttmann, Julius. "Philosophy of Religion or Philosophy of Law." *Proceedings of the Israel Academy of Sciences and Humanities* 5 (1976): 188-207 [Heb].

Hadad, Eliezer. *Torah and Nature in Maimonides's Writings*. Jerusalem: Magnes, 2011 [Heb].

Halbertal, Moshe, and Avishai Margalit, *Idolatry*. Translated by Naomi Goldblum. Cambridge, MA: Harvard University Press, 1992.

Hämeem-Anttila, Jaakko. "Ibn Wahshiyya and Magic." *Anaquel de Estudios Árabes* 10 (1999), 39-48.

Hartman, David. "Philosophy and Halakhah as Alternative Challengers to Idolatry in Maimonides." In *Shlomo Pines Jubilee Volume on the Occasion of His Eightieth Birthday*, vol. 1, edited by Moshe Idel, Warren Zev Harvey, and Eliezer Schweid, 319-333. Jerusalem: Hebrew University, 1990 [Heb].

Hartman, David. *Maimonides: Torah and Philosophic Quest*. Philadelphia: Jewish Publications Society, 1976.

Harvey, Steven. "Maimonides in the Sultan's Palace." In *Perspectives on Maimonides*, edited by Joel L. Kraemer, 47-75. Oxford: Oxford University Press, 1991.

Harvey, Steven. "Did Maimonides' Letter to Samuel Ibn Tibbon Determine Which Philosophers Would Be Studied by Later Jewish Thinkers?" *Jewish Quarterly Review* 83 (1992): 51-70.

Harvey, Steven. "The Meaning of Terms Designating Love in Judeo-Arabic Thought and Some Remarks on the Judeo-Arabic Interpretation of Maimonides." In *Judaeo-Arabic Studies: Proceedings of the Founding Conference of the Society for Jewish-Arabic Studies [Chicago, May 1984]*, edited by Norman Golb, 175-196. Amsterdam: Harwood Academic Publishers, 1997.

Harvey, Steven. "Maimonides and the Art of Writing Introductions." *Maimonidean Studies* 5 (2008): 86-106.

Harvey, Warren Zev. *Crescas' Critique of the Theory of the Acquired Intellect*. Ph.D. Dissertation: Columbia University, 1973.

Harvey, Warren Z. "A Third Approach to Maimonides' Cosmogony-Prophetology Puzzle." *Harvard Theological Review* 74 (1981): 287-301.

Harvey, Warren Z. "Crescas versus Maimonides on Knowledge and Pleasure." In *A Straight Path: Studies in Medieval Philosophy and Culture—Essays in Honor of Arthur Hyman*, edited by Ruth Link-Salinger, 113-123. Washington, DC: Catholic University of America Press, 1988.

Harvey, Warren Z. "Why Maimonides Was Not a Mutakallim?" In *Perspectives on Maimonides*, edited by Joel L. Kramer, 105-114. Oxford: Oxford University Press, 1991.

Harvey, Warren Z. "Sex and Health in Maimonides." In *Moses Maimonides: Physician, Scientist, and Philosopher*, edited by Fred Rosner and Samuel Kottek, 33-39. Northvale, NJ: Jason Aronson, 1993.

Heinemann, Yitzhak. *The Reasons for the Commandments in the Tradition*. Jerusalem: WZO, 1966 [Heb].

Hjarpe, Jan. *Analyse critique des traditions arabes sur les sabéens harraniens.* Uppsala: Skriv, 1972.

Holzman, Gitit. *The Theory of the Intellect and Soul in the Thought of Rabbi Moshe Narboni Based on His Commentaries on the Writings of Ibn Rushd, Ibn Tufayl, Ibn Bajja and Al-Ghazali.* Ph.D. dissertation: Hebrew University, 1996 [Heb].

Hourani, George F. *Islamic Rationalism: The Ethics of 'Abd al-Jabbār.* Oxford: Clarendon Press, 1971), 21.

Hyman, Arthur. "Maimonides' 'Thirteen Principles.'" In *Jewish Medieval and Renaissance Studies*, edited by Alexander Altmann, 119-144. Cambridge, MA: Harvard University Press, 1967.

Hyman, Arthur. "Interpreting Maimonides." In *Maimonides: A Collection of Critical Essays*, edited by Joseph A. Buijs, 19-29. Notre Dame: University of Notre Dame Press, 1988.

Hyman, Arthur. "Demonstrative, Dialectical and Sophistic Arguments in the Philosophy of Moses Maimonides." In *Moses Maimonides and His Time*, edited by Eric L. Ormsby, 35-51. Washington, DC: Catholic University of America Press, 1989.

Idel, Moshe. *Golem: Jewish Magical and Mystical Traditions on the Artificial Anthropoid* (Albany, NY: SUNY Press, 1990).

Idel, Moshe. *Maïmonide et la mystique juive.* Translated by Charles Mopsik. Paris: Cerf, 1991.

Idel, Moshe. *R. Menahem Recanati: The Kabbalist*, vol. 1. Jerusalem: Schocken, 1998 [Heb].

Idel, Moshe. *Kabbalah and Eros.* New Haven: Yale University Press, 2005.

Idel, Moshe. "*Sitre 'Arayot* in Maimonides' Thought." In *Maimonides and Philosophy*, edited by Shlomo Pines and Yirmiyahu Yovel, 79-91. Dordrecht: Nijhoff, 1986.

Idel, Moshe. "Hermeticism and Judaism." In *Hermeticism and the Renaissance: Intellectual History and the Occult in Early Modern Europe*, edited by Ingrid Merkel and Allen Debus, 59-76. London and Toronto: Associated University Presses, 1988.

Idel, Moshe. "An Astral-Magical Pneumatic Anthropoid." *Incognita* 2 (1991): 9-31.

Ivry, Alfred L. "Neoplatonic Currents in Maimonides' Thought." In *Perspectives on Maimonides*, edited by Joel L. Kramer. Oxford: Oxford University Press, 1991.

Ivry, Alfred L. "Maimonides and Neoplatonism: Challenge and Response." In *Neoplatonism and Jewish Thought*, edited by Lenn E. Goodman, 137-156. Albany, NY: SUNY Press, 1992.

Kaplan, Lawrence. "Maimonides on the Miraculous Element in Prophecy." *Harvard Theological Review* 70 (1977): 233-256.

Kellner, Menachem M. *Dogma in Medieval Jewish Thought: From Maimonides to Abravanel.* Oxford: Oxford University Press, 1986.

Kellner, Menachem M. *Maimonides on the "Decline of the Generations" and the Nature of Rabbinic Authority.* Albany, NY: SUNY Press, 1996.

Kellner, Menachem M. *Maimonides' Confrontation with Mysticism.* Oxford: Littman Library, 2006.

Khwolson, Daniil Avramovitch. *Die Ssabier und der Ssabismus*, vol. 2. St. Petersburg: Kaiserlichen Akademie der Wissenschaften, 1856.

Khwolson, Daniil Avramovitch. "Über die Überreste der altbabylonischen Literatur in arabischen Übersetzungen." *Mémoires des Savants étrangers* 8 (St. Petersburg: Kaiserlichen Akademie der Wissenschaften, 1859).

Klein-Braslavy, Sara. *Maimonides's Interpretation of the Story of Creation*. Jerusalem: Rubin Mass, 1987 [Heb].

Klein-Braslavy, Sara. *King Solomon and Philosophical Esotericism in the Thought of Maimonides*. Jerusalem: Magnes, 1996 [Heb].

Klein-Braslavy, Sara. "Maimonides' Commentary on Jacob's Dream of the Ladder." In *Moshe Schwarcz Memorial Volume* [= *Bar-Ilan Annual* 22–23], edited by Moshe Hallamish, 329-349. Ramat-Gan: Bar-Ilan University Press, 1987.

Kraemer, Joel. "*Shari'a* and *Nomos* in the Philosophical Thought of Maimonides." *Te'uda: Studies in Judaica*, 6 (1986): 183-202 [Heb].

Kraemer, Joel L. "Maimonides on Aristotle and Scientific Method." In *Moses Maimonides and His Time*, edited by Eric L. Ormsby, 53-88. Washington, DC: Catholic University of America Press, 1989.

Kreisel, Howard. "Judah Halevi's Influence on Maimonides: A Preliminary Appraisal." *Maimonidean Studies* 2 (1991): 95-121.

Kreisel, Howard. "Moses Maimonides." In *History of Jewish Philosophy*, edited by Daniel H. Frank and Oliver Leaman, 245-280. London: Routledge, 1997.

Kreisel, Howard. "The Love and Fear of God." In *Maimonides' Political Thought: Studies in Ethics, Law, and the Human Ideal*. Albany: SUNY Press, 1999.

Langermann, Y. Tzvi. "'The Making of the Firmament': R. Hayyim Israeli, R. Isaac Israeli and Maimonides." In *Shlomo Pines Jubilee Volume on the Occasion of His Eighteeth Birthday*, vol. 1, edited by Moshe Idel, Warren Zev Harvey, and Eliezer Schweid, 461-476. Jerusalem: Hebrew University, 1990 [Heb].

Langerman, Y. Tzvi. "Maimonides' Repudiation of Astrology." *Maimonidean Studies* 2 (1991): 123-158.

Langerman, Y. Tzvi. "The True Perplexity: The Guide of the Perplexed, Part II, Chapter 24." In *Perspectives on Maimonides*, edited by Joel L. Kraemer, 159-174. Oxford: Oxford University Press, 1991.

Lasker, Daniel J. "Love of God and Knowledge of God in Maimonides' Philosophy." In *Écriture et réécriture des textes philosophiques médiévaux: Volume d'hommage offert à Colette Sirat*, edited by Jacqueline Hamesse and Olga Weijers, 329-345. Turnhout: Brepols, 2006.

Law, B. C. "Avicenna and his Theory of the Soul." In *Avicenna Commemoration Volume*. Calcutta: Iran Society, 1956.

Leaman, Oliver. *An Introduction to Medieval Islamic Philosophy*. Cambridge: Cambridge University Press, 1985.

Levinger, Jacob. *Maimonides's Techniques of Codification: A Study in the Method of Mishneh Torah*. Jerusalem: Magnes, 1965 [Heb].

Levinger, Jacob S. *Maimonides as Philosopher and Codifier*. Jerusalem: Bialik Institute, 1990 [Heb].

Lewis, H. S. "Maimonides on Superstition." *Jewish Quarterly Review*, o.s. 17 (1905): 474-488.

Lieberman, Saul. *Hellenism in Jewish Palestine: Studies in the Literary Transmission of Beliefs and Manners of Palestine in the I Century B.C.E.-IV Century C.E.* New York: The Jewish Theological Seminary, 1962.

Liebes, Yehuda. *The Sin of Elisha*. Jerusalem: Hebrew University, 1986 [Heb].

Lobel, Diana. *Between Mysticism and Philosophy: Sufi Language of Religious Experience in Judah Ha-Levi's Kuzari*. Albany, NY: SUNY Press, 2000.

Lorberbaum, Yair. "On Maimonides Conception of Parables." *Tarbiz* 71 (2001): 87-132 [Heb].

Lorberbaum, Yair. "On Allegory, Metaphor, and Symbol in *The Guide of the Perplexed*." In *Jewish Culture in the Eye of the Storm: A Jubilee Book in Honor of Yosef Ahituv*, edited by Avi Sagi and Ilan Nahem, 396-422. Tel Aviv: Hakibbutz Hameuchad, 2002 [Heb]

Lorberbaum, Yair. "Changes in Maimonides's Approach to Aggadah." *Tarbiz* 78 (2008): 81-122 [Heb]

Lorberbaum, Yair. "Criticism of Aggadah in *The Guide of the Perplexed*." *Tarbiz* 78 (2009): 203-230.

Lorberbaum, Yair. "The 'Seventh Cause': On Contradictions in Maimonides's 'Guide of the Perplexed.'" *Tarbiz* 69 (2010): 211-237 [Heb].

Marmura, Michael E. "Avicenna and the Problem of the Infinite Number of Souls." *Medieval Studies* 20 (1960): 232-239.

Marmura, M. E. "Some Aspects of Avicenna's Theory of God's Knowledge of Particulars." *Journal of the American Oriental Society* 82 (1962): 299-312.

Marx, Alexander. "The Correspondence between the Rabbis of Southern France and Maimonides about Astrology." *HUCA* 3 (1926): 311-357.

Mascall, E. L. "The Doctrine of Analogy." In *Religious Language and the Problem of Religious Knowledge*, edited by Ronald E. Santoni, 156-181. Bloomington, ID: Indiana University Press, 1968.

Mattila, Janne. "Ibn Wahshiyya on the Soul: Neoplatonic Soul Doctrine and the Treatise on the Soul Contained in the Nabatean Agriculture." *Studia Orientalia* 101 (2007), 103-155.

Maurer, Armand A. "Maimonides and Aquinas on the Study of Metaphysics." In *A Straight Path: Studies in Medieval Philosophy and Culture—Essays in Honor of Arthur Hyman*, edited by Ruth Link-Salinger, 206-215. Washington, DC: Catholic University of America Press, 1988.

Melamed, Abraham. *On the Shoulders of Giants: The Debate between Moderns and Ancients in Medieval and Renaissance Jewish Thought*. Ramat-Gan: Bar-Ilan University, 2003 [Heb].

Michot, Jean R. *La destinée de l'homme selon Avicenne: le retour à Dieu (ma'ad) et l'imagination*. Louvain: A. Peters, 1986.

Morewedge, Parviz. *The Metaphysica of Avicenna*. London: Routledge and Kegan Paul, 1973.

Nasr, Seyyed Hossein. *An Introduction to Islamic Cosmological Doctrines: Conceptions of Nature and Methods Used for Its Study by the Ikwān as Safā', al-Bīrūnī, and Ibn Sīnā*. Cambridge, MA: Harvard University Press, 1964.

Nemoy, Leon. "Maimonides's Opposition to Magic in Light of the Writings of Jacob al-Qirqisani." *Ha-Rofe ha 'Ivri* 27, 1-2 (1954): 102-109 [Heb].

Norman, Richard. "Aristotle's Philosopher-God." In *Articles on Aristotle*, edited by Jonathan Barnes et. al., vol. 4, 63-74. London: Duckworth, 1979.

Nuriel, Abraham. "Maimonides on Parables Not Explicitly Identified As Such." *Daat* 25 (1990): 85-91 [Heb].

Nuriel, Avraham. *Concealed and Revealed in Medieval Philosophy*. Jerusalem: Magnes, 2000 [Heb].

Pines, Shlomo. *Studies in the History of Jewish Thought*, edited by Warren Zev Harvey and Moshe Idel. Jerusalem: Magnes Press, 1997.

Pines, Shlomo. "The Limitations of Human Knowledge according to Al-Farabi, ibn Bajja, and Maimonides." In *Studies in Medieval Jewish History and Literature*, edited by Isadore Twersky. Cambridge, MA: Harvard University Press, 1979.

Pines, Shlomo. "On the Term *Rūhaniyyāt* and its Origin, and on Judah Halevi's Doctrine." *Tarbiz* 57 (1988): 511-540 [Heb].

Pines, Shlomo. "Some Traits of Christian Theological Writing in Relation to Moslem *Kalām* and to Jewish Thought." In *Studies in the History of Arabic Philosophy by Shlomo Pines*, edited by Sarah Stroumsa. Jerusalem: Magnes Press, 1996.

Pines, Shlomo. "Introduction: The Philosophic Sources of *The Guide of the Perplexed*." In Maimonides, *The Guide of the Perplexed*. Translated by Shlomo Pines, lvii-cxxxiv. Chicago: University of Chicago Press, 1963.

Rahman, Faizur. *Avicenna's Psychology*. London: Oxford University Press, 1952.

Rahman, Faizur. "Essence and Existence in Avicenna." *Medieval and Renaissance Studies* 4 (1958): 1-16.

Ravitzky, Aviezer. "Aristotle's 'Meteorology' and the Maimonidean Modes of Interpreting the Account of Creation." *Aleph* 8 (2008): 361-400.

Ravitzky, Aviezer. "The Secrets of *The Guide to the Perplexed*: Between the Thirteenth and the Twentieth Centuries." In *Studies in Maimonides*, edited by Isadore Twersky, 159-207. Cambridge, MA: Harvard University Press, 1990.

Ravitzky, Aviram. "The Doctrine of the Mean and Asceticism: On the Uniformity of Maimonides' Ethics." *Tarbiz* 79 (2011): 439-469 [Heb].

Ravitzky, Aviram. "Saadia's Theology and Maimonides' Philosophy: The Characteristics of Medieval Jewish Thought." In *Religion and Politics in Jewish Thought: Essays in Honor of Aviezer Ravitzky*, vol. 1, edited by Benjamin Brown et. al., 287-317. Jerusalem: Israel Democracy Institute, 2012.

Rawidowicz, Simon. *Hebrew Studies in Jewish Thought*, vol. 1, edited by Benjamin C. I. Ravid, Jerusalem: Rubin Mass, 1969 [Heb].

Rosenberg, Shalom. "'And Walk in His Ways.'" In *Israeli Philosophy*, edited by Moshe Hallamish and Asa Kasher, 72-91. Tel Aviv: Papyrus, 1983 [Heb].

Rosenthal, Erwin I. J. "Avicenna's Influence on Jewish Thought." In *Avicenna: Scientist and Philosopher—A Millenary Symposium*, edited by G. M. Wickens. London: Luzac, 1952.

Rotenstreich, Nathan. *Experience and Its Sytematization*. Hague: Nijhoff, 1965.

Safran, Bezalel. "Maimonides' Attitude to Magic and to Related Types of Thinking," in *Porat Yosef: Studies Presented to Rabbi Dr. Joseph Safran*, edited by Bezalel Safran and Eliyahu Safran, 92-110. Hoboken, NJ: Ktav, 1992.

Saif, Liana. *The Arabic Influences on Early Modern Occult Philosophy*. Houndmills, Basingstoke, Hampshire: Palgrave Macmillan 2015.

Schwartz, Dov. *The Religious Philosophy of Samuel Ibn Zarza*. Ph.D. dissertation: Bar-Ilan University, 1989 [Heb].

Schwartz, Dov. *The Philosophy of a Fourteenth-Century Jewish Neoplatonic Circle*. Jerusalem: Bialik Institute, 1997 [Heb].

Schwartz, Dov. *Faith and Reason: On Patterns of Discussion in Medieval Jewish Thought*. Tel Aviv: Broadcast University, 2001 [Heb].

Schwartz, Dov. *Contradiction and Concealment in Medieval Jewish Thought*. Ramat-Gan: Bar-Ilan University, 2002 [Heb].

Schwartz, Dov. *Faith at the Crossroads: A Theological Profile of Religious Zionism*. Translated by Batya Stein. Leiden: Brill, 2002.

Schwartz, Dov. *Amulets, Properties, and Rationalism in Medieval Jewish Thought*. Ramat-Gan: Bar-Ilan University Press, 2004 [Heb].

Schwartz, Dov. *Studies on Astral Magic in Medieval Jewish Thought*. Translated by David Louvish and Batya Stein. Leiden-Boston: Brill, 2005.

Schwartz, Dov. *Music in Jewish Thought*. Ramat-Gan: Bar-Ilan University Press, 2013 [Heb].

Schwartz, Dov. *Messianism in Medieval Jewish Thought*. Boston: Academic Studies Press, 2017.

Schwartz, Dov. "Divine Immanence in Medieval Jewish Philosophy," *Journal of Jewish Thought and Philosophy* 3 (1994): 249-278.

Schwartz, Dov. "Rationalism and Astral Magic in Jewish Thought in Late Medieval Byzantium." *Aleph* 3 (2003): 165-211.

Schwartz, Dov. "Creation in Late Medieval Byzantine Jewry: A Few Aspects." *Pe'amim* 97 (Autumn 2003): 63–80 [Heb].

Schwartz, Dov. "The Figure of Judah Halevi as Emerging from Maimonides's *Guide* I:71." *Daat* 61 (2007): 23-40 [Heb].

Schwartz, Dov. "The Separate Intellects and Maimonides' Argumentation." In *Between Rashi and Maimonides*, edited by Ephraim Kanarfogel and Moshe Sokolow, 59-92. New York: Yeshiva University Press, 2010.

Schwartz, Dov. "Astral Magic and Specific Properties (*Segullot*) in Medieval Jewish Thought: Non Aristotelian Science and Theology." In *Science in Medieval Jewish Cultures*, ed. Gad Freudenthal, 301-319. New York: Cambridge University Press, 2011.

Schwartz, Dov. "Understanding in Context: R. Mordekhai Komitiyano's Commentary on the *Guide of the Perplexed*." *Pe'amim* 133-134 (2013): 127-183 [Heb].

Schwartz, Dov. "Philosophy as a Medium in Byzantium in the Late Medieval Period: R. Michael b. Shabbetai Balbo and R. Shalom b. Joseph Anabi." *Sefunot* (forthcoming) [Heb].

Schwarz, Michael. "The Qādī ʿAbd al-Gabbār's Refutation of the Ashʿarite Doctrine of 'Acquisition' (Kasb)." *Israel Oriental Studies* (1976) 6: 229-263.

Schwarz, Michael. "Who Were Maimonides' Mutakallimūn? Some Remarks on *Guide of the Perplexed*, Part I, Chapter 73," *Maimonidean Studies* 2 (1991): 159-209; 3 (1992/1993): 143-172.

Schwarz, Michael. "Maimonides and the Babu'ah." *Daat* 42 (1999): 5-6 [Heb].

Sela, Shlomo. *Astrology and Biblical Exegesis in the Thought of Abraham Ibn Ezra*. Ramat-Gan: Bar-Ilan University Press, 1999 [Heb].

Sela, Shlomo. *Abraham Ibn Ezra and the Rise of Medieval Hebrew Science*. Leiden/ Boston: Brill, 2003.

Septimus, Bernard. *Hispano-Jewish Culture in Transition: The Career and Controversies of Ramah*. Cambridge, MA: Harvard University Press, 1982.

Shapiro, Marc B. *Studies in Maimonides and His Interpreters*. Scranton: University of Scranton Press, 2008.

Shilat, Isaac, ed. *Maimonides' Introductions to the Mishnah*. Jerusalem: Ma'aliyot, 1992 [Heb].

Shilat, Isaac. *Between the Kuzari and Maimonides*. Ma'aleh Adumim: Shilat, 2011 [Heb].

Silman, Yohanan. *Philosopher and Prophet: Judah Halevi, The Kuzari, and the Evolution of His Thought*. Translated by Lenn J. Schramm. Albany, NY: SUNY Press, 1995.

Silver, Daniel Jeremy. *Maimonidean Criticism and the Maimonidean Controversy 1180-1240*. Leiden: Brill, 1965.

Simon, Ernst. *Abraham Ibn Ezra's Two Commentaries on the Minor Prophets: An Annotated Critical Edition*, vol. 1. Ramat-Gan: Bar-Ilan University Press, 1989 [Heb].

Soloveitchik, Haym. "*Mishneh Torah*: Polemic and Art." In *Maimonides After 800 Years: Essays on Maimonides and His Influence*, edited by Jay M. Harris, 339-355. Cambridge, MA: Harvard University Center for Jewish Studies, 2007.

Sorabji, Richard. *Time, Creation and the Continuum: Theories in Antiquity and the Early Middle Ages*. Ithaca, NY: Cornell University Press, 1983.

Stern, Josef. "Maimonides' Demonstrations: Principles and Practices." *Medieval Philosophy and Theology* 10 (2001): 47-84.

Strauss, Leo. *Persecution and the Art of Writing*. Glencoe, IL: Free Press, 1952.

Strauss, Leo. "How to Begin to Study *The Guide of the Perplexed*." In Maimonides, *The Guide of the Perplexed*. Translated by Shlomo Pines, xi-lvi. Chicago: University of Chicago Press, 1963.

Stroumsa, Sarah. "Elisha ben Abuyah and Muslim Heretics in Maimonides' Writings." *Maimonidean Studies* 3 (1992-1993): 175-183.

Stroumsa, Sarah. "The Sabians of Harran and the Sabians of Maimonides: On Maimonides' Theory of the History of Religions," *Sefunot*, New Series 7 (1999): 277-295 [Heb].

Stroumsa, Sarah. *The Beginnings of the Maimonidean Controversy in the East: Yosef Ibn Shim'on's Silencing Epistle Concerning the Resurrection of the Dead*. Jerusalem: Yad Izhak Ben-Zvi, 1999 [Heb].

Stroumsa, Sarah. "'Ravings': Maimonides' Concept of Pseudo-Science," *Aleph* 1 (2001): 141-163.

Stroumsa, Sarah. *Maimonides in His World: Portrait of a Mediterranean Thinker* Princeton, NJ: Princeton University Press, 2009.

Tardieu, Michel. "Sabiens Coraniques et 'Sabiens' de Harran." *Journal Asiatique* 274 (1986): 1-44.

Thorndike, Lynn. *A History of Magic and Experimental Science*, vol. 2. New York: Columbia University Press, 1964.

Turner, Masha. "The Structure of the Lexicographic Chapters in the 'Moreh Nevukhim.'" *HUCA* 62 (1991): 29-42 (Hebrew section).

Twersky, Isadore. "Halakha and Science: Perspectives on the Epistemology of Maimonides." *Shenaton ha-Mishpat ha-Ivri: Annual of the Institute for Research in Jewish Law* 14-15 (1988-1989): 121-151 [Heb].

Twersky, Isadore. *Introduction to the Code of Maimonides (Mishneh Torah)*. New Haven, CO: Yale University Press, 1980.

Urbach, Ephraim E. *The Sages: Their Concepts and Beliefs*. Translated by Israel Abrahams. Jerusalem: Magnes Press, 1975.

Urbach, Ephraim E. "The Laws Concerning Idolatry and the Archeological and Historical Reality in the Second and Third Centuries." In *The World of the Sages: Collected Studies*. Jerusalem: Magnes Press, 1988 [Heb].

Verbeke, Gérard. "L'immortalité de l'âme dans le *De anima* d'Avicenne: Une synthèse de l'Aristotélisme et du néoplatonisme." *Pensamiento*, 25 (1969): 271-290.

Wasserstrom, Steven. "The Unwritten Chapter: Notes Towards a Social and Religious History of Genizah Magic." *Pe'amim* 85 (2000): 43-61 [Heb].

Wolfson, Elliot R. *Circle in the Square: Studies in the Use of Gender in Kabbalistic Symbolism*. Albany, NY: SUNY Press, 1995.

Wolfson, Harry A. *The Philosophy of the Kalam*. Cambridge, MA: Harvard University Press, 1976.

Wolfson, Harry Austryn. "The Classification of Science in Medieval Jewish Philosophy." In *HUC Jubilee Volume 1875-1925*, 263-315. Cincinnati, 1925.

Wolfson, Harry Austryn. "The Double Faith Theory in Clement, Saadia, Averroes, and St. Thomas and its Origin in Aristotle and the Stoics." *The Jewish Quarterly Review* 33 (1942-1943): 213-264.

Wolfson, Harry A. "Maimonides on the Unity and Incorporeality of God." *Jewish Quarterly Review* 56 (1965-1966): 112-136.

Index

Note: Page numbers followed by 'n' refer to notes

A
Abba Mari, 97
'Abd al-Jabbār, 110, 114–117
    Kitāb al-Mughni fi'Abwāb al-Tawḥīd wal-ᶜAdl, 110
'Abd al-Muttalib ibn Hāshim, 111–112
Abraham ibn Daud, R., 19
Abrahamov, Binyamin, 52
abstract knowledge, 127n31
Abulaʻfia, R. Meir, 132
Abu Maʻshar, 110
acquired intellect (ʻ*aql al-mustafād*), 127n31, 129–130
active intellect, 59–60, 63, 64n6, 71–72, 77, 79, 82–83, 83n55, 118, 120n6, 130n36
Aderet (Rashba), R. Shlomo b., 97
Aggadah, 8, 54
Aher, *see* Elisha ben Abuyah
Akiva, R. (Akiba, Aqiba), 17–18n42, 18, 19, 20n55, 21, 24–25, 34
Alexander of Aphrodisias, 11, 34, 66, 119
Alfārābī, ix–x, 42, 43n124, 68, 120n7, 123n15, 127n31, 131, 139, 161
Allah, 110–116
analogical thought (*see also* analogy), 61–62, 70, 78, 80, 87
analogy, 70–72, 78–80, 82–83, 88–89
Andalusian intellectual tradition, xi, 55, 74, 97–98, 107, 134, 140, 160
anthropomorphism, negation of, 3–4, 24–25
apprehension, 5–6, 8–14, 17, 19–22, 24, 26n64, 29, 31, 34, 40, 42, 49, 56–57, 62, 77, 89, 123, 123n15, 144, 155, 158
Aristotelianism (*also* Aristotelian science; *see also* Aristotle), ix–x, 7n14, 12, 22, 54, 58, 61–63, 87, 91, 123n15, 125, 134, 138–139, 141–146, 145–146n31, 157, 160–164
Aristotle, 6n10, 13–14, 30, 66, 78, 84, 143–146
artifice, 5, 26–30, 42, 43n123, 44, 50

Ashʻarīyya, 134, 138, 145–146
astral magic, x, 90-104, 117, 165
astrology, 105, 108, 116
atomism, x, 135, 137, 161
attributes *see* Divine attributes
Averroes, 14, 15n36, 68
    Epistle on the Possibility of Conjunction, 82–83
    Short Commentary on *De Anima*, 15n36
Avicenna, ix, 31, 38, 68, 88, 118–126, 128–133, 139, 161
    al-Ishārāt wal-Tanbīhāt, 119
    Kitāb al-Najāt, 119–125, 128–130
    Kitāb al-Shifā, 119
Avodah Zarah, 93–94, 98, 100
Avot, 14, 39, 55, 153n50

B
Ben Azzai, 18–20
Ben Zoma, 18–20
Berman, Lawrence V., ixn4, 4, 11, 25, 42
Blumenthal, David, 52–53
bodily faculties (*al-quwa al-badaniyya kullahā*), 15–16
Book of Correspondence, *see* Moshe ben Maimon, R.
The Book of Nabatean Agriculture, *see* Ibn Waḥshīyya
Book of Prophecy, *see* Moshe ben Maimon, R.
Babylonian Talmud Hagigah (BT Hagigah), *see* Hagigah

C
cogitatio, 16n38
Commentary on Avot, *see* Moshe ben Maimon, R.
Commentary to the Mishnah, *see* Moshe ben Maimon, R.
cosmoeroticism, 30–31
Crescas, 16n40, 136n9

Index | 183

D
Davidson, Herbert A., 15n35, 16n40, 62n4, 83n55, 118n1, 119n2, 120n6, 121n8, 122n13, 126n29, 129n35, 135n2, 139n14, 142n24, 150n42, 156n 56
Diamond, James, 5
al-Dimashqī, Ibn Abī al-ʿIzz, 117
Divine attributes, vii-viii, 3-4, 7, 22, 35, 36, 42-52, 58, 66, 68, 72, 88-89, 111n28, 127n31, 141, 151, 161, 163
Duran, Profiat, 16n40, 30n73, 81, 140n19

E
Efodi, *see* Duran, Profiat
Eliezer, R., 40
Elisha ben Abuyah (Aher), 5, 18–20, 20n55, 21, 24
emanation, viii, 42, 64–66, 79–81, 107, 109–110, 116, 118, 139–140n14
"Epistle Dedicatory," *see Guide of the Perplexed*
Epistle of the Possibility of Conjunction, *see* Averroes
Eran, Amira, 5, 31–32
eros and politics, metaphysics, 30–45
    poltical movement, 41–45
    sexual movement, 30–41
essence *v.* existence, 27–29, 88–89, 161, 163
eternity of the world, viii, 3, 20, 47–48, 51, 67n15, 79–82, 111, 125, 141–146
Even Shmuel (Kaufmann), Yehudah, 56–58
ex nihilo, 64, 79–82, 111n24, 142, 149
Exodus, 92–93, 109
Ezekiel, viii, 74, 77

F
Falaquera (R. Shem Tov b. Joseph Ibn Falaquera), 13–14, 16n38, 47–48n134, 73
family, 40–41, 45
Faur, José, 90, 96n23
The Fountain of Life, *see* Gabirol, Solomon Ibn
Frank, Daniel, 147
Freudenthal, Gad, 4n2, 66n12, 95n19

G
geonim, xi, 18, 50–51, 90, 134, 140
al-Ghazālī, 10n16, 31, 38, 52, 132–133
Girondi, R. Nissim (Ran), 94
God, *see* Divine attributes
Guide of the Perplexed, *see also* separate intellects
    "Epistle Dedicatory," 7, 10n18, 147–150, 155–157, 159, 161

"Introduction to the First Part," vi–viii, 2, 34, 38, 60–62, 69–70, 78, 87, 147, 150–155, 157–160, 164
Part I, ix–x, 3–60, 70, 72, 84n59, 88–89, 98, 106, 116, 119, 126, 134–136, 140–141, 145–146, 148, 150, 160
Part II, 3, 17, 49, 51–52, 60, 62–73, 75–84, 87–88, 138–139n14, 138–147, 151, 156
Part III, ix, 2, 4, 12, 18, 23, 34, 38, 49, 49n137, 49n140, 67, 72, 74, 77, 91n5, 94–96, 105, 123, 147, 159n66
Guttmann, Julius, 4, 139, 156, 164
Guttmann, Yehiel, 90

H
Hai Gaon, 18
Hagigah
    Babylonian Talmud, 17–18, 21, 24, 30, 43–44, 63, 70, 74, 151
    Palestinian Talmud, 17, 21
    Tosefta, 17–18, 21
Halakhah, 164
Halevi, R. Judah, 8n14, 18, 97, 107–109, 115, 117, 140, 150
    Maimonides and, 160–16
    The Kuzari, 18–19, 2563, 27n67, 107–108, 115, 150, 160–162
Happiness, *see* immortality and imagination, pleasure
al-Harizi, 13
Hartman, David, 107n6, 139
Harvey, Steven, 10n16, 31, 67n17, 132n40, 148
Harvey, Warren Zev, 31n79, 120n6, 123n15, 139n14, 156n57
al-Hasan ibn Musa, 110

I
Ibn Bājjah, ix
Ibn Ezra, R. Abraham, 97, 107, 109, 117
Ibn Ezra, R. Moshe, 97
Ibn Gabirol, Solomon, x, 163
    The Fountain of Life, x
Ibn Paquda, R. Bahya
    The Duties of the Heart, x
Ibn Tibbon, R. Samuel, 13, 68n19, 126n29, 131, 132n40, 165
Ibn Ṭufaīl, ix
Ibn Wahshiyyah (ʾAbū Bakr ʾAḥmad bin ʾAlī)
    The Book of Nabatean Agriculture, 91, 97, 105
idolatry, x, 91, 93–94, 96n23, 97–99, 103–118

Laws Concerning Idolatry, 90–92, 98n27, 100–103, 106–107n6
    idolatry as mediation, x, 104–117, 165
        Jewish sources, 107–109
        Muslim sources, 110–115
        potential influence, 115–117
    immortality and imagination, 118–133
        Avicenna's concept, 125
        immortality as pleasure, 120–125
        reactions, 131–133
        substrate of immortality, 125–131
intellect in habitu, 16n40
Isaiah, viii, 43
al-Ishārāt wal-Tanbīhāt, see Avicenna

J
Jamshīd, 111
Jawzahr, 101n30
Job, 32–33, 77n37
Joseph ben Judah, R., vii, 7, 10n18, 147–149, 157, 162
Judah he-Hasid, R., 55

K
Kalām, x–xi, 2, 7, 8n14, 21–22, 33, 50–52, 67, 116, 134–135, 137–138, 140, 142, 144–146, 148–150, 155–156, 161–163
Kantian terminology, 56–58
Kaplan, Lawrence, 139n14
karet, 127–128, 133
Kaspi, R. Joseph ibn, 84–85
Kellner, Menachem, 5
Kitāb al-Mughni fi 'Abwāb al-Tawḥīd wal-'Adl, see 'Abd al-Jabbār
Kitāb al-Najāt, see Avicenna
Kitāb al-Shifā, see Avicenna
Klein-Braslavy, Sara, 5, 29n72, 38–39
Komtiyano, R. Mordekhai, 4, 20n55, 80–82, 84–86, 140n21
Kraemer, Joel, 4, 5n3, 13n32
Kreisel, Howard, 21, 22n59, 27n67, 52n141, 64n6, 107n7
The Kuzari, see Halevi, R. Judah

L
Laws Concerning Idolatry, see idolatry
Levinger, Jacob, 90
Liebes, Yehuda, 33n88

M
ma'aseh bereshit, viii–ix, 2, 63–64, 68–70, 72
ma'aseh merkavah, viii–ix, 2, 4, 17, 31, 35, 40, 44, 63–64, 68–70, 72, 74, 81

magic, see astral magic
Maimonides, see Moshe ben Maimon, R.
Ma'rifat al-Nafs, 119
material hindrances to intellectual perfection, 34–35
material intellect, 15, 16n39, 33,
material world, *also* material dimension, viin2, ix, 1, 8, 56, 63, 71–72, 75n33, 76, 77, 79, 81, 83, 86, 110n21, 114, 119–120, 122, 126, 128, 130, 141, 157
Maurer, Armand, 5
Meiri, R. Menachem, 93
metaphysics, passion for, 1–55
    apprehension, limits of, 8–22
    context, 50–52
    eros and politics, 30–45
    passion, 52–54
    political leadership and dogma, 45–50
    primary impulse, 22–30
metaphysics and creation, 64–72
Midrash, 73–76, 84–87, 94, 153–154, 159
Migash, R. Joseph ibn, 90
Moses, 78, 88, 141
Moshe ben Maimon, R.
    Book of Correspondence, 153, 154n54, 155
    Book of Prophecy, 153, 155
    Commentary on Avot, 119
    Commentary to the Mishnah, vii, ix, 31–32, 35–36, 55, 67, 91, 96, 100–103, 105, 119–120, 123, 154n54
    Guide of the Perplexed, see separate article
    Mishneh Torah, vii, 83, 90–95, 101–103, 105, 120, 124, 127, 152–155
        Laws Concerning Idolatry, see idolatry
        Laws of Repentance, 120, 124
    rationalism of, 54–55
Moshe Narboni, R., 4, 15n36, 20n55, 74, 80, 82–83, 85
Mu'tazila, 26n64, 115, 134, 138, 146
Mutakallimūn, Mustakallims, x–xi, 7, 67n15, 134–141, 145–146, 148, 150, 164

N
Narboni see Moshe Narboni, R.
Neoplatonic tradition, 27n67, 54, 66, 73, 77–78, 84, 134, 138–139, 142, 157, 162–164
Nuriel, Abraham, 16n38, 42n120, 151n44

P
pardes, 5, 17, 19, 20n55, 33n88
Perek Helek (Tractate Sanhedrin), 38, 116, 120, 123, 154n54
Philoponus, John, 135, 164

Pines, Shlomo, 4, 11, 13, 68n19, 108n12, 131n39, 157, 165
pleasure, 31, 38, 120-133
primary impulse, metaphysics, 22–30
Proverbs, 19, 32, 37–38
Psalms, 18, 72–73, 109n15, 152

Q

Qafih, R. Yosef, 29n72, 92, 94, 99n28, 102n34
qa'idah, 116

R

al-rabbānīn, 12
Rambam, *see* Moshe ben Maimon, R.
rāy, 136n7
regulative concept, 57

S

Saadia Gaon, 8, 21, 33, 162
  The Book of Beliefs and Opinions, x, 21, 33
Sabianism, *also* Sabians, 91, 96, 103–104
Samuel ben Eli, R., 132
Sanhedrin, Tractate, *see Perek Helek*
Schatzmiller, Joseph, 97n24
Schwartz, Adolf, 90
Schwartz, Dov, 8n14, 12n29, 20n55, 27n67, 32n86, 58n 150, 69n21, 72n26, 80n45, 81n49, 83n55, 87n65, 95n19, 98n26, 102n36, 104n2, 105n4, 108n9, 133n44, 141n22
scientific truth, x–xii, 64, 140, 153
Sefer Mishneh Torah, see Mishneh Torah
separate intellects, viii, 2–3, 30–31, 36n99, 37, 60–87
  emanation and creation, 79–80
  exoteric and esoteric elements in Maimonides, 63–64
  God, as mover of sphere, 83–84
  medieval commentaries on *The Guide of the Perplexed*, 80–81
  metaphysics and creation, answers, 69–72
  metaphysics and creation, questions, 64–67
  prophets and sages, 72–79
  purpose of *The Guide of the Perplexed*, 67–69
  "The World Plus One Third," 84–86
sex, 6, 30–41, 45, 52, 54–55, 124

sitrei 'arayot, 31–32, 33n88
shawq, 9–10, 35, 37, 40, 52–53, 129
al-Sha'm, 111
Shem Tov, R. Isaac ibn Shem Tov, 4,
Shem Tov, R. Joseph ibn Shem Tov, 16n40, 81–82, 87n65,
Shem Tov b. Joseph ibn Falaquera, *see* Falaquera
Sinai epiphany, 4, 108
Soloveitchik, Hayim, 90
spheres, viii-ix, 36, 42, 53, 62-66, 70-86, 99, 110, 130 *see* separate intellects
Stern, Josef, 52
Strauss, Leo, 71, 140, 147n32
Stroumsa, Sarah, 5, 20, 148
substance, 118-119, 127-131, *see* immortality and imagination

T

ta'avah (desire), 37, 53
Tchernowitz, R. Hayyim (Rav Tsair), 58, 90
Torah, vii, ix–x, 13, 24, 27–28, 32, 38, 41, 43, 70, 79, 81, 94, 98, 109, 116, 125n23, 127, 132–133, 159n66
  sitrei Torah (misteries of the Torah), 2, 6, 8, 27, 43, 46, 49–50, 69, 155
Twersky, Isadore, 90

V

vacuum, x, 135, 137
velocity, 65
verification, x-xi, 21, 51

W

al-Warrāq, Abu 'Isā, 111
Weltgeist, 56–57
Wolfson, Harry Austryn, 4, 47n133, 65n10, 135n1, 137n11, 139n15,

Y

yakūn 'afīfan, 39n107
yearning, 31, 129–130
  see also, shawq

Z

Zayd ibn 'Amr ibn Nufayl, 112
Zechariah, 75–76

www.ingramcontent.com/pod-product-compliance
Lightning Source LLC
Chambersburg PA
CBHW051117230426
43667CB00014B/2628